327.12   Copeland, Miles.   8
           Without cloak or dagger; the truth
         about the new espionage. New York, Simon
         and Schuster [1974]
           351 p.

           Includes bibliographical references.

           1.Espionage. 2.Intelligence service.
         I.Title

         327'.12   UB270.C66
                                          74-1136

WITHOUT CLOAK OR DAGGER

The Truth About The New Espionage

MILES COPELAND

SIMON AND SCHUSTER   NEW YORK

To, of course, Lennie

CONTENTS

FOREWORD

Among their reminiscences of World War II, former officers of the U.S. Army Counter-Intelligence Corps have a story of how German interrogators finally got the truth out of Major Bernie Feldman, a senior CIC training officer who was taken prisoner on a field tour when he wandered too close to German lines.

Bernie's interrogators tried everything—torture, psychological pressures, trickery, and kindness (full privileges at the German intelligence officers' club, with a seat at the "English-language table")—but they couldn't get him to drop one crumb of information about his headquarters or his favorite subject, "The Management of Agent Wireless Networks." "We think Bernie *liked* our working him over," one of the interrogators told us after the war when he was himself under interrogation. "It gave him a chance to be a hero."

But the Germans finally hit below the belt. They sent Bernie to their school for spy handlers, assigning him to an instructor who honestly thought he knew more about managing agent networks than Bernie did. Every day, Bernie had to sit at the instructor's side and listen as he preached, with Germanic confidence, misinformation to his students. One day Bernie could stand it no more. He broke down and gave the Germans a complete rundown on how American and British intelligence

9

services managed their agents' communications networks and, for good measure, threw in some sound advice on how the Germans should be running theirs.

The story is probably apocryphal (although the German instructor, now a senior executive in a Stuttgart corporation manufacturing insecticides, swore to its truth in a speech he gave to a reunion of World War II CIC officers held in Baltimore a few years ago), but I must say this: under similar circumstances *I* would probably break. As I see the flood of misinformation on spies and counterspies that is poured out to the public on television, radio and the motion-picture screen, as well as in books, magazine articles, and newspaper reports, I appreciate how Bernie felt. I become strongly tempted to tell all I know on this subject which has occupied most of my working life.

Look at it this way. The Central Intelligence Agency's "dirty tricks department"—that comparatively small segment of the CIA which manages espionage, counterespionage, and subversive and countersubversive operations—has offices and highly trained "case officers" in every major city of the world where a measure of cooperation from the local authorities is to be had. From each of these, "operations" are run across the country's border into adjoining areas that are either hostile to the United States or, for one reason or another, continuing sources of trouble to us and to the peace of the world. Unless you can believe that even a government as wasteful and inefficient as our own would tolerate the existence of a vast and costly facility which is inactive and ineffective, you must believe that it accomplishes *something*. More than that, you must believe that *most* of what it does is successful. No government, even our own, will tolerate for long a costly agency that has more failures than successes.

But in general it is the failures that are brought to the public's attention. During my years of association with the CIA, exactly *one* genuine agent is known to have been uncovered by the Soviets. Even allowing for the possibility that the Soviets actually uncovered ten times that number, turning them into "double agents" and concealing their capture, the percentage of failures represented by those captures would be small. Over the years there have been literally thousands of CIA agents in the U.S.S.R., Red China, Cuba, and other Communist countries. To have lost only one—or ten, or a hundred—indicates a record of considerable success.

Of course, most adverse criticism of the CIA arises from exposures of covert operations that have nothing to do with espionage or counterespionage: the Bay of Pigs disaster, the attempt to bribe the Malayan Prime Minister, the fairly unsecret overthrow of President Arbenz in Guatemala, and "the CIA's secret army" in Laos—which was, of course, the least secret secret army in history. All of these operations, however, are grotesquely atypical of the Agency's method of operating. The Bay of Pigs operation, for example, was launched on the orders of the President of the United States, Dwight D. Eisenhower, despite the Agency's prediction that its chances of success were doubtful; then undercut by his successor, President John F. Kennedy, who at the last minute denied the operating force the air cover that its planners had all along insisted was essential. But in most cases, the CIA's nonespionage "clandestine operations" (that intentionally imprecise term applies to all its secret operations other than espionage and counterespionage) succeed. In an election in such-and-such a country the Soviet KGB backs a candidate, the CIA backs a candidate, and the CIA candidate wins. Or a CIA-backed group of politicians or army officers overthrows a KGB-backed government, or a CIA-backed government prevents a coup attempt against it by a KGB-backed government. Such things happen regularly.

A presentation of credentials is in order. How am *I* able to write a balanced and accurate account? To start with, I was one of those counterespionage specialists of the original American secret intelligence service, the Office of Strategic Services (OSS), whose job it was after World War II to interrogate German counterintelligence officers to determine which of our spies, British and American, they had captured and executed, or turned against us. From our findings, "American intelli-

11

gence" learned what to do and what not to do in the way of managing espionage systems. I took the knowledge to the newly formed Central Intelligence Agency and helped devise the procedures and techniques by which it was possible to recruit espionage agents and organize them into efficient systems. From time to time ever since, I have been called back to the Agency to review the systems in the light of what the Agency's sophisticated counterespionage controls have discovered about "the other side's" occasional penetrations and to recommend renovations. Also, with the knowledge and at least tacit approval of the CIA, I have helped organize and activate intelligence and counterintelligence systems for a number of other governments. In short, my knowledge of the business is from the inside, and it has been sufficiently across-the-board to keep me from making the mistakes of those disgruntled CIA specialists who left the Agency to write exposés.

What about the possibility that I may give away secrets and thus endanger the systems? Specifically, I have imposed upon myself the following restraints: I will reveal no information that will give "the other side" clues to the existence of specific current American or British operations, or any information which suggests that American or British counterespionage services are aware of specific operations run by "the other side"; I will give away no British or American techniques or tricks that "Kim" Philby and others like him have not already made known to the Soviets, or any foreign techniques or tricks that "the other side" does not know the Americans or British have discovered. In addition, with certain exceptions, I have changed the details of operations and identities of the participants, so that the reader can only guess at the true cases on which I have based my account.

I must make it clear, however, that no one at the CIA, the British Secret Intelligence Service (SIS), or any other official agency has "cleared" this book or in any other way implied approval of my writing it. I have been associated with intelligence agencies long enough to realize how futile it would be for one such as myself to request official permission to publish even the most antiseptic book. When General Eisenhower submitted his memoirs, some poor security chap *had* to sit down and read every word, and be prepared to write a memorandum explaining every deletion he recommended. But I am not General Eisenhower. Any security officer to whom I could submit the manuscript for clearance would take one look at its title, ponder the possibility that he just *might* miss one potentially explosive sentence, and disapprove publication.

So I have been my own censor, and if I have included cases and information that have until now been held under tight security wraps, it is because I cannot accept the reasons for their continued secrecy. Since men like Kim Philby have already given the material to the Soviets, I see no reason why they should be kept from the American public.

WITHOUT CLOAK OR DAGGER

THE SPIES OF THE SEVENTIES

They do still exist . . .

FOLLOWING the Lambton-Jellicoe affair, in which two members of the British nobility were discovered to have been consorting with call girls, a security commission was formed to ascertain the extent to which the British Government's security had been endangered. Members of the commission, under Lord Diplock, concentrated on the question of whether or not either of the unfortunate peers might have blurted out TOP SECRETS while engaged in postcoital pillow talk—and, whether the fact that one of them was smoking pot during intercourse had a bearing. They dealt only summarily with the question of possible blackmail, since it was apparent to all of them that the lords, both basically good and honest men despite the errancy in question, would have scoffed at any blackmailer.

British security officials no doubt had their reasons for letting the report go unchallenged, but they must have been appalled by its naiveté. Some espionage services make extensive use of prostitutes—and "sex bars," massage parlors, escort services, model studios, and all the rest—but not to tease secrets out of their targets. They use such resources *only* to get their targets into compromising positions, so that blackmail can follow. As security officials well know, there was no danger whatever that either of the two lords, whether on pot or on alcohol, would give away secrets to the prostitutes. Can you imagine

Lambton, with a puff on his joint, saying, "Darling, I simply *must* tell you about the new X5-11"—or the prostitute having the faintest idea what he was talking about even if he did? The danger was not loose talk while "under the influence," but exposure to blackmail—and not blackmail by some Soho pimp threatening, "Give me a thousand pounds or I'll send these pictures to the newspapers," but by a trained "case officer" using highly sophisticated methods.

Before settling down with their findings in the Lambton-Jellicoe affair, members of the Diplock Commission would do well to study how the modern espionage service works. They may start by considering how the KGB does in fact try to penetrate our two governments, then move on to a consideration of what our two services do to penetrate the Russians' and other governments of "the other side."

Let us start with the case of "Emily," an attractive but shy lady who, one spring evening in 1950, met a kindly, handsome man of about forty whom we may call "Foster."

Emily was personal assistant to the Assistant Secretary of State, who headed a departmental bureau dealing with an important segment of the Third World. As such, she had access to all the secrets of that bureau—exchanges with the British and the French with respect to policies affecting the area, intentions of the U.S. Government in connection with the carrying out of these policies, secret agreements with leaders of governments in this particular part of the Third World, and contingency plans of a U.S. fleet in the event of conceivable emergencies. Foster was "in insurance," and he had no visible interest in international politics.

The meeting, which occurred at a tea in honor of the famous anthropologist Margaret Mead at the Unitarian Church on Sixteenth Street, N.W., Washington, D.C., took place on the same day that Emily had received bad news about her mother. Emily's mother, a whining, malingering widow of eighty years, had just learned that she *really* had cancer. The doctor had pronounced her beyond the stage at which an operation would

18

help and had predicted that she would live for a few more years and would then die a slow and painful death.

There was nothing remarkable about Emily's meeting with Foster, except that in the course of the evening he spilled vin rosé over her new dress and Emily, already upset, burst into tears. Foster apologized profusely, insisting on accompanying her to her home in Georgetown, then waited until she changed into a housecoat so that he could take the wine-splotched dress to "a French laundry I know that can remove *any* kind of spot." After one nightcap, which Foster gulped quickly upon hearing Emily's mother shout from the bedroom ("Emily! *Emily!*"), they shook hands at the door, and Foster departed.

Their friendship blossomed. It was "not the great romance of the century" as Emily later admitted, but it was "very pleasant and undemanding."

Foster didn't seem to *want* anything, not even sex, and he took no interest whatever in Emily's job. He seemed genuinely to enjoy Emily's company, and he knew all sorts of cozy little restaurants—in Georgetown, out Massachusetts Avenue, across the Maryland line from southeast Washington—where they could talk and share personal confidences. They went to plays, concerts, and the movies. Foster obviously wasn't rich, but he could afford all the simple pleasures, and he treated Emily in such a way that she had no sense of being "cultivated." Foster often called Emily "just to talk," and Emily, upon being greeted so warmly when she called Foster for the first time ("I was just *thinking* about you," he had said), put aside her shyness and called him whenever she felt lonely.

Before many months had passed, Foster induced Emily to lean on him financially. At first the amounts were small, and Foster had to use the argument "It's for your mother," a woman whom he had totally managed to charm. Later, the amounts were larger and more regular, and without realizing it Emily began to count on them as a part of her normal income. All this time Foster asked for nothing in return, except for an occasional quick kiss on the staircase—though his manner did suggest that his feelings were not *entirely* platonic. Indeed, for him not to have done so would have appeared unnatural.

Then, one day, Foster asked Emily for a small favor. Being in the insurance business in a town where an enormously high percentage of the population was government-employed, he naturally wanted to "break into the State Department market" —which, according to common belief, consists of careerists who not only receive extremely high salaries but have extensive private means. "I could make my living just selling life insurance to your friends," Foster told Emily. He then asked for a list of her acquaintances at the State Department, together with brief descriptions of their various assignments.

Emily resisted at first, arguing that the State Department publishes annually a *Biographic Register,* a *Foreign Service List,* and other such materials which are easily obtainable from the Government Book Store on Pennsylvania Avenue, but she finally gave in. Foster explained that he wanted "not the sort of stuff one would find in a register," but personal information that would indicate which employees were particularly good prospects for insurance and what would be the best "sales hooks" to use on each. "I could arrange a cocktail party and have you *meet* some of them," said Emily. "No, not yet," said Foster. "Besides, for a while we must keep it confidential. Don't tell *anybody.*"

Emily didn't understand why the information she could give Foster on her friends would be of any real help to him, or why the information should be kept secret, but she did as he asked. Soon she was gossiping freely about her associates and even about some of the confidential matters with which they dealt. There seemed to be no good reason *not* to—although occasionally, remembering her Departmental security indoctrination, after telling Foster some especially confidential item she would giggle and say, "I really shouldn't be telling you such things! You must never tell anyone I told you!" Foster assured her that he wouldn't.

Foster, an officer of the U.S.S.R.'s secret intelligence service, was putting Emily through what is known in the jargon of professional spy handlers as "prerecruitment development." Rule number one is: "Never ask the prospective agent to do anything that is beyond what his conscience will allow. The first task in developing the prospective agent is to expand his conscience gradually, so that he will eventually do what you want him to do without qualms." By the time Foster was asking Emily to bring home secret documents in the evening (to be photocopied, and replaced in the files when she returned to work the following morning), she was ready. In fact, he knew that she had become a Soviet agent.

Emily served Soviet Intelligence for fourteen years—without incident. She built up a sizable bank account in Beirut, Lebanon, and within a few years she could have retired in comfort. Foster disappeared early in her career of espionage, but an attractive, independently wealthy, intelligent woman can always uncover romantic possibilities even when she has entered her fifties.

Then one spring morning, almost fourteen years to the day after Emily first met Foster, a Soviet defector being interrogated by experts at the CIA "human library" in the Allegheny Mountains mentioned offhandedly: "We knew all along about the stuff you planted on us on the————affair." Upon being pressed by the interrogator, he described "the stuff" in some detail, and although he couldn't identify the exact source, he had inferred from the content that it came—or was *supposed* to have come—from the office of Assistant Secretary————and that the source was probably his personal assistant. He said that Soviet analysts, after many years, had come to the conclusion that much of the information was fake.

There followed what is known in Washington as a "flap"—or, in more up-to-date jargon, a "quiet flap," since the frantic inquiries intelligence agencies used to make when leaks were suspected are now a thing of the past. The investigation designed to run down this particular leak was conducted with extreme discretion, so as not to alert any suspects. It led straight to Emily. And Emily, under the kindly questioning of the State Department's chief security officer, who had been her friend for many years, confessed all.

What to do? Here was a longtime Soviet agent planted deep inside the Department's inner circles of secrecy, who had passed over to the Soviets God-knew-what information. Their behavior for the past fourteen years would have to be reinterpreted in the light of what we now realized they had known about our real intentions, as opposed to our announced ones. All sorts of reassessments would have to be made. Possibly, the harm had not been *too* great because, if the Soviet defector was to be believed, the Soviets had for some years regarded Emily's information as fake. Only one conclusion could be drawn with any degree of certainty: the harm resulting from revealing the affair to the public would greatly outweigh any advantages to be gained from bringing Emily to trial. There was simply no way to explain to the public how even the finest security system cannot prevent penetrations such as Emily's. So when a CIA expert on "disinformation" suggested that the Department exploit the Soviets' apparent belief that Emily had been a deception agent all along, the Department's security authorities leaped at it. Emily was left at her post, but during the following weeks she was made to pass the Soviets materials that would be seen through as fake but would, retroactively, increase their suspicions of the genuine materials they had received in the past.

Eventually, Emily got off scot-free—except, that is, for having to return to the U.S. Government most of the $100,000 which she had accumulated in the Beirut bank. Emily was transferred to some administrative post, and shortly thereafter, under an arrangement with the security office, she announced that she had contracted some nervous disease and would have to seek less demanding employment outside of Government. She is now a librarian in some small New England town.

THE "TRULY SUCCESSFUL SPY"

"Emily" is one kind of spy the Central Intelligence Agency's instructors in "Management of the Espionage Operation" have in mind as they train new officers. "First," begins the opening lecture in the course, "you must put out of your mind all you have read about spies. The spies you have read about, by the mere fact that you have read about them, are exceptions. The spies who interest us are the ones who do not get caught, and who therefore are not to be read about."

The lecture indicates that most spies live uneventful lives, often to retire in comfort on earnings stashed away in foreign banks. It includes the phrase, borrowed from British Intelligence, "A good espionage operation is like a good marriage. Nothing out of the ordinary ever happens in it. It is uneventful. It does not make a good story."

Naturally, teaching new officers about typically effective spies, not the bumblers who get caught, poses awkward problems. The officers study case histories of those few spies for "the other side" who were effective enough but were caught by accident. They also study histories of spies on their own side who lived out long careers without getting caught, and whom they can learn about by reading sanitized accounts from CIA operational records. There is a limit, however, to how much can be learned from reading about successful CIA spies. Since they are all of other nationalities and cultures, it is difficult for the new officers to identify with them. CIA trainers want their students to get the *feeling* of espionage, of what it feels like to be a spy, and they therefore prefer to teach case histories of Soviet spies working against American targets, since these spies are American citizens, usually of educational and social backgrounds similar to those of the students themselves. Once they get a feel for the motivations, foibles, and anxieties of these, they can move on to a more difficult step, that of understanding citizens of Communist countries who are agents of the CIA.

The spies whose case histories are first taught to students in the CIA's school on espionage management are American citizens of these categories:

1. The "Emily"—the spy who was originally spotted by a KGB recruiter, also an American citizen, who recognized his or her potential, and who was conditioned, recruited, and trained, like the original Emily, according to conventional principles of agent management;

2. The "Mickey"—the "walk-in" spy who, because of special knowledge and experience, was able to get in touch with a foreign intelligence agency and offer his services without being spotted by counterintelligence controls;

3. The "Philby"—the long-term agent, recruited in his youth, who at the time of his recruitment was outside his assigned target and took years working his way into it;

4. The "Willie"—the spy who is actually working for one intelligence service (e.g., the Soviets') but who, for at least part of his career, is led by his "principal" to believe that he is working for another (e.g., an industrial-espionage organization, a credit-investigation organization, or a newspaper columnist).

The case histories that most conveniently illustrate these categories are cases of Soviet penetrations of Western targets, but they are with only minor differences also illustrative of Western penetrations of Communist targets—or of penetrations of any country's secret installations by the espionage service of another.

THE CASE OF "MICKEY"

"*Even* the CIA can have its penetrations," said defensive members of that Agency when they heard about Emily. "*Only* the CIA could have penetrations like Mickey's," retorted State Department officials when, months later, they learned of the CIA's most serious known penetration. "Mickey," as we shall call him, was a "walk-in" agent who could never have made his initial contacts with the Soviets without his CIA background and skills. Having decided that he had information for which the Soviets would pay large sums, he figured out a basic operational plan for extracting the information from CIA files, and then made contact with the Soviets. His professional training made it easy to avoid traps that invariably catch the amateur "walk-in," and once he had made contact he set his own terms. Soviet Intelligence could take them or leave them. It accepted.

Mickey was a mad Irish-American who felt strongly about politics only when he was drinking, and even then his feelings were such a mixture of extreme right-wing conservatism and leftish resentment of the CIA's "Ivy League dilettantes" that his best friends, when they were questioned just after his capture, were unable to give any clues as to where he stood on the major political issues of the day. In all probability, security analysts eventually decided, he had *no* political views: certainly, when he eventually tried to justify his behavior in terms of political convictions ("It will look better for you if you appear to have been moved by ideology rather than simple financial greed," his legal adviser had told him), he could speak only in clichés, and these were interspersed with emotional outbursts totally incompatible with the politics of his Soviet employers.

When Mickey approached the Soviets, he was a senior member of a CIA unit that received "raw information" from all the U.S. Government's sources—published materials, reports from diplomats and intelligence "stations," technical gimmickry, and liaison with friendly governments. His unit then processed the material into "finished intelligence" summaries that were sufficiently dependable, timely, and brief for the President of the United States. Mickey had virtually all the TOP SECRET security clearances; he attended top staff meetings not only of the CIA itself but, on occasion, of various bureaus of the State and Defense departments. His closest friends were CIA officers who dealt with the Agency's most sensitive problems. He knew as much as it was possible for one man to know, given the U.S. Government's "need to know" policies,* about how our Government saw the rest of the world, mainly Soviet Russia. Although he was excluded from discussions of policy, he was able to observe policymakers' reactions to the intelligence they received, and so could accurately estimate the policies they would recommend. For the U.S. Government, he was a topflight intelligence analyst; for Soviet Intelligence, he was a topflight espionage agent. "Had he not been caught in the end," said one of his superiors, "he might have received service decorations from both sides."

Mickey died "of a heart attack" late in 1964, just as his interrogation was ending. The penultimate paragraph of the report of Mickey's interrogation, the one entitled "Financial Arrangements," was never finished; but the paragraph on "Mode of Operation" was complete, if chillingly brief. It said simply that at irregular intervals, perhaps as often as three to five times a month, Mickey took secret documents home with him in the evenings (as do many senior officers of the CIA), photocopied them, and returned them to his office the following morning. To avoid being detected in the course of the security office's nighttime spot checks of the files, he habitually substituted dummies for those documents he had removed. He met his Soviet case officer at bimonthly intervals, and his weekly deliveries of photocopies and written reports were made via dead-letter drops and "brush" contacts in public places—the men's room of the Mayflower Hotel, a neighborhood movie house, the locker room of a public athletic club, a clump of woods on a municipal golf course.

---

* In government agencies housing particularly sensitive information, general carte blanche TOP SECRET clearances do not exist. Regardless of the trust placed in any employee, he is allowed to know only what he needs to know in order to carry out his job. Moreover, these agencies are so organized that their secrets are tightly compartmentalized. Even the Director of the Central Intelligence Agency is "protected" by need-to-know regulations which keep from him all information that is not essential to his job—and this would be almost all of the detailed information held in his organization.

All was routine; nothing out of the ordinary ever happened. There was no "story." In all the many years that Mickey worked for the Soviets, there were only two "incidents." The first occurred when, through elaborate special arrangements, Mickey crossed into East Berlin to meet "headquarters officers" who were curious to see such an exceptionally productive agent; the second was the one instance when a check of the files by the security office took place on the one night when Mickey forgot to substitute dummies, and particularly sensitive documents were found to be missing. This latter incident led to an investigation. While it is not unusual for documents to be missing from files of officers who insist, despite regulations, on doing "homework," it became increasingly evident that Mickey's comments and behavior did not reflect the kind of knowledge he would have had were he doing "homework" on the missing documents rather than merely copying them.

Mickey's successful and uneventful career as a Soviet agent lasted just under thirteen years, from early 1952 until late 1964. "There is literally *nothing* extraordinary to be found in his case history," the chief investigating officer told Admiral William Raborn, then Director of the Central Intelligence Agency. His motivations, insofar as they could be determined from the interrogation, were unremarkable—in fact, they were shared by numerous other Agency officers any one of whom, under conceivable similar circumstances, might have been moved to sell out to the Soviets. There was nothing ingenious about his "walk-in" approach; there was nothing in his behavior that could have been prevented by any reasonable security precautions. After all, the security office could not possibly keep every member of the CIA under twenty-four-hour surveillance. There was not even anything remarkable about his financial situation: he was not in any particular financial difficulty when he first approached the Soviets, and the $100,000 or so he must have collected from the Soviets was not reflected in his spending habits. (That money is probably still intact in some Swiss bank, to be picked up one day by his heirs.)

Like the Emily affair, the Mickey case was hushed up. Nothing would have been gained by calling public attention to the fact that such an important penetration had taken place, particularly since circumstances suggested that similar penetrations might still be in progress.

AND WHAT ABOUT "KIM" PHILBY?

Kim Philby, the Soviet agent who penetrated the British Intelligence Service, is a "famous spy," but his fame resulted from a fluke, as did his discovery. Had he not escaped to Russia, he would almost certainly have been liquidated (as Mickey was) or neutralized (as Emily was) and the world would have heard nothing of him. He meets our qualifications for men worth studying as a "real" spy. He was of proved effectiveness; he was caught really by chance; and his personal history indicates that he was not unique—that there may be others like him still planted in Western governments.

Like the careers of Emily and Mickey, Philby's life as a Soviet agent was uneventful. If discriminating writers have managed to write whole books about him it is because he was interesting as a man, not as an agent. He had an unusual childhood as the son of the famous Arabist St. John Philby; he had an adventurous career in the Spanish Civil War; he held a variety of important posts in British Intelligence. He initially gained widespread publicity as the result of rumors that he was the "third man" in the Burgess-Maclean affair. After being discharged from British Intelligence because of these lingering suspicions, he traveled widely as a newspaperman. So the "events" of his life that are interesting enough to write about had little or nothing to do with his spying. While he was gallivanting about in the pursuit of adventure he was of little use to his Soviet masters. Despite Philby's own claims,* it was only when he was working quietly and uneventfully inside British official installations that he could produce information

---

* See *My Silent War*. London: Hodder and Stoughton and New York: Grove Press, 1968.

28

of importance to the Russians. Needless to say, the means by which he delivered the information were entirely normal and unspectacular.

The Philby case has some, but not much, relevance to modern-day espionage. During the Thirties, when Hitler was on the rise and the economic depression in the West was at its worst, the Soviets recruited to the cause of Communism scores of young men and women—Americans, Britons, Europeans—who had not yet chosen their careers. Of these, a percentage were instructed, first, to "go underground" and conceal their Communist sympathies; second, to seek employment in their respective governments. Of these, the majority fizzled out—either because they decided to come into the open with their Communist views, or because they lost interest in the cause altogether, or because they were unable to find government employment that fitted both their personal interests and those of the Soviets. Of those who did remain undercover, with their Communist convictions frozen (as were Philby's *), a few were

---

* Graham Greene and other admirers of Philby, including Philby himself (see Philby's My Silent War, introduction by Graham Greene), believe that he was motivated by strong ideological convictions. I am told, however, that the mass of biographical data on Philby which British Intelligence has by now assembled supports a more cynical view—that expressed by John Le Carré, himself an old intelligence officer, in his introduction to the Insight team's Philby (London: André Deutsch, 1968): "I do not much believe in the political motive of Kim Philby; but I am sure that the British secret service kept it alive as no other environment could have done. The British intelligence world described here is apolitical. Once entered, it provides no further opportunity for spiritual development. The door that clanged behind the new entrant protected him as much from himself as from reality. Philby, once employed, met spies, conundrums, technique; he had said goodbye to controversy. Such political opinions as sustained him were the opinions of his childhood." This is certainly my view of Philby's political motives, and I knew him as well as anyone did—especially during the period just before he fled to Moscow. Like others who have combed their memories for clues to his pro-Soviet sympathies, I can only recollect remarks of his that were as uncharacteristically naive as they were pro-Soviet—and I do not believe he could have been dissembling. In any case, when used to designate a category, our "Philby" refers to spies who became committed to a cause early in life, and whose minds remained "fossilised," as Hugh Trevor-Roper says.

caught and convicted; a few more landed in SUSPECT files and were thereafter unable to obtain the necessary security clearances; and a few more were detected but were quietly "doubled" or left their jobs without fuss. The remainder could still be functioning—just as Philby, Burgess, and Maclean were up to the day they were removed from their governmental posts. According to what J. Edgar Hoover told a Congressional investigating committee in 1969, FBI files contain the names of "between thirty and forty" U.S. Government employees who fit the "profile" that FBI experts believe applies to persons who *could* be Soviet agents, but on whom there is insufficient evidence to warrant the withholding of most routine security clearances. These files also contain the names of "a hundred or so" officials of British and European governments who might be Soviet agents. The CIA and British Intelligence are less pessimistic, but they believe that there are "probably a few Philbys" high in the governments of the United States, Britain, and the other NATO countries who regularly furnish the Soviets with extremely important secret information, and who may never be caught. Thus, Philby is not unique. There is still such a thing as a "Philby-type" agent, and it is a type that must be taken seriously.

The "Philby" is entirely a feature of Soviet Intelligence. Our intelligence services never had the opportunity to develop a political movement behind the Curtain, and even had they been able to do so it would have been practically impossible to maintain the kind of contact with them necessary to sustain their enthusiasm over the years.* More important, with

---

* Israeli Intelligence may have succeeded where others have failed in planting "Philbys" in the Soviet Government. There are indications that a principal reason for the sudden wave of anti-Zionism which recently swept the U.S.S.R. was the discovery in various Soviet Government offices of Israeli agents who had been recruited and trained by underground Zionist organizations before Israel became a state and had penetrated sensitive areas of the Government long before the outbreak of the 1967 war. Certainly, Israeli Intelligence has been extremely well informed on the inside workings of the Soviets' agencies concerned with Middle Eastern affairs.

"Emilys" and "Mickeys" being a dime a dozen behind the Curtain, there has been no need for Western intelligence agencies to go to the expense of developing "Philbys."

The "Philby" is not only peculiar to the Soviets; he is also peculiar to the "old espionage." Today, although the Soviets still waste considerable time and money on persons who just *might* one day work their way into targets of importance, they find that Philby's young counterparts are as anti-Soviet as they are anticapitalist and anti-"imperialist." Besides, these students seem incapable of sustained activity either as Soviet Intelligence agents or as employees of the targets they are supposed to penetrate. Still, the Soviets try—in American, British, and European universities. Their success has been so slight that Western security agencies have all but discontinued their "doubling" of the few who succumb. Most are so feckless as counterspies that they could be of little help to the Soviets as spies. So why bother? "Philbys" are worth our serious attention only because a few older ones are *already* in our governments.

THE PLAGUE OF "WILLIES"

In 1952, when "McCarthyism" was at its height, a sensationalist Washington columnist one day received a letter of unquestionable authenticity giving highly confidential information about the State Department's harsh treatment of employees accused of Communist sympathies. The letter was a violation of security regulations, but the intention behind it kept it from being a contravention of the nation's espionage laws. The writer had no thought of communicating the information to a foreign power, but only wanted to make the public aware of what he honestly thought to be an injustice.

Although the letter was signed simply "a patriotic American," it took only an hour or so of discreet inquiry for the columnist's chief investigator to determine the author's identity. Without informing the columnist of his intentions, the investigator approached the employee, swore him to secrecy, promised him monthly "expense money," and made arrangements for him to continue to indulge his patriotic impulses by furnishing weekly reports. Some of the reports would be published as having come from "a source close to the State Department," with details altered to mislead the Department's security officials as they tried to run down the leak; the rest would be kept in the columnist's office as "background material" to support other stories. It was a satisfactory arrangement to both men—if not to the columnist, who was not told about it.

The investigator, it happened, was not only a reporter; he moonlighted as a "principal" of the Soviet KGB. As an investigator he was able to use the columnist's good name—or rather, his reputation as a crusader—to employ informants. Some remained mere informants, happy in the belief that they were merely exposing to the public deficiencies of the bureaucracy. Others, after careful development, became regular Soviet agents—in other words, "Emilys."

Those who remained unaware that they were reporting to a foreign power were "Willies"—i.e., agents who don't know they are agents. They wouldn't think of working for an enemy government, but their sense of morality is not offended at the idea of furnishing information to private companies or individuals, or even to "friendly" governments. They grow like garden weeds at times when the public believes official-secrets acts are being used to hide the bureaucracies from well-informed criticism, and when for any other reason there is disrespect for security laws and regulations.

After the suspicions of the "Willie" have become aroused, he is, like any of the other types, more likely to continue his espionage work than to turn himself in. Most security officers believe that hundreds of uncaught "Willies" may exist in Western governments. Certainly thousands exist in governments of the so-called "Third World," having been planted there not only by Soviet Intelligence but by our own intelligence services. They even exist in the Soviet Union. One Willie thinks he is giving tips to an industrial concern seeking government contracts; another, that he is giving information on his co-workers required for purposes of credit investigations; another, that he is keeping a right-wing religious group informed of "left-wingers" in his office. The stickiest Willies are those who think they are working for Congressmen or prominent newspaper columnists, because in many cases they *really are*—except for the fact that the principals who collect the information give it not only to their respective Congressmen and columnists, but also to Soviet Intelligence. In any case, termination of a Willie is normally awkward, as "termination with extreme prejudice" (i.e., liquidation) of Willie cases is frowned upon by most security services.

IS THERE A "STANDARD" AGENT TYPE?

To the CIA's espionage specialists, agents can so easily be typed as "Emily," "Mickey," "Philby," and "Willie" that variations of these names are used to categorize new cases of foreign agents and even, sometimes, to categorize agents of our own. "We have managed to plant an Emily in the Algerian Foreign Ministry," a CIA espionage specialist might tell a colleague. The British have similar categories; so do the Soviets—although, of course, they are more in line with national characteristics. A review of the operational files of any espionage branch, however, would surely reveal that fewer than half its agents fit these categories. There is a wide range of agents who fit no category except "miscellaneous."

THE "MISCELLANEOUS" AGENT

Even the most disciplined, textbook-minded espionage officers are occasionally unable to resist the temptation to recruit agents who do not fit the accepted patterns. For example, there is "that silly little sub-lieutenant," as British security officers call David Bingham, the Navy officer who had his wife "walk in" to the Soviet Embassy in London to offer his services. Before the working day was over, the British security authorities knew of the approach and had set about making arrangements whereby Bingham would have access only to material, genuine and fake, that British Intelligence "disinformation" experts had cleared for passing. Meanwhile, the Soviets, presumably realizing that so naive an approach would have been spotted by British surveillances, only set up expandable operational facilities for the Binghams—and, no doubt, assumed that the material they delivered was generally fake.

Why did they bother? "The temptation to follow up on such an approach just to see where it will lead is irresistible," a CIA case officer once told me apropos of a similar case. "We spend far too much time on such matters." Why, then, do the courts make such a fuss over cases like the Binghams? There are a number of reasons, all centering around the fact that *important* detected Soviet spies rarely reach the courts, and it is essential to make the most of the "miscellaneous" ones who do. In sentencing Sub-Lieutenant Bingham, Mr. Justice Bridge of the Winchester Crown Court described the officer's action as "a monstrous betrayal of your country's secrets," adding, "The damage you may have done to these interests is incalculable," while counterespionage analysts estimated that most of the Binghams' information could have been obtained by technical intelligence or inferred from overtly obtainable publications.

It is the fact that there are *some* "miscellaneous" agents (certainly more than the professionals think there *should* be), whom the courts are allowed, when they get caught, to make a fuss over, that gives writers of spy books and the general public the impression that they are what the espionage business is all about. Perhaps it's just as well. Many professionals no doubt think it useful for the public to have such a false impression. But there is one aspect on which I think it important that the public be set straight. This is that most spies are not oddballs like the Binghams. It is not their peculiarities upon which spymasters play to recruit them, but what CIA psychologists have come to call "normal vulnerabilities."

34

2

ESPIONAGE—THE INTELLIGENCE AGENCY'S LAST RESORT

. . . but what is left for them to do?

CRITICS of the CIA who object to the fact of its existence, rather than its supposed ineffectiveness, forget that the United States was the last major power to have a proper intelligence service, and that in its predecessor organizations, as in the CIA itself, espionage has always played a minor role. At the time of Pearl Harbor, "military intelligence" was not an organization but a staff function performed by "G-2" units attached to military commands, from the Company level up through Battalion, Division, Corps, Army, Army Group and Theater commands, with only the barest supervision from the Assistant Chief of Staff, G-2. The Navy had a similar arrangement under the Office of Naval Intelligence; so did the Air Force—which, incidentally, began life in World War I as *the* intelligence service, performing only reconnaissance in the earliest days of the War before its combat potential was recognized. The State Department was, as it is now, an "intelligence organization" of sorts, but its "intelligence officers" were for the most part highly individualistic and opinionated ambassadors whose reporting didn't lend itself to the kind of processing necessary to produce coordinated estimates for policy purposes.

Until 1947, the only centralized intelligence activity of the U.S. Government was the cryptography performed by the War Department's "Black Chamber" founded by Herbert Yardley;

even that was dissolved at the insistence of the Secretary of State, Henry Stimson, who argued that "Gentlemen do not read other gentlemen's mail." Mr. Stimson was not just voicing a personal view but expressing an attitude that prevailed throughout the State Department and the armed services. There was no objection to intelligence, but it had to be "fair" —it didn't involve "peeping into the other fellow's hand," as Mr. Stimson put it. It took Pearl Harbor to make us realize not only that we needed more effective intelligence, but that we couldn't afford to be squeamish over how we got it.

The International Telephone and Telegraph Corporation (ITT), which earned so much notoriety at the time of the Chilean elections in 1972, did its part in shaking Mr. Stimson off his high moral pedestal. The story has been kept so secret that the present top executives of ITT didn't know it, and therefore couldn't revive it to use as a rebuttal to allegations that it was trying to use improper influence on the CIA to get it to prevent a Communist candidate from winning Chile's 1971 elections. It will one day be presented in its entirety as an important chapter in the history of American intelligence. For the present, it is to be found only in summary form as a case history used by CIA for training purposes.

According to this abbreviated version, just after Mr. Stimson made his remark about not reading other gentlemen's mail, in 1933, the British began bombarding the State Department with information intended to shake us out of our apparent refusal to take Hitler seriously. They shortly succeeded in convincing us that we had better keep track on him in any way we could —even by reading other people's mail if that proved necessary. Somewhere along the line, the British Foreign Office admitted that its principal agent in European rightist circles was Juan March, the smuggler-turned-financier who was largely responsible for bringing Francisco Franco to power in Spain. March established contact with Admiral Wilhelm Canaris, chief of the German Abwehr (military intelligence), and later brought him into contact with the British MI-6. Although stories about Canaris' later activities are confusing, his work for the British during the Thirties produced intelligence which, when passed to the U.S. War Department, convinced even Mr. Stimson, who had become Secretary of War by that time, that *he* needed a March and a Canaris, complete with accessories.

The mood of Washington being what it was at that time, the State and War Departments felt that we were less in need of a high-level espionage arrangement which would tell us of Hitler's bad points than of one which would give us a dependably balanced picture—including points in Hitler's favor, if any. Several approaches to the problem of setting up such an arrangement were considered, and the most practical one seemed to be the use of ITT. Sosthenes Behn, then head of ITT, had just visited Hitler along with some other American businessmen, and had taken time out to write a lengthy TOP SECRET report to Mr. Stimson giving him his impressions. We are not yet allowed to know whether the impressions were favorable to Hitler or unfavorable, but the result was to convince President Roosevelt that we should keep an eye on the rise of Hitler but meanwhile keep our options open.

In those days, ITT was a small company—a fraction of its present size as a gigantic multinational corporation—and its top executives had a greatly exaggerated notion of the extent to which the company's success depended on the goodwill of the U.S. Government. Sosthenes Behn was anxious to please. In the years following his first report to Mr. Stimson, he and one or two of his top lieutenants met with Hitler, Goering, and other top Nazi figures and wrote lengthy reports on them which were more comprehensive than any others the U.S. Government was receiving at the time—and which were regarded as highly reliable, since they pointed to conclusions roughly the same as those of the much-respected U.S. Ambassador in London, Joseph P. Kennedy. It seemed both to Mr. Behn and to Mr. Kennedy that Hitler's chances of coming out on top in a European war were better than even, especially since the British Government was not acting on its own alarmist intelligence. Although such reporting did not endear either of these gentlemen to President Roosevelt, Washington's budding intelligence community gave them both credit for honestly "calling it the way they see it," as Mr. Stimson told the President.

When the National Archives finally agree to declassify Mr. Behn's prewar reporting, we will probably learn that Mr. Behn was somewhat more sanguine about Britain's chances than Mr. Kennedy was—or, possibly, that he was more disillusioned with the Germans. Unlike recent popular accounts of the ITT's wartime record, the case history of the CIA's training department indicates that Mr. Behn at first conducted his business affairs in Germany in exactly the way he would have conducted them had he believed that Germany was eventually going to lose the war, and that he adopted more bullish policies only at the insistence of the U.S. War Department. Anyhow, Mr. Behn kept the U.S. Government informed in painstaking detail of all his business activities in Germany, and his reports were available to anyone in the State Department who had appropriate TOP SECRET security clearances and the patience to read them. They were given a super–TOP SECRET classification, and locked away in Mr. Stimson's personal safe, when the British began denouncing Mr. Behn and his company.

Behn came unfavorably to the attention of the British as a result of Mr. Stimson's challenging British intelligence reports on the basis of information that could have come only from ITT sources. By that time, Mr. Stimson was not only reading other people's mail but, thanks to ITT's technical entrée into Europe, listening to their telephone conversations as well. "The ITT became Mr. Stimson's private intelligence service," reports the Office of Strategic Service's historian who wrote the report that is presumably the basis of the CIA case history. "This was one 'operation' he wasn't going to let the British in on." This was at a time when the newly formed OSS had no assets of its own and was in the middle of its humble beginnings under the tutelage of the British MI-6.

Apart from the ITT operation, and one or two others which the OSS director, General "Wild Bill" Donovan, developed from among contacts of his New York law firm, the OSS was entirely a wartime affair, organized without any thought of its becoming a peacetime intelligence agency. Therefore, when we were finally ready to get into the business of centralized intelligence, including a centralized espionage organization independent of the military and diplomatic services, we had some very definite advantages: we were able to start from scratch, with brand-new personnel, ideas, and equipment, while the intelligence organizations of other great powers were stuck with their old arrangements and couldn't bring themselves to scrap them. "We are now the oldest service," CIA Director Allen Dulles once said to a British friend, "because we've been in the twentieth century the longest." He went on to remark that before long the British intelligence setup, which the CIA had begun by imitating, would soon be imitating the CIA—and so would the Soviets'.

Things haven't *quite* turned out as Mr. Dulles predicted, but it is true that the new CIA's clandestine services concentrated so intensely on the development of method that they were soon leading other countries in what the CIA's Chief of Training called "philosophical depth" and modern management methods. As a result, the CIA has been increasingly able to confine its espionage branch to those tasks which only an espionage branch can perform. Unlike the espionage branches of the other great powers, the CIA never uses spies to get information that can just as well be obtained by other means. The CIA is *not* an espionage organization. It only has a (very small) section that handles espionage.

"WHAT, NO ESPIONAGE SERVICE?"

The CIA almost got under way without having an espionage section at all. The idea of an espionageless intelligence service was attractive not only to three secretaries of State (James F. Byrnes, George C. Marshall, Dean Acheson), but to a great many intelligence experts, including many who had stayed in the Government after serving throughout the war in key positions in the OSS. The State Department people were leery of espionage partly on moral grounds, but more because of a fear that some of our spies were bound to get caught; they felt the resulting embarrassment would cause more harm to international goodwill than the information they could produce would be worth. The intelligence specialists were unenthusiastic about espionage simply because they thought it was unnecessary. In 1946 a group of management advisers reviewed informational material going into the IN baskets of the President, the Secretary of State, the secretaries of War and the Navy, and other top policymakers of the Government and found that almost all of it came from newspaper reports and ordinary diplomatic cables and dispatches and that anything which could have been added by an espionage service wasn't missed or needed. This was just after the war and before the Cold War, of course; but if the antiespionage people had had their way, today's espionage would probably have been pretty much of an improvised affair instead of the highly systematized effort that it has turned out to be.

There are several stories in the CIA's secret annals to explain how the dispute was settled, but although they "make better history," as Allen Dulles used to say, they are only half-truths and much less consistent with the ways of government than the true one. Old-timers at the Agency swear that the anti-espionage people would almost certainly have won out had it not been for the fact that an Army colonel who had been assigned to the management group charged with the job of organizing the new Agency suborned secretaries in the FBI, the State Department, and the Defense Department and organized them into an espionage network which proved not only the superiority of espionage over other forms of acquiring "humint" (i.e. intelligence on what specific human beings think and do in privacy), but the necessity for its being systematized and tightly controlled. The colonel was fired, as were the secretaries, but by that time General John Magruder, then head of the group that was organizing the CIA, had in his hands a strong argument for creating a professional espionage service and putting it under a single organization. Also, thanks to the secretaries and their Army spymaster, he had enough material to silence enemies of the new Agency— including even J. Edgar Hoover, since Magruder was among the very few top bureaucrats in Washington on whom Mr. Hoover didn't have material for retaliation.

What was left of the wartime Office of Strategic Services' espionage in those days was in the hands of an independent section, administered by the Department of Defense, known as the "Strategic Services Unit." The SSU consisted of three cadres: a group of specialists inherited from the OSS's counter-espionage division, "X-2"; also from the OSS's espionage divisions, "SI"; and a miscellany of administrative, sabotage, para-military, black propaganda, and political-action types who had been waiting to see the great new peacetime intelligence agency that General Donovan had promised. The only really busy people in the SSU's temporary quarters were the counter-espionage specialists. These, naturally, came to dominate the unit. SI's agents were low-level informants scattered through-out Western Europe, where targets were easy enough to spot with the naked eye, but X-2 had as agents a number of pro-fessional intelligence officers belonging to the most effective police, security, and intelligence agencies in the world. X-2 officers tended to hold SI in contempt, and some X-2 officers firmly believed that a national espionage service was unneces-sary, since secret cooperation with foreign services would pro-duce all the information needed.

In 1946, an X-2 officer known within the organization as "Mother" took a lot of information on Palestine from *The New York Times*; spooked it up a bit with fabricated details, places, and claims of supersecret sources; and sent it to the head of SI, Stephen Penrose,* for appraisal. After studying it carefully,

---

* Steve Penrose was a highly moral man of missionary background who, after suffering X-2's psychological warfare against him to the breaking point, first transferred to the job of Assistant to Secretary of Defense James Forrestal; then later went to Beirut, Lebanon, to become President of the American University there. He and various other top people in SI

Penrose and his assistants decided that the material was "genuine," that its source must be very deep inside secret Zionist and Arab terrorist groups, and that arrangements should be made for developing the sources into a regular espionage network. Mother then negotiated with Penrose for a budget, meanwhile leading the SI officers through a maze of fake names, fake background reports, and the like, and finally established that SI would be willing to pay as much as $100,000 a year out of what was left of OSS funds. Mother then confessed that the whole thing was a hoax and that the information could have been acquired for 25 cents through the purchase of five issues of *The New York Times*. He thereby demonstrated not only the naiveté of our nation's only existing group of espionage specialists but the value of ordinary *New York Times* reporting on matters regarded as being of high-priority intelligence interest.

The standard example usually dragged out by antiespionage factions in intelligence organizations was the case of "Alpha" in World War II. This operation, the first to be run by the OSS independently of the British SIS, was a network of American and French agents operating in the general neighborhood of Clermont-Ferrand, about halfway between Paris and Marseille, whose sole job was to report on the state of rail transportation from the south of France to the north. It was launched on twelve wireless-transmission sets with spare parts, one boxcar load of weapons and explosives, and enough medical supplies and canned food to keep as many as one hundred persons in complete hiding for three months. By the end of the war, it had lost thirty-odd men and women, some of whom were tortured to death by the Germans without revealing any information of significance. Another thirty or so—about half of those who managed to survive the war—received military decorations and commendations. The American officer who started it, one Jules Knowland, was promoted from second

---

(with a few conspicuous exceptions, such as Richard Helms, who defected to X-2 and went on to become the CIA's Director) were generally thought to be "too Christ-like for the spy business," as Mother put it.

lieutenant to major in less than two years, and by the time of his discharge from the Army he had won the Silver Star, the Legion of Merit, the Bronze Star, and the French Croix de Guerre. In the final appraisal of the Office of Strategic Services' espionage operations submitted to Supreme Headquarters Allied Expeditionary Forces (SHAEF) just after VE-Day, "Alpha" was judged to have been "one of the most successful espionage operations of World War II."

It was, in fact, almost totally useless. At least once a week, but usually more often, the network radioed to OSS headquarters the results of every Allied bombing raid on bridges and terminals on railroads running between the Mediterranean coast and Paris, and the progress of German engineers in repairing them. When the reports reached the Evaluations desk at OSS, they were marked "A-1," meaning they were both valuable and reliable, and passed to the Research and Analysis office. There they more often than not went straight into the wastepaper basket. One Walter Levy, who has since become world-famous as a petroleum economist, already knew all our Air Force needed to know about the state of rail transportation in that part of the world simply from studying photographs taken by our bombers as they made the raids, and by watching changes in the price of oranges on the Paris market. The price invariably went up just after our bombs had destroyed the means of their being transported to Paris; it plummeted dramatically when the means were restored.

Stories about "Alpha" were all over Washington; every intelligence officer, whether an ordinary diplomat at the State Department or a map-room orderly in the Pentagon, had his favorite way of showing that a competent person could easily enough discover the most secret item on his "requirements" list by reading some obscure Soviet medical journal, by properly interpreting a lot of photographs acquired innocently by a maiden aunt touring the U.S.S.R., or by expertly interpreting ordinary news items. In August, 1947, one month before the CIA was activated, a group of scientists proved to the Secretary of Defense, James Forrestal, that scientists trained to the

level of Soviet physicists could by then have inferred all they
needed to now about the current state of our atomic research
simply by reading *Scientific American* and various other publications, and that American scientists could do the same on
Soviet atomic research from the study of Soviet publications.*
About the same time, a group of Army officers undergoing a
"strategic intelligence" course at the Pentagon showed that
by using the new "game" methods of analysis they could have
predicted not only the attack on Pearl Harbor, but also the
place, the time, and the forces that would be used.

Even so, the SSU's cadres plugged ahead, determined to
carve out a niche for themselves in the great new intelligence
system. While high-powered debates were taking place on
"the Hill," the office of the interim caretaker unit in the old
Naval Hospital building on E Street, the Pentagon, the FBI,
and a group of SSU officers with internal names like "Jojo,"
"Mother," and "the Fisherman" were building a capability
that would at least *seem* indispensable to the planners on
"the Hill." "Penetration begins at home," Mother said, "and
if we can't find out what's going on in the offices where our
future is being planned, we don't deserve to be in business."

---

* Months later, the lawyers of Klaus Fuchs were trying to find some way
of using the findings of these scientists to support the argument that
Fuchs had given the Soviets only information that they could have
acquired from overt sources. The Government agency employing the scientists took evasive action, however, and it was not until Fuchs had
served his sentence that the CIA openly admitted that, with the maximum
allowable security controls in a democratic country, trade journals, Ph.D.
theses, and other easily attainable scholarly works would inevitably make
available to the Soviets, or to anyone else employing skilled analysts, all
they would conceivably want to know about our scientific advances.

When General Bedell Smith was Director of the CIA, he commissioned
a group of college professors to put themselves in the shoes of Soviet
intelligence analysts, and to see how complete an appraisal of American
military strength they could get by studying only published information,
mainly from Congressional hearings. In weeks, the professors produced
findings which, in the words of General Smith, "could not be improved
on, either in detail or in accuracy, by the addition of information obtained
by other means."

Books, magazine articles, and newspaper stories have been written about the formation of the CIA, and even today there are publicized debates about all the policy considerations that placed the CIA atop the "intelligence community." Especially in recent years there has been a wide range of publicized comments about the CIA's alleged failure to predict this or that coup d'état, its supposed incorrect evaluation of the comparative strengths of American and Soviet missiles, and its questionable role in the Vietnam war. Also, there have been assaults on the CIA by columnists and politicians who, believing the CIA to be only an espionage service,* have asked for its curtailment on moral grounds. But until James Schlesinger took over the CIA in 1973, the unit that had begun as the SSU remained virtually untouched.

LIMITS ON THE USE OF ESPIONAGE

The success of the old SSU cadre in perpetuating itself has been due in part to an extraordinary capacity for Byzantine intrigue,† but to a larger extent to the discipline that its mem-

---

* In 1947, *The New York Times*'s senior military strategist, Hanson Baldwin, wrote: "There is still a native repugnance to the permanent establishment of a peacetime intelligence system: it smacks too much of duplicity and hypocrisy, and poses hidden dangers to the social system." A few years later, the U.S. Ambassador to the United Nations, Adlai Stevenson, objected to the use of "secret intelligence methods" by the U.S. Government because he believed that they would "corrupt not only the spy but those who employ him, and those who give official approval to his use." He went on to say that he would rather deal with a hostile government that has integrity than with a friendly government that is corrupt—meaning that when you employ spies in the government you damage it in two ways: you purloin its secrets, and you undermine the loyalty of its employees and, therefore, its integrity.

† This intrigue was used mainly to keep "the Hill" off its back. The Director of the Central Intelligence Group, as the CIA was called before it was legalized by an act of Congress, Admiral Sidney Souers, and the first two Directors of the CIA, General Hoyt Vandenberg and Admiral Roscoe Hillenkoetter, were straightforward military types who had little understanding of clandestine operations but who were sensible enough to

bers have imposed upon its operations. Through all the Agency's organizing and reorganizing—first when X-2 and SI were combined to form a single espionage and counterespionage unit known as the Office of Special Operations (OSO); later when OSO and a "clandestine operations" unit known as the Office of Policy Coordination (OPC) were combined to form a single secret-operations unit; and still later when the OPC was castrated following the infamous "Bay of Pigs" operation—the original SSU nucleus, expanded by the recruitment of like-minded spirits, has retained an almost monolithic integrity. It has had no penetrations, no important leaks, no "blown" operations of size to embarrass the Government, and a string of successes that testify to its efficiency.

Since it started operations in 1947, it has never undertaken an assignment to acquire a particular kind of information (a "requirement") unless its planners believed that, in the event of costly exposure, they would be able to justify the operations as having been absolutely vital to national security.

One would think that, in view of all the "native repugnance" to espionage, the CIA would never have to apply the first of these disciplines: its "customers" themselves would refrain from asking for information by spying unless it was a matter of preventing a nuclear attack. To the contrary, soon after the CIA had formally opened its doors, with the OSO looking after its espionage operations, requests began to flow in from

---

allow the units that ran them a free hand as long as they were satisfied that the units were not up to mischief which might embarrass the intelligence community. Heads of the units found that giving the right assurances was no more than a matter of skillful briefing. When a Director was appointed—General Bedell Smith—who took their briefings with a generous seasoning of salt, they connived to have one Lyman ("Kirk") Kirkpatrick, one of the most effective briefers in Government and a trusted aide of Smith's, to be assigned the job of keeping an eye on them. Kirk was sublimely honest, but he had a great reputation for being able to see through "operators," and he was believed to be a match for Machiavellians such as Mother, Jojo, and the Fisherman. He was, but it worked out to their advantage. Within weeks he had become their champion, and their principal shield against attack. When he was moved to CIA headquarters as Inspector General, his place was taken by Richard Helms, who was himself one of the SSU originals.

even the most puritanical elements of the U.S. Government. One of Mother's assistants tells me, for example, that he was once called to Admiral Hillenkoetter's office to meet with two gray-flannel-suited members of the U.S. Government's Mission to the United Nations. As he waited, expecting to have to sit through a lecture on how the mere existence of an espionage unit within the U.S. Government could severely damage international goodwill, he was surprised to learn that the gentlemen had come to request a penetration of some Arab government's mission to the United Nations in order to steal an advance copy of a speech its representative was to make the following week. The OSO accepted the requirement, knowing that all it had to do to get a copy of the desired speech was swap off to the Arab representative a copy of the speech the U.S. delegate, Mrs. Eleanor Roosevelt, was to make right afterward, but the request nonetheless shows how, even on this point, the espionage specialists have to provide their own restrictions.

An example is the case of the CIA's penetration of the Iraqi Assyrians. As one reconstructs the story, it appears that some incidental information the CIA's Chief of Station in Baghdad sent in on the "Assyrian Council" got rave notices from the State Department, together with a notation on the Evaluation Memorandum: "Please, urgent, more of same." Penetrating a political-religious organization that was *begging* to be penetrated was hardly a great feat of espionage, but for all the State Department knew it might have involved enormous risk. It was later learned that the urgent request was motivated by nothing more than a desk officer's desire to enliven the dissertation on Assyrians he was doing for his Ph.D.

Early in the game, the Requirements staff of the OSO learned the advisability of assigning one officer specially to deal with lunatic requests—from State, from the Pentagon, or even the White House. The Kingfish was the first to be assigned the job—partly because of a wartime reputation for being good at handling drunks and partly because of an often-repeated story about how he once defused a poor madwoman who came to General Eisenhower's Grosvenor Square headquarters claiming that she was being tortured via short-wave by the Gestapo. He soon learned that the job was to be taken seriously. Kingfish's trick was not to turn away an impractical requirement but to accept it and then carry it out in his own way, getting the information from *The New York Times* and dressing up the results so that it would appear to have come from an extremely difficult espionage operation. I was working in "K" building at the time, and I can personally testify that there were at least a dozen "operations"—complete with agents, principals, cutouts, secret inks, and all the rest—which were run entirely within the confines of Room 2213, "K" building.

From something of a joke, Kingfish's small unit grew into one of the most important developmental sections in the CIA. The unit didn't fabricate information—only the means by which the information was supposed to have been produced. The information was, in fact, more detailed and accurate than any that could have been produced by spies during those postwar years. Until the CIA's espionage branch developed its modern methods, spies were universally unreliable.* We all knew at the time that 100 percent of the German spies in Britain reported to their headquarters only what was fed to them by British "disinformation" experts, so we had every reason to suspect that at least *some* of our agents behind the Iron Curtain would be similarly controlled by the Soviets.

In those days, the world was infested with what came to be known as "paper mills"—émigré groups, special-interest groups, or simply groups of former CIA informants who fabricated masses of information and sold it to the highest bidders. Their products were so pervasive that they showed up in gen-

---

* In 1947, when the CIA station chief in Beirut chided his colleague across the mountain in Damascus for fabricating his reports, the colleague in Damascus asked, "What's the difference between my fabricating reports and your letting your agents do it? At least mine make sense and are correct." Headquarters' reactions confirmed that this was so. Until it was taken over by a more orthodox chief in 1950, the Damascus station consistently got the highest evaluations of any station in the Middle East.

uine espionage operations, at local intelligence services with which the CIA conducted liaison, and even in diplomatic communications. CIA station chiefs themselves sometimes resorted to "paper," either to befuddle other intelligence services or to punish U.S. military attachés or other American officials who dared to venture into their preserves.

There is the case of the American military attaché in Syria, in the early days of the CIA, who used funds from his enormous entertainment allowance to recruit a "special source" who, unbeknown to the attaché, was already a native employee of the CIA station chief. The employee, frightened at the demands of the military attaché, asked his CIA employer for advice. The CIA man told the employee not to worry: *he* would furnish the information sought by the military attaché. He did. For the year that followed, the military attaché received from his "special source" a series of reports, all fabricated by the CIA man, which made sense at first but gradually became wilder and wilder and eventually led his superiors in Washington to doubt his sanity. The final report, a masterpiece of "disinformation," convinced the attaché that the Syrian Deuxième Bureau was at last on to him, and that he should flee the country. He did, and was replaced by another officer, to whom the CIA station chief told the whole story—with a warning.

Apart from the fun of punishing overeager military attachés, the organizers of the CIA regarded the use of "paper" as a problem, not a contribution. When the Kingfish first opened his "lunatic projects" unit, most of the Agency's espionage specialists felt that he should clean house, and that in the meanwhile it would not be worth the trouble to refine the low-grade information then coming from spy sources. "If there is to be any fabricating to be done around here," said the Kingfish, "we'll do it ourselves rather than leave it to amateurs and crooks."

But the period during which the CIA's espionage branch had to "snow" its customers—State, the Pentagon, and even other units of the CIA—didn't last long. The confidence of its

49

members soon grew to a point at which they no longer felt they had to humor every little GS-11 who dropped in to demand information. The OSO was beginning to acquire some modern spies, and the Kingfish's unit had become so adroit in developing "alternative sources" that its officers no longer had to deceive its customers. A desk officer from State, requesting that the OSO plant a spy in the Afghan Foreign Ministry to get the details of a supposed secret agreement with the Soviets, would be treated to a stimulating review of all the possible ways besides espionage of getting that information, and would leave "K" building feeling he had been enlightened without being patronized.

THE "ALTERNATIVE MEANS"

High on the Kingfish's list of "alternative means" were American journalists. OSO officers learned early in their experience that while newspapermen had no place in espionage operations, they often knew far more than their printed reports indicated. Moreover, a journalist, unless he is extremely shortsighted, knows that he's got to keep a confidence and that it is therefore safe to exchange information with him on an off-the-record basis. In addition, the press can go places, see people, and ask questions that are out of bounds to U.S. Government officials, while, for all sorts of reasons, the President of the United States, the Secretary of State, Congressmen, and even the Director of the CIA himself will read, believe and be impressed by a report from Cy Sulzberger, Arnaud de Borchgrave, or Stewart Alsop when they won't even bother to read a CIA report on the same subject. A CIA station chief in a European capital tells me that he spends long hours in the company of leading American and British columnists who visit his country, giving them large amounts of confidential information and his interpretations of it. His purpose is to ensure that when his own reports reach Washington they will have maximum impact on his superiors—

who, he knows, will already have been swayed by articles of the columnists. Happy was the station chief who was "Robin Armbruster" when reporting under his pseudonym as CIA station chief, but was able to use his highly respected real name as he wrote pieces in his cover job as columnist for a leading syndicate. In his CIA reporting he antiseptically reported the facts, and in his columns he presented analyses which made the facts palatable. His bosses knew the station chief and the columnist were the same man, but this somehow didn't reduce the effectiveness of the one-man "team."

There is also the question of readability. President Kennedy once admitted that he based his opinions largely on what he learned from reading *The New York Times*, *The Washington Post* and *The Christian Science Monitor* over his morning coffee. Like President Eisenhower before him, he found journalists, with their freedom from bureaucratic disciplines,* much easier to read than official news summaries. President Eisenhower would rarely read an official report that was more than one page in length, yet would happily curl up with a long piece in *Foreign Affairs* or read the whole international-affairs section of a Sunday newspaper. "I wouldn't dare be even slightly discursive in my own reporting," a CIA station chief told me, "but I can give my views to someone like Jim Hoagland of *The Washington Post* or to Juan de Onis of *The New York Times*, and he can combine them with his own and write them up in a long piece mixing fact, conjecture, and opinion, and my boss in Washington will read every word."

Simple lack of courage is also a reason why many diplomats and intelligence officers pump their information and opinions through newsmen. "Our officers see Zionists, Irish nationalists, or Nationalist Chinese around every corner," a retired American ambassador told a graduate seminar at Georgetown Uni-

---

* President Kennedy once became so annoyed with the stiffness and wishy-washiness of diplomatic reports that he instructed William Atwood, then U.S. Ambassador to Kenya but previously editor of *Look* magazine, to write a booklet instructing members of the diplomatic service how to write more interesting and less ambiguous cables and dispatches.

versity, and a week later another retired American ambassador told an audience at a Middle East Association banquet, "Any diplomat who dares to suggest in his reporting that Israel is not one-hundred-percent right and the Arabs one-hundred-percent wrong is taking his career in his hands."

Whether justified or not, the fear is general. James Keeley, Minister to Syria in 1948, was demoted to the post of Consul General in Sicily for commenting "disrespectfully" on the Zionist movement; David Nes, Deputy Chief of Mission in Cairo at the time of the Six-Day War, was removed from his post and forced to resign because he chided the Department for its "uncritical" support of Israel; a young officer who remarked that Golda Meir looked "like President Johnson in drag" was reprimanded not for a slur on President Johnson but for a slur on Mrs. Meir; two senior diplomats in Arab capitals were forced to resign because of charges of moral turpitude brought to the State Department by Congressmen who had obtained them from "unnamed sources" who, upon investigation, turned out to be Zionists. There have been at least five cases, two of them involving CIA station chiefs under State Department cover, in which cleverly fabricated cases of sexual misbehavior or financial malfeasance were made out against officers who were generally believed to entertain an anti-Zionist bias.

Our diplomats' and intelligence officers' fears of Zionist influence are great; so are their fears of other nationalist lobbies. "Our diplomatic and intelligence officers hold their punches as they report on subjects which would touch on the sensitivities of minorities in this country," Allen Dulles told the CIA's Senatorial "watchdog" committee. At the same time, they release their frustrations by giving their most sensitive information to reporters such as *The Christian Science Monitor*'s John Cooley, who is not only a man of unassailable integrity but an independent reporter who can write as he pleases without fears for his future.

The special relationship the U.S. Government has with the

world's leading journalists encompasses not only the Americans, but also those of other countries, including some that are cool to the United States—for example, Mohammed Heykel of Egypt. A journalist can be as harshly critical of American policy as he likes as long as he is generous with his own information and does not misuse the information that the embassy gives him in return. Some of Heykel's most bitterly anti-American articles were based on information given him freely by the U.S. Ambassador in Cairo—but on an understanding under which Heykel reciprocated by giving the Ambassador details of other relevant information in his possession, complete with explanations as to how he got it. "In all my dealings with Heykel," Ambassador Lucius Battle told his successor, "Heykel has never on a single occasion played unfairly with me." There are "Heykels" in other capitals of Africa and Asia where anti-American sentiments prevail, and the benefit of exchange-of-information arrangements with them has in almost all cases greatly outweighed any harm to our interests that might have resulted from our enhancing the quality of their anti-American outpourings.

Anti-American outpourings bother our diplomats much less than journalists, both American and foreign, imagine they do. The officials of an embassy are rarely so stupid as to discriminate against a journalist simply because they disagree with what he writes; but the reporter who misuses "background information" given him by an embassy will from that time on get only the cold shoulder or "the party line." The same is true of the guessers who, whether irresponsibly or maliciously, report falsehoods about the Government, especially items that are supposed to be secret. The word goes out, and afterward our diplomats are on the lookout from Lima to Tokyo.

The late Drew Pearson was a favorite victim of U.S. officials who took delight in punishing journalists who wrote irresponsibly. Once, when Pearson was attending an Embassy dinner in Teheran also attended by Justice William O. Doug-

53

las, the Justice told the Ambassador a long story about how he had encountered a "Major Lincoln" during a recent expedition to the wild Kurdish country in northern Iran. According to the story, as Douglas was skewering a piece of lamb over the campfire, a man dressed as a Kurd stepped out of the darkness, introduced himself as "Major Lincoln," gave him a short oral message for the Ambassador, then disappeared as quietly as he had come. Justice Douglas then pretended to whisper the message into the Ambassador's ear. On the basis of what he overheard, Pearson wrote a piece in his column, *Washington Merry-Go-Round,* which was picked up by many leading newspapers in the Middle East. At the time, I was serving as political attaché in the U.S. Legation, Damascus, Syria. Since the French Embassies in the Middle East knew from their intelligence records that I had used the alias "Major Lincoln" during World War II,* they promptly assumed that it was I whom Justice Douglas had seen wandering about northern Iran in fancy dress; their inquiries to the Iranian, Turkish, Iraqi, and other security services brought the suspicions of the whole world of Middle East intrigue onto me. I diverted the suspicions by passing the word through friends in the Syrian, Lebanese, and Egyptian security services that the real "Major Lincoln" was not myself but my friend Colonel Steve Meade, a CIA officer-at-large operating from Beirut; but until the word was spread I was under intensive surveillance, and sometimes in danger of being kidnapped or killed.

All journalists who pride themselves on being crusaders and specialists in exposés, and who exploit leaks from disgruntled government employees, are constantly the victims of hoaxes, some even more farfetched than the "Major Lincoln" story but most of them much more credible and subtle. The journalist of good reputation, though, who is helpful to our embassies is handled almost as though he enjoyed a TOP SECRET

---

* When I later chided Justice Douglas for having used my old cryptonym, "Major Lincoln," he said he had forgotten this had been my alias, and that he had just used the first name that popped into his head. Possibly it had bubbled up from his subconscious.

security clearance—a "need to know" clearance, that is.* Once he gains acceptance, he learns something that those who remain on the outside find it hard to imagine: that the ordinary embassy officer has at his fingertips more important inside information in one day's cable traffic than even the best journalist could pull together in six months. From then on, what he gets in exchange for his helpfulness is more than a fair bargain.

The Kingfish was quick to recognize the value of good relations with reputable journalists. Shortly after his unit began work, he convinced his superiors that they should direct CIA station chiefs to set up means for systematically filing the by-products acquired by embassies from the journalists with whom they were in contact, and work them into periodic summaries to be sent to Washington in suitably classified and sanitized form. The system not only made available to the CIA masses of information from the world's most skilled observers, but gave our diplomatic reports stores of footnotes which they could use to support their own reporting. The system was of great benefit to the journalists themselves as well: just after the coup d'état in Iraq in July, 1947, the leading American and British newsmen in Beirut came to the Embassy seeking back-

---

* The British are extremely class-conscious in their differentiation between journalists: for example, reporters from the sensationalist press, typified by "Tullback Brown" in Nicholas Monserrat's *The Tribe That Lost Its Head,* are received coolly by British Embassies, while such journalists as Robert Stephens of *The Observer,* David Holden of *The Sunday Times,* Paul Martin of *The Times,* and Clare Hollingworth and John Bulloch of *The Telegraph* are dealt with as though they are visiting royalty, and the exchange of confidences with them is at a very high level. Kim Philby, when he was in Beirut reporting for *The Observer* and *The Economist,* was so treated. If he got confidential information from the British Embassy it was as a trusted journalist, not as a former member of SIS or some kind of "double agent." Moreover, he got the information strictly on a "need to know" basis—that is, he was told only what it suited the purposes of the Embassy to tell him in order to improve the quality not only of the one-tenth he would report, but of the nine-tenths that he would make available to the Embassy. It happens, he wasn't told much. If his Soviet masters were impressed by it, they were truly hard up for information.

ground information on the two unknown leaders of the coup, Abd-el Kerim Kassim and Abd-el Salam Aref. The CIA station chief was able to give it to them—on the basis of information the journalists themselves had turned in on earlier trips to Baghdad and had then forgotten.

The OSO started the "by-product" project and held on to it for some years. Although it was hardly an appropriate function of an espionage organization, the Kingfish and his superiors liked to control it because they could then milk it for "operational data"—i.e., information that is required in the planning of operations, especially espionage operations. In time it became one of the most fruitful "alternative means" of getting intelligence information and, therefore, a strong factor in their campaign to cut the requirements on espionage down to reasonable proportions. Although this was little realized at the time and has now been forgotten by OSO old-timers themselves, the OSO spent considerable time in its early days thinking of ways to beef up the effectiveness of "alternative means" for no purpose other than to get out of having to exercise its specialty, espionage.

At that time the researchers at State, the Pentagon, and the CIA were already doing very well without the Kingfish's help. They had learned that scientists—even Soviet scientists—can't be kept from publishing, and that even the most carefully censored public documents, including such simple items as printed instructions on mechanical objects, even toys, inevitably include clues to secrets. It took the OSO to discover and to point out how the tightest security controls imaginable cannot entirely conceal the movements of personages who have any social life at all, and that masses of harmless personal chitchat, when analyzed by a computer, reveal patterns of personnel assignments and movements which the Soviets may be trying to keep secret. It was also the OSO's experimenters who discovered that we all have unique, undisguisable habits of speech and writing which, if studied, become as recognizable as fingerprints. By examining masses of printed materials, they were able to conclude who was writing what, even when it was signed with pen names.* Today, it is at least partly thanks to the Kingfish and his assistants that the study of nonsecret trade journals, directories, official memoranda, and the like is one of the most productive means of acquiring secret information.

The Kingfish, and the others who helped start his "lunatic projects" unit, also deserve credit for having brought the Agency's art of "creative intelligence" to its present high degree of effectiveness. "If this is so, then that must be so" has long been a standard reasoning tool of the intelligence analyst. But the Kingfish's experts, drilled through the war years in the art of deducing the secret activities of German spies by studying their overt "cover" behavior, were able to add new dimensions. In a CIA classroom exercise, students were each given a key, a doll, a sheaf of shipping papers held together by a paper clip, and two or three more such objects and asked to develop "creative intelligence" by examining them. The students, all experienced researchers, listed an extraordinary range of inferences. Then they were shown the list of inferences developed by the Kingfish's unit from the same objects. It had on it detailed conclusions with respect not only to where the items had come from, but to where the raw material had originated, how they had been manufactured, and the technical capabilities such manufacture represented. In addition, conclusions were listed on the psychology, personality, character, and intentions of the instructors who chose the objects.

Then there was "gaming." Various independent units throughout the intelligence community, including those offi-

---

* Some years later, after the National Security Agency had taken over this kind of analysis (by counting word frequencies and studying habitual sentence structures—with computers, of course), application of the technique applied to a series of three articles in *Playboy* magazine pointed unmistakably to an outwardly somewhat straitlaced Washington bureaucrat writing under an alias. Also, by way of demonstrating the effectiveness of the technique, NSA experts correctly identified the author of some humorous materials written over an assumed name by the economist John Kenneth Galbraith, then Ambassador to India.

cers in the strategic-intelligence school, were experimenting with mathematical and nonmathematical game theories for the purpose of figuring out what completely rational governments would do under given circumstances. The theory behind most of these experiments was that each national "player" would do whatever was in his national interest. The Kingfish and his group introduced the idea that every "player" is playing not one game, but three: the international game: the United States versus the Soviets versus France versus Britain versus all the other nations of the world sitting around a sort of Chinese checkers board; the domestic game: Republicans versus Democrats, or Conservatives versus Labor, or one Communist faction versus another; and a personal game, in which each man advances his own interests. It was suggested that many moves in the international game—indeed, *most* moves in that game—are not genuine moves in that game at all but mere reflections of moves in the domestic game which may, in turn, be at least partly reflections of moves in various personal games.

With these thoughts in mind, the Kingfish's unit introduced the element of "Method acting" into game play. Instead of figuring out, by computer and other impersonal methods, what a national leader *should* do, the players should put themselves in the shoes of the real-life "players" in the way a "Method" actor puts himself in the shoes of a character he is playing. Using extremely sophisticated character studies of the world's key leaders at the time—Konrad Adenauer, Charles de Gaulle, and the like—the CIA players were given leads upon which they could build their assumed characters. With a bit of "creative intelligence" thrown in, they would wind up with a combination of impersonations in their game rooms that could simulate real-life international conflicts, which included domestic and personal conflicts, with amazing accuracy. The CIA "peace game center" that emerged * was by no

---

* See my book *The Game of Nations*. London: Weidenfeld & Nicholson, 1969; New York: Simon and Schuster, 1970.

means an OSO project; it was not even a CIA project, although a CIA officer presided over it. But the Kingfish and his assistants can take credit for having raised it to the highly sophisticated level it finally attained, and for continuing to supply it with the data that made realistic impersonations possible.

The CIA's espionage branch, in order to divest itself of all but really essential requirements, contributed as much as any other element of the intelligence community to the development of "alternative means." We cannot pass the subject without mentioning the particular contribution of the OSO chief Lyman Kirkpatrick, known to his subordinates as "Kirk" or "our aging bright young man." When Kirk was put in charge of the espionage branch (in 1950, by General Bedell Smith), he introduced to its weird world of Byzantine cunning real no-nonsense managerial talent of a kind this type of organization rarely sees. While he placed no curb on all the intriguing, he did systematize it and put an end to the intrigue-for-the-sake-of-intrigue that is endemic in any espionage organization. He so effectively backed the Kingfish's efforts to develop "alternatives" that the OSO's assignments could thenceforth be confined entirely to those which were indisputably essential to national security, and which were within the CIA's recognized capabilities.

Various books about the CIA and its so-called "invisible government" have alleged that the CIA attempts to make "spies" out of ordinary citizens who are about to travel abroad, by swearing them to secrecy and telling them to be on the lookout for certain information. In its early days, the CIA was without espionage assets or any other means for getting even the simplest information from areas denied to official travelers. Zealous officers would take advantage, in any way they could, of tourists, students, and businessmen who were planning trips into those areas and who might, in the course of their travels, observe items of intelligence interest. It didn't take the Agency's operations staff long to learn, however, that approaching travelers *before* they left for the U.S.S.R., Poland, Yugoslavia, or wherever had certain dangers. One elderly couple—missionaries, if I remember correctly—were so horrified at being asked to become "common spies" that they went first to their Congressman, then to a crusading columnist, and once again the Agency's jittery top officials were treated to vilifying headlines over their morning coffee. Another traveler, a young man, went to Russia, played James Bond all over the place, and came back to go on a tour with a lecture, "I Spied for Uncle Sam." (I am told that he didn't even bother to drop by the Agency for a debriefing.) Another, not so lucky, got drunk in a Moscow bar, confided in a stage whisper to a KGB girl who had been assigned to him that "I'm really not a student at all, but a G-man," and spent a few weeks shoveling salt in Siberia before the U.S. Consul obtained his release. All in all, the Agency's attempts to get information from travelers on a basis of prior briefing brought more grief than worthwhile results.

Before coming to the OSO, Kirkpatrick had been head of an Agency division that was responsible for all contact with Americans traveling abroad, and he had so systematized the procedures that the dangers were removed. When he came to the OSO, he issued orders that from then on the OSO would use only genuine agents even for the simplest observations behind the Iron Curtain. Since there were regulations already in effect that forbade the employment of U.S. citizens as agents, with rare exceptions which had to be cleared by the Director himself, Kirkpatrick's order took the OSO out of the tourist business altogether. As he imposed the orders, he passed on highly imaginative and constructive suggestions as to how the Agency's overt-contacts division—and the State Department, and all others in contact with travelers—could upgrade the quality of travelers' information without making the travelers liable to the charge of espionage in the countries they visit.*

---

* If a traveler is briefed by his country's intelligence agency before he goes abroad, his observations may constitute espionage in some countries even if what he sees is in no way secret. If he is not so briefed, however,

In another measure that eased the burden of requirements placed on the OSO, Kirkpatrick changed the "cover" role of OSO personnel serving in embassies and consulates. While it can hardly be said that Kirk ever became the darling of the State Department, most of the Department's officials who were directly concerned with State–CIA relations had to admit that he had done more to improve these relations than any other one person. Until he took an interest in the problem, CIA station chiefs were virtually independent of their ambassadors, and they made no pretense of carrying out any of the regular embassy duties that were to provide their cover. During Kirk's tenure, all CIA station personnel began not only to take their cover functions seriously, but to use their CIA work to enhance the effectiveness of the embassy. Instead of using their cover assignments as entrée to local officials they might recruit as agents, they were instructed to use their know-how and special knowledge to enhance the ambassador's chances of developing these same officials as regular diplomatic sources.

Since Kirkpatrick's motives were hardly altruistic, the co-operation worked both ways. An ambassador and a station chief working closely together would sometimes find it more in the interest of the U.S. Government to keep an official of the local government entirely on a "straight" basis, even though he might happily have become a CIA agent if asked, and at other times would find that one or another of the ambassador's "straight" contacts should be turned into a long-range career agent.

It is often alleged that the CIA allows—or instructs—its station chiefs to take actions without the knowledge of their ambassadors, and that the ambassador's authority is a "polite fiction." I would agree with Seymour Freidin and George

---

but is merely interviewed upon his return, he is not made retroactively guilty of espionage. The OSO has developed ways of so stimulating travelers before their departures that, without knowing that they will later be interviewed, they will be on the lookout for items they might otherwise not notice.

Bailey's rebuttal to this allegation * and say that those who made it could not be acquainted with very many American ambassadors. If there is ever a facade of independence covering a CIA station, it is always for some reason with which the ambassador sympathizes. Take, for example, the situation that existed in Egypt during the two years I was assigned to advise President Gamal Abdel Nasser's security services. CIA cooperation was required, because some of the techniques and equipment could be provided only by the CIA. Nasser appreciated this, and so did the U.S. Ambassador, Jefferson Caffery. However, it suited the purposes of both Nasser and Caffery to keep the arrangement entirely apart from Egyptian–American diplomatic relations. The CIA station chief told Caffery all he wanted to know about the CIA's aid program, but it wasn't much. When Caffery was succeeded as Ambassador by Henry Byroade, the situation changed: Byroade wanted to be kept informed on a day-to-day basis, and he was. In both cases it was the Ambassador who decided what degree of independence the station chief was to have, not the station chief himself.

The innovation with which Kirkpatrick most dramatically reduced the requirements load on espionage was the "sneaky." In early 1952, the OSO personnel officer received a telephone call from a mysterious voice which said, "Stand back from your wall clock. It's about to blow up." In seconds, it did. The explosion was only a light *pfft!*—but it could just as easily have been as powerful as the explosion of a letter bomb. It had obviously been set off by remote control from outside the office, by someone who could time it to the second. Later in the day, a member of the OSO staff who was Kirk's gimmickry expert and who was known internally as "Jojo" repeated the demonstration in Kirkpatrick's office, showing that a miniature bomb, planted in a split second with a piece of chewing gum, could be set off by a radio signal given from an automobile a

---

* See *The Experts* by Seymour Freidin and George Bailey. New York: Macmillan, 1968.

quarter of a mile away.* Admittedly, it would have been somewhat harder to get inside a really important office than to get into Personnel, where dozens of noncleared people come every day for interviews, but it wouldn't be *much* harder, since almost any executive office of the Agency receives *some* outside visitors who don't have security clearances.

A week or so later, a Japanese electronics expert who was a longtime friend of the CIA station in Tokyo invited Jojo and some of his staff to his suite in the Mayflower Hotel, on Washington's Connecticut Avenue, to see what he called "an exhibition." After he had shown them into the room and served them drinks, the Japanese asked, "Well, what do you think of them?"

"What do we think of what?"

"Look for yourself."

Jojo and his assistants, all skilled in gadgetry and the art of search, saw nothing even after they searched the room. They gave up. The Japanese then pointed out twenty or more items —ashtrays, lamps, pens, etc.—that contained means of emitting radio sounds which could not be detected by counterintelligence devices then in use. "They are to transistors what transistors are to radio tubes," Jojo later told Kirkpatrick.

Eventually, the Japanese and his exhibit were sent along to the National Security Agency, the intelligence organization that has primary responsibility for electronic gadgetry. But before doing so, the man instructed Jojo and his staff to look into other small, out-of-the-way devices that were within the country's scientific capability but were not being manufactured

---

* In 1954, when Egyptian engineers were completing the construction of a tower that Nasser had ordered built as a means of throwing $3 million back in the faces of his CIA friends (see *The Game of Nations*), CIA technicians on hand managed to smuggle into the tower's basement a wad of explosives attached to a radio receiver which, upon a signal sent from a radio transmitter on a ship far out in the Mediterranean, would blow up the whole structure. Two years later, when the U.S. Government was cross with Nasser for his seizure of the Suez Canal, Secretary Dulles ordered that the explosives be set off, but they had been found and defused by an officer of the Egyptian *Mukhabarat*.

because there was no commercial demand. The results were astounding; they included not only electronic items but medical, chemical, and even psychological items. Within months, devices developed by the OSO's own technicians, on the basis of inventions that IBM, General Electric, Westinghouse, Du Pont, Squibb, Pfizer, and other such companies had buried deep in their copyright safes because they were of no immediate commercial value, included the following:

—A chemically treated handkerchief which, after one minute of exposure to the open air, would pick up traces of factory fumes that could later be accurately analyzed and identified;

—Desk sponges (for wetting stamps) which would pick up traces of "body chemistry" so accurately that, upon later analysis, they would reveal what persons (or what kind of persons) had been in the room during the period of exposure;

—Really effective truth drugs, which would dramatically lower a persons "discretion threshold" without his being aware of it;

—Wireless and batteryless sending sets which, although too weak to transmit intelligible voice sounds, would emit tones that could reflect changes in the nature of activity in areas where they were planted;

—Undetectable chemicals and bacteria which would induce anything from a mild headache to a hallucination, and which could be transmitted in an ordinary letter;

—Several variations of LSD;

—A variety of minuscule microphones, virtually undetectable, except by experts who know exactly what to look for.

And a dozen others. By the time Kirkpatrick was ready to release the finds to the NSA, dozens of practical uses had been devised for them—most of which would involve "technical espionage" of kinds that were only partly the province of the OSO.

Kirk left the OSO in July, 1952, having come down with a serious case of polio contracted during a trip he and I made through the Middle East and Southeast Asia a month earlier, but before doing so he left explicit instructions that before OSO planners accepted an espionage requirement, they would "assume the role of devil's advocate and *prove* that the requirement cannot be fulfilled by alternative means." The "alternative means" he specified were:

1. The press, trade journals, and other published materials plus any incidental information that can be obtained in interviews with the authors;

2. Common sense—referred to professionally as "creative intelligence";

3. Diplomatic reporting and official liaison—"Before you decide to spy on the Ministry of Defense, at least have the military attaché call on some official there to see if he can't get the information legally";

4. The National Security Agency;

5. The *Encyclopaedia Britannica*—an "alternative means" of which Kirkpatrick was especially fond, presumably because he is one of its contributors on military history, military science, and one or two other subjects.

Only after satisfying themselves that these "alternative means"—to be applied by intelligence units other than the OSO—could not sufficiently fulfill the requirement, would OSO planners give the go-ahead for the development of an espionage operation.

SO WHAT WAS LEFT FOR SPIES TO DO?

Even after the most drastic cutting of OSO requirements, there were enough assignments left to give espionage operations more than they could handle. The priorities have shifted back and forth during the past twenty-odd years, but the main categories of requirements heaped upon the OSO are these:

Information on foreign espionage activity: Partly because the OSO started out under the domination of X-2's counter-espionage specialists, partly because the OSO is now the *only* intelligence unit with facilities to acquire information under this category,* and partly because of the string of spy scares that have persisted throughout the years, this item has remained near the top of each year's list of priorities. The OSO, like the espionage services of Great Britain, the U.S.S.R., and France, spends more time spying on the spies of other nations than it does on Soviet missile installations. Kim Philby's book, *My Silent War,* gives an excellent picture of the way in which spies spy on spies, admitting that his main contribution to the Soviet intelligence effort was the identification of Soviet agents who were identifying British agents to the SIS. And the contribution of Michael Goleniewski, the CIA agent who eventually exposed Philby, was the identification of Soviet and other Bloc agents who were identifying CIA and SIS agents to the Soviets. All this incest seems hardly justified until from time to time a spy is uncovered who has broken the circle and is operating against some scientific or military target, or until there is a mix-up that Mother, or his British or Soviet equivalent, can parlay into a system of crossed wires and then control for puposes of "Deception," as described in Chapter 5.†

"Pieces": This term, presumably derived from that misleading phrase "pieces of the jigsaw puzzle," was used frequently by intelligence analysts before the jigsaw-puzzle analogy was proved to be inexact. A "piece" is an item of information which, although seemingly unimportant in itself, is required to make some other piece of information clear or to verify some possibly misleading bit of evidence obtained through

---

* The FBI relinquished its overseas counterespionage posts to the OSO in 1945.
† Philby, who knew Mother well and who hinted at his identity in his book, is reported to have told his Soviet debriefers that "Foreign agencies spying on the U.S. Government know exactly what one certain person in CIA wants them to know, and no more and no less."

some means other than espionage. The CIA once directed the OSO to "find out the purpose of that mosquelike tower next to the communications center at Karaganda in Kazakhstan," because one possibility that occurred to interpreters of satellite photographs at the National Photographic Center was that the center wasn't an ordinary communications center at all, but something vastly more important. It turned out that the tower had been constructed by the Soviets specifically for the purpose of flushing out the OSO and SIS spies in the vicinity—but this is nonetheless a valid example of the kind of "piece" that espionage operators might be asked to seek out.

Another "piece" would be the present whereabouts of some Soviet scientist known to have unique qualifications; such information would indicate that, regardless of external appearances, a certain type of scientific inquiry is going on at the place in question. The OSO was once ordered to determine the type of electric current, the type of sockets, and the electrical peculiarities of a remote Siberian village on which such information was strangely missing. The reason was that a team of NSA technical specialists had to get into the area secretly, attach some special equipment to local outlets, then get out before they were observed. On another occasion, the OSO was required to plant an agent in a Soviet supply depot just to count the ups and downs in the supply of white mice to a nearby military laboratory—such a statistic being an important "piece" in the picture of Soviet biological-warfare capabilities.

Information on denied areas: Some of these examples suggest that there are many OSO agents who do not penetrate targets in the manner of the Soviet Emilys, Mickeys and Willies, but who roam at large in denied areas. Although "alternative means" gather almost all the information our Government needs on factories, missile sites, military sites, and other such targets which are outside of capitals and metropolitan areas, the OSO still has to use on-the-ground observation. Although for this purpose it does not require espionage

67

of the conventional sort, it often uses "agent" personnel of a kind that can best be recruited, trained, and supported by the OSO. Since in recent years pressures have so increased on other intelligence agencies (mainly the Defense Intelligence Agency) to stop dropping American personnel into denied areas such as China and the U.S.S.R., the OSO is now the only intelligence unit in the U.S. Government that regularly takes on this requirement.

Drawing boards: Only a few years ago, scientific espionage —peeking at the other side's drawing board—was item number one on the priority list of any great power's espionage service. Fuchs, Coplon, May, and most of the other publicized Soviet spies of the Forties and Fifties were after atomic secrets. So were the unpublicized American and British spies in the Soviet Union. By now, each side is so aware of the other's capabilities that "alternative means" are quite sufficient to keep track of most of what each country needs to know about the scientific progress of the others. *Plans* for progress are another matter. No satellite or "sneaky" can get into the mind of a scientist—or even, except in rare cases, see his drawing board or "classified waste" basket. So the OSO, like all major intelligence services, directs a considerable amount of effort at what amounts to "industrial espionage" and employs techniques much the same as some business firms use in spying on their competitors. In obtaining American or British scientific plans, the Soviets use industrial-espionage organizations as fronts, and any poor "Willie" who thinks he is spying on Company X for the benefit of Company Y will do well to contemplate the possibility that he is actually an agent of the Soviet intelligence service.

There are no private corporations inside the Soviet Bloc, so American and British espionage services are unable to use exactly the same approach. They can, however, take advantage of the extent to which Bloc agencies spy on one another, and use approaches remarkably similar to the Soviets' use of industrial fronts. In 1956, when there was mounting anti-Soviet feeling in Czechoslovakia, the CIA station chief in

Prague used one of his senior agents, a colonel in the Soviet military mission, to organize a complete network of agents in the Czech industries, making them think they were working for a special section of the KGB. The ostensible mission of the network—the one the agents thought they were performing for the KGB—was to monitor Czech scientific establishments to detect instances in which the Czechs were concealing their inventions and their progress from the Soviets; their real mission—the one they were unknowingly performing for the CIA—was to acquire details of Czech–Soviet exchanges of secret scientific information. Since the Czechs were far ahead of the Soviets in many fields of science, penetration of scientific offices of their industries could have produced information of enormous value. It didn't, because the operation was blown at the time of the Soviet invasion, but it survived long enough to prove that the concept was sound, and it has subsequently been imitated elsewhere. A senior officer in the OSO's Eastern Europe Division boasted to his counterpart in the SIS that the CIA's industrial operations run "under KGB cover" were far superior to the KGB's real ones, which he knew about from having penetrated them. "If we could somehow teach the KGB to improve their methods," he said, "we would be able to get rid of these tiresome Willies."

Operational data: One alternative means, the use of sneakies, sometimes requires ordinary espionage agents either to guide their placement or actually to install them. Since many sneakies require a certain amount of upkeep, including in some cases the recharging of batteries, OSO agents are often used on a continuing basis to maintain them. "Crash units"— groups of technicians who sweep into a place commando style, install sets of sneakies, then get out again the way the "plumbers" were supposed to do at Watergate—are often specialists who are brought in from outside the espionage services. Since upkeep requires constant access which can be maintained only by techniques peculiar to the straight espionage business, the job of maintenance is almost always assigned to the espionage branch.

Assignment to one of these crash units, it happens, is a very popular one. The OSO technicians who move into and out of Georgia, Armenia, and Azerbaijan are of course natives of those republics, and they enjoy visits "back home" with the relatives who hide them out, while spending their off hours in comfortable living quarters in Turkey or Iran. The technicians who service installations in China have a harder time of it, because they are ordinarily parachuted in from faraway bases and otherwise have greater risks to run. All the same, like their Russian counterparts, they are able to visit relatives, and to smuggle food and luxuries to them, and sometimes to smuggle out objects of value which bring good prices in Hong Kong. I am told that the major disciplinary problem of these crash units is not smuggling but bigamy. Several cases have been uncovered of technicians' keeping wives inside the U.S.S.R. or China while there are other wives waiting for them in Ankara, Teheran, or Seoul. After spending three years in a Russian jail—for smuggling, not for espionage—an agent in a crash unit on the "milk run to Samarkand" demanded back allowance for *three* wives, arguing that, as an Uzbeki and a Moslem, he was entitled to at least that many.

Early warning: Finally, there is the Pentagon's system of "early-warning signals" which involves requirements for *all* the U.S. Government's information-gathering agencies, the OSO included. No matter what secrecy a great power is able to maintain, there are certain actions it *must* take before launching a major military action. Our intelligence system maintains millions of dollars' worth of electronic equipment, from high-powered detectors which are to radar what radar was to telescopes all the way down to swarms of sneakies so numerous and so well hidden that "the enemy" could never find them all or jam even a fraction. Yet there are certain "signals" that can be seen only with the naked eye—for example, hour-by-hour movements of persons in "enemy" governments, not necessarily top decision makers, who are the ones involved in "pressing the button." Since agents used for the purpose of fulfilling the early-warning requirement, like any observers on "long watch" duty, tend to grow lax, the OSO assigns them missions just to keep them busy and alert. But the justification for their continued employment is to maintain an up-to-date ability to spot the "early warning signals" assigned to them.

THE ESPIONAGE BRANCH'S MONOPOLY

The "requirements" of an intelligence organization are the ends it is supposed to achieve; its "operations" are the means. Since the considerations that have made OSO operations what they are also affect every nation's espionage branches, the following types of operation might be said to be typical of them all:

1. *Conventional espionage:* By "conventional espionage" we mean espionage conducted by recruiting of career agents who are *inside* their assigned targets (like "Emily," "Mickey," Philby and "Willie") to regularly photocopy secret documents of unquestionable authenticity. In almost every modern country, the responsibility for conducting operations of this type is entrusted to a single agency. Other intelligence agencies, despite the sometimes tremendous pressures on them to do so, are normally restrained from engaging in espionage beyond the level of employing casual informants—and the espionage branches of the great services resist even this form of competition. This is certainly true in the American and British intelligence communities, and, increasingly, in the Soviet. In the United States, the CIA is constantly battling with the Defense Department because this or that military attaché has employed an "informant" in such a way as to jeopardize the OSO's true espionage operations. If the military attaché really needs an espionage operation to cover his assigned targets, he is supposed to work with his OSO colleague in setting it up. He may participate in the operation as a "cutout" or "case officer," but the appropriate OSO officer retains control of the operation, and integrates it into the overall operation pattern of the area to which he is assigned. The military, air, or naval

71

attaché who wants to play James Bond is a menace—not only to the CIA's espionage branch, but to the whole intelligence effort of his government. Fortunately, he is only a routine menace: CIA station chiefs long ago figured out ways of booby-trapping overeager service attachés so that they hang themselves before they cause any real trouble. The less squeamish Soviets and the French—and even the British— deal with "unauthorized espionage operations" more directly.

2. *Counterespionage:* The espionage branch normally has exclusive responsibility for "positive" counterespionage operations—that is, the active penetration or manipulation of foreign espionage systems, as opposed to the purely defensive, preventive measures that come under the headings of "security" or "counterintelligence." In some intelligence organizations, "counterespionage" includes the security of the organization's own espionage operations—for example, all those measures required to ensure that the operations have not been penetrated by the opposition's counterespionage operations. In other countries this kind of security is the responsibility of the organization's security branch that deals with *all* its security problems. The reason for this more conservative approach is a fear that the espionage branch may be tempted to cover up its own bloopers or, in the interest of "getting things done," take chances that it might not take were an outside security branch looking over its shoulder. The espionage branch's counterespionage ("CE") specialists have their hands full with the task of simply confounding foreign espionage services—or, ideally, of ensuring that the foreign services acquire only such information as the branch's superiors wish them to have.

3. *"Third World" operations:* This category of operation conducted by the espionage branches of the American and British services and, in its own way, of the Soviet service is frequently incredible. As is generally now known, the CIA often receives assignments that lie outside its charter simply because it is one of the few U. S. Government agencies with unvouchered funds at their disposal. (Subsidizing student

72

groups is an example: the CIA has only marginal, if any, direct interest in such groups.) Within the CIA, the espionage branch (OSO) often finds itself saddled with responsibilities that are far removed from the conventional operations to which it would like to devote its full attention.

Although it would be impossible for me or anyone else to convince the numerous governments of the Third World that the great Western and Soviet powers do not consider them worth penetrating, the fact is that were it not for the "struggle for the Third World" which Third World politicians actively encourage and exploit, there probably wouldn't be a single intelligence station in South America, Africa, or most of Asia. When President Harry S. Truman let it be known that the fifth paragraph of the National Security Act which created the CIA was to be interpreted broadly, and that the United States was to hold its own in all aspects of the Cold War, many Third World officials began figuring out ways to play the United States and the Soviets against each other. Since they had to do their "playing" secretly, it was normal procedure for them to make contact with both sides via their intelligence services. The CIA, like the British, the French, and the Soviet services, set up a separate "political action" branch (the OPC) —and, for obvious reasons, kept it separate from the espionage branch, at least at the operating level. It wasn't long before the espionage branch had to open field stations of its own just to acquire the information needed to guide the political-action operations. As the CIA's operations in the Third World expanded, so did those of the other countries.

At present, the CIA's espionage branch has some sixty "stations" in Third World countries, the Soviets about the same number, and the British and the French each about half of that. They are all up to their ears in espionage operations which are largely useless except as a means of tying up a lot of Third World politicians who might otherwise be occupied in really harmful activity. They are obvious exceptions to the "vital to national security" restrictions, but nobody seems to care—least of all the local governments.

73

4. *Special Operations:* In spite of the desire of most espionage specialists to deal only in conventional operations, irresistible opportunities to run effective unconventional operations do occasionally arise. While Kirkpatrick was goading his espionage specialists to figure out ways in which the intelligence requirements of the U.S. Government could be fulfilled by nonespionage methods, he was also pressing them to figure out new—and less costly and less dangerous—ways of conducting ordinary espionage operations. Under such encouragement, two shortcuts were developed: the use of espionage operations run by various émigré groups (Ukrainian, Lithuanian, Cuban, or whatever), and the broad-net approach to potential defectors. Under the latter, a general appeal would be made to literally *all* Soviet, Bloc, and Chinese officials and officials of certain other countries urging them to pull up stakes and flee to the West. Both these shortcuts involve headaches that the old professionals particularly dislike, but they work reasonably well and they are comparatively inexpensive, both in financial cost and, if properly handled, in security risk.

5. *Liaison:* A comparatively inexpensive and safe means of conducting espionage operations is to induce local security agencies to run them for you. The major Western services all encourage local services—not only in Europe and Japan but also in Third World countries—to run operations against Soviet and Bloc installations in their countries and to turn over the results. The Soviets, wherever possible, follow a similar policy, although they apparently are less successful. They have difficulties even in countries whose governments' policies are in tune with their own, because security officials in *all* countries tend, like army officers, to be right-wing politically, and generally suspicious of what they understand of Soviet ideology. They do, however, have a measure of success in those countries whose security services are run by sly types who believe they can operate with both sides at the same time—e.g., Algeria and Egypt. They sometimes have more success than they believe. A friend of mine in the KGB office in Cairo

74

admitted to me his belief that the CIA secretly controlled his liaison arrangements with the Egyptian general intelligence agency—the *Mukhabarat el-Aam*—and manipulated it to the advantage of the U.S. Government, although the truth was that the CIA was oblivious of these arrangements until the KGB officer admitted them to me. In fact, the CIA station chief refused to believe they existed until some bumbler in the *Mukhabarat* mixed up the tapes of telephone taps the Egyptians had done for the CIA with similar ones it had made for the KGB. It was only when he ran the tapes and heard the Western twang of the Administrative Officer scolding the native kavass for having washed the coffeepots in the urinal that he realized I had informed him correctly.

THE ESPIONAGE BRANCH AND REVOLUTION

Whether staffed by leftists or rightist personnel, intelligence and security services tend to be counterrevolutionary forces. Although it is fashionable in some countries to call them "a weapon to seek out and destroy enemies of the revolution"— or a "counter-counterrevolutionary force" *—the fact is that their functions are related to the preservation of the government in power, whatever its political leanings. They are firmly a part of "the establishment."

The fact that an espionage service is both counterrevolutionary and secret calls up memories of the secret police used by totalitarian regimes to combat dissenters: arrest without warrant, detainment without trial, the use of torture. One should remember, however, that in a democratic country the obligation of the service is not to those in power as persons but to the offices they hold. A service has no obligation to report to individuals what they want to hear, or to report to them what they need to keep them in power.

That the FBI and the CIA see their obligations in this way was brought out clearly in the Watergate hearings. As Presi-

---

* to quote Libya's Colonel Qadhafi.

dent of the United States, Richard Nixon was concerned about the wave of riots, campus disturbances, and other forms of violence that had been sweeping the nation, and he wanted to determine whether or not there was any pattern to them and any backing from abroad. It would have served his purpose as the Republican candidate for President to have proof that there *was* a pattern to all the violence, that it was backed by foreign powers, and that its perpetrators were sympathetic to his political opponents. The FBI and the CIA were happy to oblige Nixon as President of the United States but not as Republican candidate. To start with, they were able to find but little concrete evidence to support their suspicions that terrorist groups in the United States were tied to one another or to foreign governments. They reported their findings to the President—*as* the President. Then, when it became apparent that White House aides were making no distinction between Mr. Nixon's informational needs as President and his needs as a Presidential candidate, they began to withhold what little information they *did* have.

According to various journalists at the time of the Watergate revelations, the CIA reported in 1969 and again in 1970 that radical groups in the United States had no connection with similar groups in other parts of the world, received no support from abroad, and were "homegrown, indigenous responses to perceived grievances and problems that had been growing for years." The fact is, however, that the CIA has consistently argued that there *must* be working arrangements between the most important terrorist groups abroad, that there are overwhelming indications that this is the case (including detailed information on many terrorist actions that would have been impossible without international cooperation), but that it has so far been unable to determine the exact nature of this cooperation. The FBI has reported substantially the same with respect to domestic terrorist groups, and in the last months of his life FBI Director J. Edgar Hoover made several public statements on their dangers, calling attention to the fact that they would not have been able to operate as they did without international connections.

The CIA and the FBI have not belittled President Nixon's fears of radical groups; the thrust of their reporting is not that the groups are essentially harmless and independent of one another, but that we need to know more about them. Whatever they may have said in their few public statements on the subject, both agencies believe that extremist groups hiding within the so-called "New Left" are a much greater danger to the security of both the United States and Britain than the old Soviet-directed Communist parties ever were.

As the New Left fights the American "establishment," it is the FBI and the CIA that fight back. There are three features of the assault of New Left extremists on our institutions that make it difficult for the FBI and CIA side.

The first is that there is no single international New Left "organization" susceptible to penetration with Emilys, Mickeys, Willies, and agents of other standard types. "New Left targets don't sit still long enough to let us penetrate them," a CIA case officer told his superiors. The old Communist Party, penetrated from the top to the bottom by the FBI, had cells with permanent membership, command channels through which orders were received from Moscow, and informational channels through which bits of information were passed back up the line. In addition, there were sidetracks leading to KGB representatives in various Soviet and satellite diplomatic installations in the United States and neighboring countries. Despite all its secrecy, the FBI had no difficulty in planting agents at all levels of the system. Similarly, by the late 1950's the CIA had penetrated most Communist parties throughout the world, as well as the KGB espionage units that were their outgrowths. Extremist groups associated with the New Left, however, are made up of intellectual transients who receive their "instructions" unilaterally from "sources of inspiration" rather than organizational leaders, and who commit their acts of terrorism not in obedience to orders passed down from above but as a matter of ad hoc planning. Even their "sources of inspiration" often don't know who they are.

The second difficulty of intelligence and security services as they try to keep track of New Left extremists arises from the fact that a high percentage of their spokesmen, and even of their activists, are by no means agents of foreign powers. It has by now been established, by the "word-count" method I mentioned earlier, that what New Left leaders say and do in the United States and Britain is closely related both in content and in timing to what New Left leaders are saying and doing elsewhere in the world. There is unquestionably a well-coordinated "people's war against imperialism and capitalism" from which the Soviets and the Chinese—or both—benefit. Moreover, all New Left leaders, whether they are paid agents of the Soviets or intellectual independents, behave exactly as though they were playing key roles in a unified movement. Singling out the genuine "baddies," however, is extraordinarily difficult. In the days of Senator Joseph McCarthy, the ratio of dupes to Communists taking orders from Moscow was about five to one. According to recent information, however, the agents of foreign powers make up less than one out of a hundred members of New Left organizations, and they are not conspicuously in the forefront of these organizations. To keep ninety-nine innocents under surveillance in order to identify one Soviet, Chinese, or Cuban agent is a security job that is not only costly but distasteful.

Finally, there is the fact that prevention of terrorist acts committed by leftist extremists is more difficult than containment of terrorism by nationalistic rightist extremists and cannot be accomplished by ordinary defensive means. Following the example of the Palestinians' Maoist groups, the militant New Leftists everywhere have decided that anybody or anything which aids or encourages "capitalism and imperialism" is their target. It can be an office of IBM or the Bank of America; it can be the home of a well-known industrialist or the well-known industrialist himself. It can even be Olympic

Games athletes. Protecting every conceivable target would mean a "police state" effort exactly of the sort the extreme left would like to see us exert in order to have an obviously "fascist" enemy to war against. Besides, it wouldn't work. Even in the grossest police state, an attempt to protect all targets the terrorists might conceivably strike would spread protection so thin that it would be easy to penetrate.

Already, this applies to international airliners. There are *no* means of search yet devised that can prevent a determined and well-trained hijacker from taking onto an airplane sufficient explosives to blow it up. He can carry enough in a tube of toothpaste to destroy the largest airplane, and he can carry a detonator in his ball-point pen, so cleverly made that even an X-ray won't detect it. If he wishes, he may connect the detonator to the explosives; attach the two of them to a radio receiving set concealed in his electric razor or some other such appliance; disembark, leaving the apparatus behind; and then blow up the airplane with a radio signal sent from the ground.

In short, except for spotting the hijacker who is an individual criminal or lunatic, physical searches of passengers are next to useless. The *only* effective way of preventing politically motivated hijackings is to know about them in advance, or to identify potential hijackers before they board airplanes as members of terrorist groups. This is possible only as the result of information that cannot be obtained except by spying. Unfortunately, the nature of leftist extremists being what it is, it necessitates spying on a lot of innocent people.

The CIA, in cooperation with internal-security services the world over, has already managed to put together sufficient information on members of terrorist groups, and persons who may be used by them, to enable checkers at airports to determine within seconds by computer whether the name, number, and physical description on a particular passport match those in some SUSPECT file.* By so checking potential hijackers, air-

---

* Most security services of the free world have directly or indirectly supplied the CIA with information on members of their respective terrorist groups—enough, anyhow, to relate the information to passport holders of

port officials all over the world have already caught would-be hijackers who would probably not have been detected by a physical search. For this reason, some airports have eliminated baggage and body searches and are relying entirely on the identification system.

We have, therefore, a new item on the CIA's list of intelligence objectives that can be achieved only by spying: the spotting of terrorists and backers of terrorists among groups of the extreme left fighting "the people's war against imperialism and capitalism." The fact that acts of violence are perpetrated by only a small minority of the citizenry does not make them less dangerous. Techniques of leftist "urban guerrillas" are such that a maximum of disruption may be achieved with a minimum of effort.

In the face of current criticism, the argument in favor of *some* spying by the FBI (internally) and the CIA (externally) is that we must do a certain minimum in order to protect our institutions. Given this fact, our agencies believe that this mini-

---

cooperating governments. It is extremely difficult, if not impossible, for even the best forger of passports to match a name, a number, and a physical description so that they will tally with the centralized, computerized record kept at any major airport. Forge the name "John Jones" onto a passport, and the computer will turn up a dozen John Joneses—but not with the right number and description. Or make up some unique name, and the computer will turn up the fact that the number on the passport fails to match that name but does match the name of someone else—or doesn't exist at all. What if the passenger holds the passport of Czechoslovakia, South Yemen, or some other country that hasn't contributed to the informational "bank"? In such a case the passenger may be told politely that he must undergo a thorough physical search—not the fault of the security authorities at hand, but the fault of those of the passport holder's own country because they refused to take part in the international effort. Or if he bears a passport of the Soviet Bloc, he is allowed to go straight through without search because the Soviets and their allies maintain their own controls, much tougher than ours, over the passports they issue. Remarkably, even including Indians, Pakistanis, and travelers from other such heavily populated countries, the total number of passports in the system is only twenty million. Names, serial numbers, identifying marks, and "remarks" of only twenty million entries can be kept in computer storage occupying no more space than a broom closet, and any one entry may be retrieved in less than a second.

mum must be left entirely in the hands of highly qualified professionals whose integrity is above question, and who are controlled by organizations so constructed and so backed by legal protection that they are beyond corruption—even by the directors of the organizations or by the President of the United States.

THE SPY GAME

What, in this day of advanced gadgetry,
is espionage all about?

JoJo, describing a period when he was making a special study of Soviet intelligence resources in Europe, tells of a diplomatic cocktail party in Vienna where the American, British, French, Soviet, and Egyptian espionage service chiefs chatted easily to one another, quite ignored by the regular diplomats. As he visited other European capitals attending similar cocktail parties, he noticed the same phenomenon. Although all the espionage officers were under cover—one as an economic counselor, another as assistant military attaché, another as an embassy legal officer, and so on—they seemed to gravitate together simply as the result of some mutual attraction in their chemistries. Certainly, American and British intelligence officers get along better than do American intelligence officers and American career diplomats, and the same holds for British intelligence officers and diplomats. This is true also of their French counterparts, and even officers of small, neutral countries. I claim that I can spot officers of the Egyptian *mukhabarat* from across the room at any diplomatic gathering they may be attending. My friends in the CIA and the SIS say they can do the same with both Egyptian and French intelligence officers under diplomatic cover. The Egyptian gives himself away by calling an American or British colleague by his first name and the Frenchman by instinctively *tutoi*-ing an American or Englishman he senses is a colleague.

During an evening of drinking in Beirut, I once remarked to Kim Philby that I knew the top KGB officers in both Beirut and Cairo and found them better company than at least half the diplomats in the Anglo-American colony. For reasons that later became obvious, Philby had studiously avoided public contact with Soviet diplomats; yet he heartily agreed. After Philby fled to Moscow, I recalled the exchange and told a friend in British security about it. "How clever of Philby!" he said—meaning that it would be perfectly natural for a loyal British intelligence officer to admit liking his Russian colleagues, but that a British officer who was spying for them would presumably be afraid to do so for fear of giving himself away. Philby saw the subtle distinction.

I have yet to meet a CIA or SIS officer who works directly against the KGB in Europe or elsewhere who did not actually like many of his adversaries. While the straight Soviet diplomat is afraid to be seen alone with an American, a Western European, or any non-Communist (at official functions, the only kind they are allowed to attend, they circulate in twos), a Soviet station chief and some senior members of his staff often behave pretty much like diplomats of European countries, even to the extent of engaging in friendly arguments about Communism. With other members of the intelligence community—American, British, French, and others—they sometimes go much further than that. It is an essential part of the espionage specialist's "game player" makeup for him to be able to fight his adversary tooth and nail, yet feel no hostility toward him—and even, as far as the espionage "game" allows, occasionally show a bit of sportsmanship.

When the "Mercury" operation * blew, the KGB station

---

* As reported in the Teheran press, "Mercury" was a senior Iranian security official who convinced the CIA station chief in Teheran that he had suborned the wife of a Soviet military attaché and that she was regularly furnishing him with highly secret information on Soviet intentions toward Iran—which information, upon being checked on the Iranian side, en-

chief in Teheran took every advantage of it he could, but he saw no particular point in causing personal damage to his CIA opponent. He therefore so arranged the exposure that the operational mistakes of the CIA officer were concealed, and so that his bosses would find that "it could have happened to anybody." Being a man of integrity, the CIA officer told his headquarters the whole story without trying to play down his own incompetence, but the KGB officer's attempts to help him emerged. "Thanks to your Russian pal," an inspector told him later, "you could easily have gotten away with claiming it was an unpreventable catastrophe, and not your fault."

In a similar manner, CIA case officers often befriend KGB opposite numbers whom they defeat in battles of "dirty tricks." Sometimes their so doing is just another dirty trick—i.e., they want to gain a hold which may later be used to induce a defection—but more often their motives are pure professional camaraderie. The warmth of feeling that tends to exist between British and American intelligence officers and their KGB opposites is to be seen in the exchanges of "calculated indiscretions" that sometimes occur in secret Soviet-American drinking bouts in out-of-the-way places such as Kabul, Conakry, and La Paz. Even in Cairo, where the two sides are at each other's throats, and the Egyptian Government exploits the fact, I once heard a CIA officer and an SIS officer comparing notes with the local KGB chief on how each service gets on with its "straight" colleagues in its respective embassy. British intelligence officers, it appears, intimidate their straight colleagues by being of a higher social class; CIA officers, by going over their heads to Washington; and the Soviets, by sending anyone who displeases them to Siberia. Needless to say, the Soviet way was the envy of the others. Mother was

---

tirely made sense. "Operation Mercury" was eventually developed into a huge "network" of the traditional kind, complete with cutouts, drops, secret links, wireless transmitters—and huge sums of money, furnished by the CIA station chief. When it blew, it turned out that the whole thing was a fabrication, laid on by the Iranian official with the help of the Soviets and with the approval of the Iranian government.

only halfway joking when, at a meeting in Vienna a year later, he told his Soviet opposite number, "We deplore your objectives, but we think your methods are first-rate."

In public discussions, the question sometimes comes up: Do the British and Americans spy on each other? Anyone who has been in a confidential position in either government will know that the CIA might spy on the State Department or the SIS on the Foreign Office, but never would either one spy on the other. The CIA and the SIS might team up to spy on the State Department and the Foreign Office together. This did happen during the Suez crisis of 1956. A sensationalist newspaperman claimed that the U.S. Government had had advance knowledge of the Anglo-French-Israeli attack on Suez as the result of having spies in the British Government. The truth is that a member of British intelligence who was a totally loyal British citizen with no special ties to the CIA took it upon himself to *tell* his CIA counterpart, and afterward to tell his superior that he had done so. The superior agreed that he had acted wisely and responsibly. Later, the CIA and the SIS cooperated to undo the mistakes of U.S. Secretary of State John Foster Dulles and British Prime Minister Anthony Eden.

In such "intelligence centers" as Lisbon, Beirut, Geneva, and Rome, senior intelligence officers recognize one another and make little pretense of hiding. The newcomer who insists that he *really is* his embassy's "potable water attaché" finds himself distinctly unpopular among the rest of the intelligence community. The standard British tip-off is the word "actually." "Well, *actually* I'm the Potable Water Attaché." It is not unknown for, say, the French station chief and one or another of his counterparts to get together to work deals on their own headquarters. There is the story of the Soviet intelligence officer who offered his French colleague $25,000 for photocopies of the previous week's secret despatches to Paris. Amused, the French officer cabled his headquarters and received the reply, "Ask for more money." He went back to his Soviet friend and pointed out that $25,000 was hardly sufficient reward for betraying one's country, whereupon the

Soviet operative offered $50,000. After more exchanges between the two officers, and more cabling back and forth between Beirut and Paris, the Soviet offer rose to $125,000—causing the French officer to cable his headquarters requesting immediate transfer *"parce qu'ils vont bientôt être dans mes prix."* In plain English, "They're getting dangerously near my price."

"INTELLIGENCE" AND "ESPIONAGE"

However diligently intelligence officers may try to appear like normal diplomats—or normal salesmen, travel agents, or whatever their cover—they have their own ways of conducting personal relationships, looking at things, and communicating their ideas. They avoid specific jargon, but a kind of special language is implicit in their conversation when they talk with each other or even when they discuss their work with nonprofessionals: it is jargon in that it sounds meaningless yet carries a special meaning to others similarly "in the know." They may use such terms as "intelligence," "espionage," "agents," and "spies" just as loosely as everyone else, but actually they attach very precise meanings to these words.

It is particularly irritating to an intelligence officer to hear laymen, especially government officials and journalists who ought to know better, confusing "intelligence" with "espionage." To an intelligence officer, these words are by no means synonymous. He regards "intelligence" as strictly a management term. It is sought by governments, armies, private corporations, and individuals—usually by means remote from "espionage." Before setting its goals, the Eureka Soap Company surveys the economic environment in which it is to operate in order to determine what goals are practical; before deciding what product to make, it surveys the market to determine what product is wanted—and, naturally, the extent to which the product is already being supplied by rival manufacturers; before purchasing the raw materials, it surveys all the possible sources of supplies, and studies all economic, social, and political trends that may affect the continued availability of those supplies; before deciding where to build its plants, it surveys local conditions to determine that there will be continuing sources of dependable labor.

A major oil company must necessarily concern itself with intelligence. In order to develop guidelines by which to conduct its worldwide range of activities, it must estimate what the world will be like five, ten, twenty, and thirty years from now—its population, changes in standards of living that will affect needs for energy, the long-range ability of the company to hold on to its concessions or which needs will have to be met by changes in concession arrangements, and a host of other problems requiring "intelligence." Without intelligence it would make mistakes which would lose profit for its shareholders and endanger the interests of all mankind.

In short, "intelligence" is no more than looking before you leap. It is an everyday activity essential not only to corporations, but to governments, armies, crime syndicates, football teams, and private individuals. "Each morning when you look out the window to see what the weather is like so you can decide what clothes to wear," the CIA's Director of Training Colonel Matt Baird used to tell his students, "you are engaged in intelligence." It is sometimes no more than examining a weather report, checking a position on a street map, or reading the newspapers—*anything* you might do to increase the likelihood of your making the right decision and correctly estimating its consequences." * "Intelligence" spells the difference

---

* The definition of "intelligence" accepted by most governments is the one set forth by Sherman Kent, the first head of CIA's "national estimate" group, in his book *Strategic Intelligence*. Used as an unmodified noun, "intelligence" can mean (1) *knowledge*—as in "What intelligence do we have on Syria?"; or (2) an *organization*—as in "Intelligence hasn't come up with the answer to our question"; or (3) an *activity*—as in "Espionage is but one of the many kinds of intelligence." "Raw information" must be processed into "finished intelligence." Thus, in the intelligence community it is incorrect to say "We have received lots of intelligence from that source." Intelligence (as knowledge) is produced *only* at headquarters. Even reports from a high-ranking ambassador are, technically speaking,

between success and failure for almost any activity that does not depend on pure skill.

From such a description, it should be easy to imagine what sort of people are involved in intelligence. "Espionage," if it comes into "intelligence" at all, will occupy only a very small corner of the field and will employ a type of personnel quite different from the personnel involved in the ordinary pursuits of intelligence. Popular writers on "intelligence," who invariably have *governmental* intelligence in mind, somehow assume that the operations of governments are vastly different from those of other organizations. And so, perhaps, they are. But *fundamentally* the division of responsibilities is the same as in a large organization of any other kind, and, therefore, those who work at its intelligence are merely the governmental counterparts of those who work at intelligence in corporations. *If* espionage plays a proportionately higher part in governmental intelligence, it is because a government has problems of national security which sometimes call for extreme and unorthodox measures. In any case, it would be fair to say that the part espionage plays in a governmental intelligence setup is no greater than the part it plays in corporate intelligence that makes use of industrial espionage. There is only one difference: those who supervise governmental espionage operations are not involved in breaking the laws of their own country, while those who involve themselves in industrial espionage are.

THE "INTELLIGENCE OFFICER"

A review of the tables of organization of all U.S. Government offices reveals that as many as 200,000 employees are engaged in what might legitimately be described as "intelligence." Of

mere "raw information" until some processor at State or the CIA has sprinkled holy water on it in the form of footnotes, cross references and possibly comments. What if the President takes the original and makes a decision based on it? "Well," Sherman Kent would say, "in such a case he would be doing his own processing."

these, between 70,000 and 80,000 are engaged in intelligence related to the national security. It is this second number which prompts the occasional half-informed journalist to chide the U.S. Government for employing "tens of thousands of spies." The fact is that any government employee who is an "officer," by whatever definition, and who is directly engaged in the collection of information for intelligence purposes is an "intelligence officer." This includes ambassadors, attachés (military, naval, air, civil-aviation, commercial, petroleum, agricultural—the whole lot), and all the members of embassies other than those who are doing administrative or consular work. It also includes those U.S. officials who are sent out from Washington to do open-and-aboveboard field investigations of various kinds.

It is this last category of officers that has given us the "James Bond" myth. The American and British governments try to use only their best officers for delicate jobs in foreign countries, but inevitably a few overzealous types, attracted by the glamour of "troubleshooting," manage to work their way in. Retired British intelligence officers who knew Ian Fleming entertain the theory that he built his "Bond" stories around one James Boone, a Foreign Office administrative inspector whose real job was to examine inventories of supplies on hand at British diplomatic missions in the Middle East and Africa but who pretended to his girlfriends that it was only cover for more glamourous missions. A strong and healthy man, though practically brainless, he got into nightclub scrapes in a few of the capitals he visited, and in Teheran he tangled with a drunk who was molesting his girlfriend and killed him with a single karate chop. It turned out that his victim was a well-known heroin smuggler, wanted in five countries, so he emerged as a hero. From then on, he lived a Walter Mitty existence, halfway convincing himself that his invented exploits were the true ones.

He appears to have halfway convinced Ian Fleming, who told stories about the man to Allen Dulles, then Director of the CIA, when the two men dined together on the yacht of a

Greek shipowner in 1960. Dulles countered with the story about how some of his underlings had maliciously spread the word among South American security services that a certain member of the State Department Inspector General's staff was not what he claimed to be, but a special representative of "the Dulles brothers" making the rounds of South American countries in search of military leaders capable of taking over their respective governments and willing afterward to "stand up and be counted" on the capitalist side in the Cold War. Instead of getting into the kind of trouble the CIA pranksters had in mind for him, he was warmly received by military leaders and ambitious politicians of many of the countries he visited, some of them with carefully developed coup d'état plans to present for his consideration. From then on, until his superiors put an end to the practice, he actually used the phrase "I'm on sort of a James Bond mission" as he approached South American politicians he had reason to believe would be friendly.

It is true that when John Foster Dulles was Secretary of State and his brother, Allen, was Director of the CIA, the use of high-level troubleshooters and fact finders was prevalent. Men such as Averell Harriman, Robert Murphy, and Robert Anderson had one quality which the Dulles brothers thought essential and which, by definition, a secret operative would lack: prestige. More recent secretaries of State and directors of Central Intelligence subscribe to the theory that our ambassadors have quite enough prestige for almost all purposes, and that visits of Great White Fathers might damage it irreparably. They send special investigators from Washington only when there are jobs requiring specialists not normally kept on local staffs, and these are all jobs that can be performed in an open-and-aboveboard manner. There are rarely if ever any *secret* missions that can be better accomplished by a visiting specialist than by a local officer, and there are therefore no intelligence officers with duties approximating those of James Bond. Writers of spy thrillers looking for real-life models must satisfy themselves with stationary intelligence officers, since there are none who move from assignment to assignment in the Bond manner.

THE CIA "STATION CHIEF"

In many U.S. embassies in the world, there are small groups of CIA personnel who constitute what are known in the CIA as "stations." Each "station" is under a senior CIA officer, suitably "covered" by some misleading title,* whose job is to supervise his "case officers" and other station personnel, to provide general supervision and administrative support to the CIA "operations" run outside the embassy, to keep Washington informed of the progress and problems of these operations, and to satisfy the ambassador (who will rarely want to know details) that the operations are running smoothly and are not likely to embarrass the U.S. Government. To name but a few, the British, Soviet, French, Egyptian, and Israeli embassies have "stations" inside them comparable to those of American embassies, and "station chiefs" whom "the other side" spends a great deal of time trying to spot.

Naturally, the station is under "cover"—"light," "deep," or something in between. Sometimes the station is all together in a single part of the embassy building; more often, the officers are scattered—for example, one in the military attaché's office, another in the consulate, another in the commercial attaché's office, and so on. As a rule, intelligence agencies go to a tremendous amount of trouble to cover their stations, even in nonsensitive areas, because once an officer's cover is "blown" there is no dependable way of getting it back again. All the same, there are infallible ways of spotting intelligence-station personnel, whether they be American, British, Soviet, or of any other nationality.

---

* Any title will do, as long as it is sufficiently senior and does not describe a position that can be filled only by a regular career diplomat.

Journalists spot the American (CIA) station chief and his principal assistants merely by getting to know all those in the embassy who are of the appropriate rank, since only the Bloc services can get away with putting high-ranking personnel under such low-ranking cover as that of chauffeurs or gardeners. Newsmen can then single out those who have certain characteristics: the CIA officer ordinarily has a less impressive academic background than his State Department colleagues (although more impressive than those of his Defense Department colleagues), a keener grasp of the local political situation (although he is *less* likely to speak the local language than his State and Defense colleagues), and a kind of confidence and easy manner that others in the embassy rarely have. He knows exactly what he can tell newspapers and what he can't. He doesn't jump when the ambassador and others above him speak to him. Although the ambassador is legally his local boss, his efficiency report is written by his superiors at CIA, who couldn't care less what the ambassador thinks of him. His position is such that he doesn't have to worry about protocol and most of the diplomatic niceties. He is likely to dress in tweeds, when the rest of the embassy are in gray flannels, and he calls newspapermen by their first names. He also entertains more and better, if more informally, since he has a bigger expense account and will have hired the best cook in town.

One of my favorite CIA station chiefs deliberately plays up all the above qualities, although he knows they single him out, because he is afraid that those who count in the local scenery might *not* figure out who he is, and take him for a regular career diplomat. Even if he doesn't "blow" himself by his carefree manner toward cover, the wives of embassy officers will do it for him. Wives of British diplomats, attachés, consuls, and clerks are rarely able to learn which of their husband's colleagues are intelligence officers, but if they do and if they drop some hint of their knowledge outside the embassy, they are sent home and their husbands disciplined. The same is true of Soviet wives, and the wives of all other service personnel I know about. But not so with the Americans.

"CHINESE CHECKERS" IN THE INTELLIGENCE
COMMUNITIES

In Washington, the term "intelligence community" means the whole complex of intelligence organizations—the CIA, the FBI, the National Security Agency, the Pentagon's DIA (Defense Intelligence Agency), the Atomic Energy Commission, and so on. In those other capitals of the world where the "Big Game," as it is called, is being played, the term applies exclusively to the "espionage club": the station chiefs of all the espionage services plus those of their staffs who are senior enough to "come out"—i.e., deal with the local authorities and some intelligence personnel of other nationalities without pretense of cover.

After World War II, the Big Game, like chess and football, was for two sides only: the Americans and the British on one side, with degrees of cooperation from the French and smaller powers, and the Soviets and their allies on the other. With the advent of Nasser and his "positive neutrality," the principal countries of the Third World began individually and collectively to play the two major sides against each other and, with considerable success, to force the two major sides to compete for their favors. Still later, the French discontinued their cooperation with the Americans and the British (it was limited and fairly untrustworthy anyhow) and entered the Big Game as an independent player. Various countries in the Soviet Bloc did likewise. The "intelligence community" became multipolar, and "the Big Game changed from chess to Chinese checkers," as an instructor in the CIA school put it.

Despite occasional signs that indicate otherwise, the Americans and the British work closely together as a team: the espionage branches of the CIA and the SIS are certainly closer and better coordinated with each other than, say, the CIA and the FBI. The British "station" is almost identical with that of the CIA, except, perhaps, that it is normally smaller, better covered, and better integrated into the embassy to which it is assigned. Also, it is poorer, its budget normally being about a third of the budget of its American counterpart. For this reason, it is in most parts of the world a primary duty of the British station chief to use his superior prestige and cunning to persuade his CIA colleague to join with him in joint Anglo-American operations, for which he supplies the brains and the CIA colleague supplies the funds.

That brings up another difference between CIA and SIS stations. The mission of the SIS is largely positive—to *do* something, and to do it properly. The mission of the CIA station, however, is normally negative—to stay out of trouble. The CIA station chief never runs an espionage operation except to achieve an objective that is absolutely vital and that cannot be achieved in any other way, and unless the chances of avoiding exposure are virtually 100 percent. Once the operation is started, he thereafter spends a high percentage of his working day developing "contingency plans" to implement in the event exposure seems imminent. Since most would-be spies prefer employment by the CIA to employment by other services, because of better pay and better security, the CIA station is likely to wind up with more and better operations than other intelligence stations. All the same, the cautious CIA station chief, the kind who gets ahead in his organization, more often than not prefers to back British operations (or Turkish, Spanish, Greek, Dutch, Egyptian, Japanese—anything but French) rather than run his own.

Surprisingly, the Soviet "station chiefs" are almost as timid as the American. Although they have larger "stations," the largest of any of the great intelligence services, they spend less time than is imagined in running espionage operations of their own. Like their American counterparts, they prefer supporting the operations of others (the Czechs, the Poles, etc.), to running operations of their own—in the developmental stages, at any rate. The difference is that instead of mere financial support, such as the Americans provide their partners in joint operations, the Soviets furnish administrative, technical, and "disciplinary" support. And increasingly, there is another difference:

their partners, who are becoming more and more independent, sometimes take pleasure in thwarting Soviet disciplines just for the sake of it. In recent months, there have been several cases of Bloc services' discharging members who have been Soviet agents spying on them for years, and at least two cases of Bloc agents having been spotted by the Soviets in their own intelligence establishment. American and British station chiefs are beginning to think they can deal with the various Bloc services as targets in their own rights, not as mere adjuncts of the KGB.

As espionage services of the smaller countries have become more independent, their characters have changed dramatically. The day of the Gestapo, NKVD, or "secret police" type of intelligence unit is almost over, not only in the Western and Bloc services but in the smaller countries as well. The Israelis, as would be expected, have topflight officers who are both intellectual and tough-minded. So do the Egyptians, who cleaned out their few remaining "baboons" (as "secret police" types are called by their more civilized colleagues) following a coup d'état attempt against President Anwar el-Sadat a year or so ago, and the Turks, the Greeks, the Lebanese, and the governments of other small countries which for one reason or another, sensible or unsensible, believe themselves to have international interests. The Arabs, possibly, upgraded their intelligence-station personnel so as to match the Israelis. Some Arab services still have a few baboons attached to their various stations—again to match the Israelis, who need this type of operative to combat the Black September menace—but on the whole, their officers are of extremely high quality.

Naturally, the tasks of the small services differ greatly from those of the major services. Primarily, their stations are concerned with keeping tabs on their own nationals who form émigré groups abroad to stir up support for dissidents back home. Except to the extent that the various great-power services use their activities for purposes of their own, they live in a world apart, normally unmolested by the local security services as long as they don't break the law. When the Egyptian station chief in Rome got caught in the act of smuggling a doped double agent to Cairo by air freight, he probably would have been let alone had it not been for the fact that some busybody in Alitalia had reported to his superior that he had heard a *rumore curioso* coming from the freight compartment of one of its airplanes and the superior, with the prestige of his company in mind, had reported the matter at such a high level in the Italian Government that it couldn't be swept under the carpet.

THE STATION CHIEF'S NEW HEADACHE: TERRORISM

Although it is too soon to see the full picture, no description of the typical community of intelligence stations can be complete without reference to the new problem now confronting these stations: the ad hoc terrorism. Right-wing terrorism is usually nationalistic, and therefore local and of a sort that can be dealt with by the local police. Leftist movements, however, are generally internationalist in outlook, although they may lack the resources to make effective international connections. As early as 1968, the major intelligence services began to notice that some leftist groups were gaining the resources and making the connections. Leftist terrorist movements were becoming "internationalized," and by 1970 the world's major intelligence services had built sizable files on their members who moved from country to country. By 1973, the records were so complete that would-be bombers, hijackers, riot organizers, and assassins could be spotted as they were en route to their targets and thwarted.

The CIA knew that a breakthrough had been reached when, in early 1973, it was able to predict moves of the Maoist "People's Front for the Liberation of Palestine" simply by matching television pictures of its members and contacts— taken in airports, bus terminals, and other transportation centers—against "profiles" held in "Octopus," the computerized files in Langley, Virginia. The relationships between the "subjects" and the coincidence of their movements formed a recognizable pattern. The "eye" that covered the taxi center in downtown Beirut spotted Wadie Haddad, the PFLP's planner of airplane hijackings, as he took off for his hideout in the Lebanese mountains, where he customarily stayed while an operation was in progress. The "eye" at the Beirut airport spotted a known PFLP "messenger" as he passed through the controls to board a plane for Paris, and a member of the Lebanese Sûreté noted the number and false name on his passport; French security authorities spotted him as he arrived at Orly airport—just after they had spotted two members of the Japanese Red Star whom the Japanese security authorities had reported to be in touch with Palestinian extremists. An agent inside an Arab diplomatic service reported the shipment to Paris of operational supplies through air-freighted diplomatic channels. All these items, and more, were radioed to "Octopus" within seconds of the moment they occurred, and within seconds "Octopus" had analyzed them, along with information already in the files on targets in the area and the equipment and talents required to attack them, and had radioed the alarm to the Franco-American counterterrorist team in Paris. When the terrorists were picked up and accused, they were flabbergasted at being presented with plans they hadn't yet made.

"Those are the plans we *would* have made," one of the terrorists told his interrogators, "but we hadn't yet had enough time. Were you reading our minds?"

"Knowing what you were after," the interrogator replied, "we figured they were the only plans you *could* have made." He didn't tell the terrorist, but the figuring had been done entirely by "Octopus," in microseconds.

By now, the CIA and other major intelligence services are well on their way to bringing such groups as the Palestinians' PFLP under control; but there is a new type of movement which has introduced problems that are far beyond the reach of "Octopus." Typified by the Palestinians' "Black September," they are not "organizations" at all but small "commands" using terrorism for simple purposes which are easily understood and agreed upon. While ideologically motivated terrorists of the extreme left fight with each other over minor points of doctrine, and build organizations which are easily penetrated by enemies, these "commands" know exactly what they hope to achieve, and what energies and talents are required to achieve it, and they find persons with those energies and talents who can be recruited on a straight contract basis. Black September, the prototype, recruits its terrorists, operation by operation, in the countries where its targets are located. Originally, it accepted only simple adventurers who were without political interests or connections. It has relaxed this policy out of necessity, but still has managed to avoid use of the sort of persons on whom there might be long entries in "Octopus." Its targets are "any person, organization, institution, or place that supports Israel"—a range of possibilities as wide as that of those who fight "the people's war against imperialism and capitalism." By the opening months of 1973, this type of movement was upstaging organizations such as the PFLP, and what *Time* magazine called "the deadly battle of spooks" was under way.

Libya's fanatical leader, Colonel Muammar el-Qadhafi, announced that "all Libyan embassies everywhere" were "at the disposal" of Black Septembrists on the run after their terrorist attacks. In the following weeks, he sent Libyan "intelligence officers" to his embassies in Rome, Paris, and several other places for the specific purpose of providing "diplomatic support" to Black September operations planned for Europe in 1973. These were replaced by bomb-disposal experts when it became apparent that the main effect of his announcement was to draw the fire of Israeli "counterterrorist operators." Other African and Middle Eastern embassies were shortly, at Libyan expense, housing small units to take over the functions originally assigned to the Libyan "intelligence officers." Some of these embassies (e.g., the Algerian and the Egyptian) only pretended to cooperate, while actually directing their intelligence staffs to uncover Black September personnel and plots and to lead them into traps or otherwise defuse them.* But there has been enough genuine cooperation from some Arab embassies to ensure that Black September will be a continuing problem.

The reaction of Western services—and, for that matter, of Soviet and Bloc services, since Black September is as anti-East as it is anti-West—has been mixed. As targets, movements such as Black September are even more awkward and distasteful to professionals trained in conventional espionage techniques than the New Left movements ever were. Moreover, they necessitate the mixing of espionage and "positive" operations (i.e., "counterterrorism"), and this is against the basic tenets of the intelligence game. Still, the job has to be done.

As the prominence of Black September grew, with imitators popping up in various parts of the world, the first reaction of the CIA was to avoid any central role in solving it. On the recommendation of Richard Helms, Director of the CIA, a special interdepartmental antiterrorist task force was set up with Armin H. Meyer, former Ambassador to Lebanon (and later Japan), in charge. Ambassador Meyer, a diplomat of great charm and competence, was liked and trusted not only by the CIA's and the FBI's experts on counterterrorism but by chiefs of the various Middle Eastern security services whose cooperation would be required. From the CIA's point of view,

---

* At one point, the Algerians, hoping to humor Colonel Qadhafi, gave the Black September movement (through al-Fatah, the principal Palestinian organization) fifty blank passports to fill in as its leaders wished—and then promptly tipped off the French intelligence service (the Service de Documentation Extérieure et de Contre-Espionage, or SDECE) that it had done so. Since the advent of Black September, the Egyptian Government has openly refrained from criticizing Black September and has even expressed a degree of sympathy for it. At the same time, Egyptian intelligence stations have been among those working most effectively against Black September—on the theory, shared by most thoughtful Palestinians, that Black September is the greatest setback to their cause since the actions of President Nasser's that led to the 1967 war.

the arrangement was entirely satisfactory—until, that is, operating teams of experts were formed of personnel drawn from a number of agencies other than the CIA, and CIA station chiefs began to have visions of teams of clandestine operators in their countries over which they would have no control. The latest move is to send out teams of specialists who are under the control of the station chiefs, but kept separate from their regular staffs—an arrangement which, so far as is known, is already used by the KGB. The British are following suit—reluctantly. The necessity for dealing with the Black September phenomenon, an SIS officer told me, will "lower the tone of intelligence communities everywhere." My friends in the Egyptian and Algerian services, who suffer enough headaches from the baboons they *already* have attached to their various stations, would be the first to agree.

THE HEADQUARTERS "DESK OFFICER"

Using security as an excuse, the old-time professionals in the espionage branch of the CIA have resisted suggestions that professional organization and management experts be called in to overhaul its outdated administrative structure. Consequently, an abomination known as the "area desk officer" still persists in its table of organization. The theory behind the "desk officer" is that the station chief of each major country should have, back at headquarters, "one man who is *my* man, whom I can look to on any problem from getting me a new automobile to pushing through approval for a new operation," as the influential CIA station chief in Rome once put it. But the theory overlooks the fact that an officer who is clever at cutting through red tape to get a new automobile is rarely the sort of person who can speak up effectively for the station chief on problems such as the political situation in the station chief's assigned country. And since the desk officer is normally being groomed to replace the station chief at the end of his tour of duty, he is likely to give greater attention to showing up well when he is called to "the front office" than he is at arguing with the administrative sections over automobiles. Moreover, since the concept of "delegation" is little understood at CIA, he finds it easy to have "delegated" to himself the task of drafting orders to the station chief for the signature of the division chief; he often winds up being, in effect, the station chief's boss.

Unfortunately, there are a few senior officials in the espionage branch of the CIA who have read a book or two on organization and management, and who have mastered enough of the jargon to impress those at the very top of the organization to whom the espionage branch isn't very important. These officials have been successful in perpetuating the desk-officer system. The British and the Soviets, however, as well as a dozen or so small intelligence services throughout the world supported by CIA, have removed administrative and policy functions from their equivalents of the CIA's desk officers, and their "desk officers" are now responsible only for acting as their station chiefs' liaison officers at headquarters. They see that the station chiefs get all the information they need to run their operations effectively, and they speak up in their behalf when superiors have questions to ask.* In these services as well as in the American, however, the "desk officer" is an important cog in the system's wheel. Moreover, the job of desk officer is an important step in the career of any intelligence officer specializing in espionage. Every espionage specialist spends a high percentage of his formative years in such assignments. And since the efficiency he displays is reflected in his promotions, the various intelligence services wind up being run by officers who meet the criteria by which their respective desk officers are judged—the CIA by "good company men," the British SIS by true professionals whose authority comes from reputation and prestige, and the Soviets by true professionals who know how to be as ruthless in internal

---

* See Appendix A for a description of the organizational setup of an espionage branch of an intelligence agency.

politics as they are trained to be in dealing with the outside world. *

THE "CASE OFFICER"

A function that is common to "desk officers" of all espionage branches is that of maintaining operational records of all espionage projects. The record of each project contains all known personality data of the agent, a detailed account of his recruitment and training, a detailed account of all meetings with him, all instructions given to him, all actions taken by him in the course of his operating duties, and any personal troubles that might crop up.

The responsibility of the desk officer is an administrative responsibility: to ensure that the records do exist, that they are conscientiously kept up by those in the field stations who are operationally responsible for them, and that there are no items in them which may signal possible trouble for the espionage branch.

---

* Members of the CIA, like members of any American corporation, tend to be what sociologists call "upward mobiles." The chief of the CIA station in, say, Beirut, looks forward to the day when he will be promoted to Ankara, then to Athens, then to Paris, then to London, then to the position of division chief back at headquarters, and so on. As he takes over a new station, he discards most of what his predecessor built up before him ("You should have *seen* the mess I found when I got here," he tells his colleagues) and starts all over again; consequently, with exceptions, the CIA station is rarely more than two years ahead of the game. The British officer, by contrast, makes a career out of being *the* last word on some given area. For example, I know an SIS officer whose ambition was to be the world's greatest authority on Afghanistan—and who spent his whole career, except for occasional assignments given him for purposes of developing his perspective, alternating between jobs in London dealing with Afghanistan and assignments in Kabul, first in the British Embassy and later as "resident." At the time of his retirement, his professional standing in the eyes of his own service was at least as impressive as the organizational standing achieved by his American counterpart who had started out with him in Kabul twenty-five years before and who had worked his way up from being chief of the Kabul station through a dozen stations finally to become chief of the CIA espionage branch's South America Division.

While the desk officer's responsibility with respect to these records is mainly "to keep the division's nose clean," as he would say, there is an officer in the field whose responsibility it is to originate the records, to see that they are complete and up to date, and to ensure that they reflect operations which are moving along as they should. This officer, known as a "case officer," pores over these records for hours at a time, trying to sniff out some irregularity which may indicate that an agent has been "doubled," or has begun to fabricate information, or has merely begun to show signes of laxity. Ideally, a case officer is responsible for no more than one operation. If a station has three operations, it should have three case officers —all being supervised in a general way by the station chief, but each directly responsible for the "health" of his particular operation. Practically speaking, however, most ambassadors frown on the possibility that members of the intelligence station may outnumber other members of his staff, so it is only the very large embassy that can support a station with more than two or three case officers—and normally, the station chief is himself a case officer.* Consequently, a case officer may be called upon to keep the records on two or more operations— and in some cases, to run one or more operations himself.

THE "RESIDENT"

Traditionally, the mainstay of the espionage system has been a figure known as the "resident." This individual, under com-

---

* Assuming, that is, that the station has *any* operations. I once made an inspection tour of CIA stations in the early Fifties to find that as many as *half* the stations I visited had *no* operations, and no chance of getting any. I am told that most totally inactive stations have by now been closed down, but that it is not at all unusual for an American or British officer to take over a station in some country, spend two years there, and return home after not having recruited one single agent or made any ripple on the local scenery. And we know from Soviet defectors that in more than one European country Soviet intelligence has squads of case officers, "residents," and other elements of the ordinary espionage system—but no spies.

mercial or other nonofficial cover, is a secure member of the community—financially, socially, and in every other way. Although he does not engage directly in espionage operations, he is often exposed to those who do. He must therefore enjoy such a position that he can ride out any difficulties which may arise from these operations if they are "blown."

The function of the "resident" is to act as a link between the case officers and their espionage operations. Typically, he is a national of the country whose service employs him, and he lives not in the country where his targets are located but in the one next to it. For example, the SIS resident who links one or more case officers to operations in Syria could be a middle-aged or elderly member of the British community in Beirut—perhaps the owner-manager of an import-export company, a college professor, an archeologist, or a retired diplomat or army officer. He would break no Lebanese laws, he might have excellent relations with the Lebanese Sûreté, even though they might have strong suspicions about his intelligence role, and he would rarely, if ever, go to Syria. His contact with operations in Syria would be through "principal agents" or "cutouts," although he might deal directly with those of his agents who are influential enough to be able to get out of Syria as they wish without exciting suspicion. He would maintain no records and keep no equipment. A search of his premises would reveal no wireless sets, secret-writing materials, or purloined documents. Any surveillance that would be sufficiently effective to pick up incriminating conversations between him and his principals, cutouts, or agents would involve use of equipment that is illegal in Lebanon except when used by the Lebanese authorities; and the Lebanese authorities would hardly use such sensitive equipment to monitor conversations that would be incriminating only in the eyes of the Syrians. As this book is written, there are at least three Syrian security investigators languishing in Lebanese jails for having used such equipment in attempts to ferret out imagined American, British, French, and Israeli agents. The last-named of course, would be as much of interest to the

Lebanese as to the Syrians, but the Lebanese Sûreté would need no assistance from the vastly inferior Syrian Sûreté in dealing with them.*

There are only slight differences between the ways in which the Americans, the British, and the Soviets use their residents. The CIA has heard so many complaints from American businessmen residents abroad over embarrassment caused them by the general suspicion that some of them might be "CIA agents" † that it has all but discontinued the use of American citizens as residents except in areas where they can be set up in cooperation with the local authorities. The British, with their older and more compact business communities abroad, appear to have no such problem, and the use of British residents continues. The Soviets, having no unofficial communities abroad except of kinds that would hardly serve the purpose, use either citizens of the countries in which they operate or Soviet citizens who have legally or illegally attained citizenship in those countries. Smaller countries—Israel, Egypt, etc. —choose their residents on whatever bases best suit their purposes. Since there are fortunes to be made from having access to diplomatic bags, intelligence services of these small countries have no difficulty in recruiting competent residents who lend considerable panache to the intelligence communities.

---

* While it pains me to disillusion my many friends in the Syrian security services, I must say that I very much doubt that either the British or the Americans—or any other nation, possibly excluding the Israelis—have enough interest in Syrian targets to bother.
† In many countries abroad, there are large and amorphous American business communities which include not only representatives of large American companies but hordes of promoters, "business consultants," free-lance reporters, and others who can offer only unclear explanations of how they earn their livings. At a cocktail party in Beirut, I once asked a young man what his business was, and when he launched into a long, abstruse explanation which I didn't understand, I interrupted him to say, "Look, my young friend, I have long ago learned that anyone who can't explain what he does in one sentence is a CIA case officer under deep cover." This shut him up. Minutes later, after he had regained his composure, he pulled me aside and whispered angrily into my ear, "I think the lowest thing in this world is a CIA man who will blow another CIA man's cover."

THE "AGENT"

The word "agent" is one that is so misused as to cause mutual bewilderment when intelligence officers talk to laymen, even informed politicians and journalists. Frank Wisner, when he was head of the CIA's "dirty tricks department," once told me he had to read popular literature about spies "just to find out what everybody meant." He said a member of a Senatorial committee once asked him, "Is it true that in every American Embassy you have at least one agent?" For an uneasy moment Frank thought the Senator was implying that the CIA spied on the State Department. "No, Senator," he said. "We only put agents in embassies of Communist countries."

Then he realized that the Senator was talking about regular employees, not agents, and he had to explain that he would promptly fire any of his employees who got themselves directly involved in "agent" work—i.e., spying. The Senator, having been indoctrinated by a lot of popular literature, didn't get the point and continued using the word "agent" as before. All the same, intelligence officers must stick to proper usage. So must anyone who would understand the intelligence business. Loose use of the word obscures understanding of what the business of intelligence is all about.

The "agent" is a member of the espionage system who actually "spies." He is, in fact, the *only* one who spies. That is to say, his acts are the only ones that are in contravention of the espionage laws. When he is caught, those who are caught with him—his principal, his cutouts, the resident (if he is in the country), and all others—are guilty either of "aiding and abetting the act of espionage" or of conspiracy. In the properly organized espionage operation, arrangements will have been made whereby those caught with the agent will have plausible bases for pleading ignorance of the true nature of what they were doing. Even the agent can occasionally be so protected—e.g., claiming, when captured, that he believed himself to be working not for a foreign power but for a local political group, an industrial-espionage organization, or a crusading newspaperman.

In any case, it is the agent who is on the firing line; it is he upon whom the whole operation depends; and as with the front-line soldier in the army, for every one of him there are five persons backing him up, from the principal agent to whom he reports to those at headquarters who handle his administration. And whatever the precautions, it is he who is most likely to get into serious trouble in the event his operation is blown.

This brings us to a misconception that is especially annoying to intelligence professionals. When some investigator in the course of the Watergate hearings referred to Howard Hunt and James McCord as "former CIA agents," an Agency spokesman flatly denied that either one had ever served in an agent capacity. Hunt had been a staff officer, with duties comparable to those of an officer of the Interior Department's Fish and Wildlife Service who deals in the processing of information, and McCord had served as head of the Security Division team that makes the rounds of CIA offices after working hours to see that all the safes are locked, all the secret papers removed from desk tops, and so on. Since they were not empowered to act in such a way as to obligate the CIA (a dictionary definition of "agent"), and since they were not by the widest stretch of the imagination "spies" (the professional definition), the CIA spokesman was being entirely truthful.

The FBI employs officials who are agents according to the definition found in the dictionaries: they are empowered to arrest, and to take other actions, "in the name of the law." The CIA has no such powers, however, and employs "agents" only as the word is used in the professional sense. Incidentally, the CIA only rarely, if ever, employs American citizens as agents. American citizens only rarely, if ever, have the necessary qualifications.

In discussions of espionage the question always comes up:

"What are the qualities required of the espionage agent?" Writers on the subject frequently enumerate such qualities as "ability to remain cool under pressure" or "unobtrusiveness" or, in the famous words of President Franklin Roosevelt, "a passion for anonymity." The answer any professional intelligence officer would give, however, is that only one quality is truly important: access to the target. A prospective agent with all the cool, unobtrusiveness, and anonymity in the world would be useless unless he can get inside his assigned target.

Unless he *is* inside his assigned target. There are all sorts of books on spies which allege that the CIA and the SIS pick a number of highly qualified nationals of their own countries, teach them to speak impeccable Russian and to behave like a Russian, give them forged identity documents, then send them to Moscow to spy on the Kremlin. Since even the most primitive security services can usually spot an outsider—not because there are flaws in his accent or because he eats with the fork in his right hand but simply from the fact that he *is* an outsider—such an approach would promise little chance of success. It is rare that an espionage service *needs* to send in outsiders. Why go to all the trouble to teach some American to speak Russian and to eat with his left hand and send him to penetrate the Kremlin when the Kremlin is chock-full of native Russians who already have access to the Kremlin's secrets and who would be delighted to spy for the CIA if properly propositioned?

The CIA's spies, like the spies of other intelligence services, are in 99.99 percent of the cases citizens in good standing of the countries in which the CIA's targets are located, and are in most cases ensconced in or near the targets which they are to penetrate. From the mere fact that a person is an American citizen you may safely infer that he could *not* be a CIA agent. He may be a Soviet agent or some other kind of agent, but not an agent of the CIA. The same goes for any British citizen you may suspect of being an SIS agent or any Soviet citizen you suspect of being a KGB agent.

THE "DOUBLE AGENT"

We can get an idea of the true nature of the "agent" by having a look at that prominent feature of spy books, the "double agent." Originally, he was a spy who enjoyed such confidences of both sides that he knew the secrets of both, and could report them back and forth as he wished. Czarist Russia's Ievno Aseff, for example, was a true double agent: as a member of the Social Revolutionary Party's "Battle Organization" in 1906, he was able to report to the Czar's secret police all the plans and movements of that organization; as a member of the Czar's secret police, he was able to keep the "Battle Organization" informed of all the counterrevolutionary plans of the Czarist government. Such an arrangement presupposes two sides' being naive enough to allow a known agent access to their secrets.

Such naiveté no longer exists. For example, once Kim Philby became a Soviet agent, the Soviets saw to it that from that moment on he had no access to Soviet secrets. He had access to British secrets since he was a British intelligence officer, and he could report such secrets to the Soviets. But as a Soviet agent all he knew of the Soviet side was the identity of his case officer (or his principal) and the nature of the questions he was given to answer. These could not be particularly important items in any case. When it is considered that some of the case officers who managed him in the course of his career were under false identities, and that many of the questions he was asked were red herrings, it is easy to see that it would hardly have been worthwhile for the SIS to *plant* Philby on the Soviets.

Philby was in no sense a double agent: he was a British intelligence officer, but he was an agent only to the Soviets. It was only to the Soviet side that he had the one essential quality of the agent: access to the target.

THE "PRINCIPAL," THE "UTILITY OPERATIVE," AND THE "CUTOUT"

There is a great distance between the case officer and the agent. Not only are the two of different nationalities; they are usually of different social classes, occupations, and economic circumstances. In cases in which they are closer together in these respects—for example, when the case officer is the assistant military attaché in his embassy and the agent is a colonel in his country's ministry of defense—a direct relationship between them might needlessly draw attention to the operation. In either case, the gap is closed by a variety of undercover personnel, of whom the main one is known as a "principal agent"—or, in recent parlance, simply a "principal."

A principal, who is usually of the same nationality as the agent and who is in all cases in a position to associate with him normally—as a social acquaintance, or as his teacher, doctor, dentist, psychiatrist, or whatever—is the one who maintains the direct contact with the agent necessary to recruit him, train him, and keep him on a strait and narrow path operationally. With agents of long standing (e.g., our "Emily" of Chapter 1), there may be a turnover of principals, beginning with the one who did the recruiting and leading through a whole series of managers. In other cases, the principal is dispensed with altogether. Once it has been established that an operation is virtually foolproof, the resident may be tempted to take over the agent directly. Where the agent is free to travel out of his country to some "safe area" (i.e., a place where participants in an espionage operation are immune to local surveillance and arrest), the case officer located in or near to that safe area may take over the operation directly.

Very often, a good principal is developed into what is known as a "utility operative" and is removed by his resident or case officer from contact with all espionage operations. Instead, he is assigned the totally legal task of acquiring nonclassified information such as is required in the planning of espionage operations. If a member of the Soviet intelligence service located in Washington, D.C., were to attempt openly to acquire a list of State Department employees who are delinquent in their payments to the departmental credit union he would draw unwanted attention to himself. In acquiring this and other nonclassified information he would be better off making his inquiries through a "utility operative" who was a credit investigator, an insurance claims investigator, or the like. If he wanted a prospective agent kept under surveillance during a trial period (and keeping any person under observation is not against the laws of the District of Columbia, unless illegal means or harassment are involved), he would certainly want to use some innocuous-appearing third party with good excuses for the surveillance, rather than conduct it himself and run the risk of blowing the operation before it started.

A utility operative is an employee of the resident or case officer, whose work is not illegal and who is breaking the law only in those countries where it is illegal merely to be in contact with a foreign national or to pass *any* information to a foreign national, whether classified or not.* To put it more broadly, a utility agent is one who performs for a resident (or a case officer, or even a station chief) all those chores which a foreign national cannot perform without drawing attention to himself.

Then there is a low-level subcategory of the utility operative known as the "cutout." Cutouts are members of an espionage system who have but one function: the passing of messages between an agent and his principal—or case officer, or even station chief—with the agent usually not knowing the source of the message coming to him or the ultimate recipient of the messages he sends. In the beginning stages of an operation an agent gives his messages directly to his principal, who passes them to the resident, who passes them to the case officer. As

---

* In the United States, anyone who receives pay from a foreign government for any purpose must register with the Justice Department, but there are dozens of completely legal ways to get around this requirement.

soon as practicable, however, contacts between the agent and the principal, the principal and the resident, and so on up the line, are kept "clean"—i.e., free of any incriminating materials. That is to say, as soon as an operation is functioning properly, without the need of constant supervision, arrangements are made for all incriminating materials to be transmitted through a cutout specially set up and trained for the purpose. In many cases, where "dead-letter drops" are possible, the cutout can himself be eliminated. But an operation usually requires a cutout or two, at least in reserve, because he has the advantage of mobility: a "dead-letter drop" is normally a stationary place, and even when it is a roving one (e.g., a train or airplane lavatory) cutouts are normally needed to service it.

THE ESPIONAGE "OPERATION"

There was once a time when an agent worked as part of a team, a "network," which comprised not only those in the direct line between the agent and the case officer but other agents whose spying complemented his or who otherwise helped out in a team effort. The famous spies of the Forties and early Fifties—Allen Nunn May, Klaus Fuchs, Philby, etc.—were all part of "networks," and to catch any member of a network was to clean up the whole operation. In modern espionage the network has all but disappeared, and the term "network" has fallen into disrepute because it implies a kind of operation of which espionage experts disapprove. The network, in its classic form, now supposedly exists only in what we call "special operations." In various parts of the U.S.S.R., for example, there are "networks" of agents which operate pretty much as French resistance networks operated during World War II. Even in such places, though, the linear espionage operation is favored wherever it is possible.

A strict linear operation consists of one case officer who handles one resident, who handles one principal, who handles only one agent, with one or more cutouts servicing this operation and no other persons involved. It is the ideal espionage operation. In practice, a case officer may handle as many as three or four operations, and he may use his resident and his principals to handle more than one operation each, and he may use his utility operatives "across the board" to service *all* his operations. This is necessary, at whatever the cost to security, not only for budgetary reasons but for purposes of keeping the case officer busy: handling only one strictly linear operation would necessarily involve long waits between actions, and there is always the danger that the idle case officer will become so absorbed in his cover duties that he will be unprepared to behave efficiently when the time for action arises. "The best case officer is the busiest case officer" is a maxim taught in the espionage specialists' management course. All the same, no matter how many operations a case officer may handle he must fight a continuing battle to ensure that each remains as compartmented as possible and that none of them shapes up as "networks." *

A CIA espionage operation—or one by the SIS, or probably even a Soviet espionage operation, since the Soviet KVD has at long last entered the Seventies—might shape up as follows:

1. A single *agent*, one with access to target;
2. A *principal*, someone who is on intimate terms (openly or clandestinely) with the agent and who can face him directly from time to time—originally for purposes of development and recruitment, and later for purposes of morale and discipline;
3. A *cutout*, ideally known to the agent only by sight, whose only job is to pick up documents from the agent, deliver them to the resident, and return them to the agent after they have been photocopied;

---

* What is important is that agents working in the same department be kept apart and unaware of one another. Philby, Burgess, and Maclean, all Soviet agents inside the British diplomatic establishment, knew all about one another. But this sort of "network" camaraderie is no longer allowed, not even by Soviet intelligence—except, of course, in longtime operations where it already exists and the harm cannot be undone.

4. The *resident*;
5. The *case officer*.

In addition, there will ordinarily be an assortment of "utility agents"—messenger boys, private investigators, travel agents, etc.—who are kept apart from the operation once it has been properly started and "verified"—but who, without being aware of any specifics of the operation itself, are used to collect the data on which it is based and kept functioning. It is this assortment of "utility agents," plus whatever is at the disposal of the station chief locally in the way of cover organizations, which gives birth to the impression of an omniscient "espionage system" which is supposedly the mark of the great intelligence agencies. The chief of an active station can often cover a whole capital city or port with stationary surveillances. When the CIA's station chief in a certain Middle Eastern capital said, "No cabinet minister in Cairo can go to the bathroom without my knowing about it," he was exaggerating only slightly. But this does not mean that, from this "third-country base," he was covering Cairo in such a way that when the Egyptian security forces pick up one utility agent they can sweat out of him the details of the whole system. The linear operation is still the mainstay of espionage work.

CONVENTIONAL ESPIONAGE

Well, there are ordinary spies "penetrating targets" . . .

INSTRUCTORS in intelligence schools like to believe that there is but one kind of agent worth having, and but one set of methods by which to develop, recruit, train, and manage him. Every station chief dreams of having just one "Emily": ideally, he would like to have *only* Emilys. But a review of the operating files of a cross section of station chiefs—CIA, SIS or KGB—would certainly show that many stations have no Emilys or agents of conventional types at all, and that *all* their agents are "exceptions."

Still, since the Emily remains an ideal, it is appropriate for us to consider how the Emily operation is conceived, planned, and set up. With modification, the same procedures are also used in operations that do not fit the standard pattern.

THE TARGET

Any espionage operation begins with a consideration of what is known to intelligence officers as "the target." An intelligence target may be defined as anything containing information that is not only secret, but accessible only by means of espionage. It can be a whole country: for example, all of Syria is a target to the Israeli intelligence service, just as all of Occupied Europe was a target of Allied intelligence during World War II. It can be a large geographical area—as, for example, areas of the U.S.S.R. which contain military sites, factories, and scientific installations that are inaccessible to outsiders. It can be an office: everything that is said and done in the office of the U.S. Secretary of State is of interest to Soviet intelligence; hence that office, as such, is a target. More often it is a filing cabinet containing classified information, or a laboratory containing classified substances—or substances that indicate the nature of secret activities conducted by the laboratory. Even a classified-wastepaper basket may be designated a target—as may be a nonclassified-wastepaper basket into which telltale scraps of classified material occasionally find their way.

A target is something physical. It cannot be the mind of a person, but it can be the person himself. You cannot expect an agent to answer such a question as "What does Tito think about Sadat's visit to Moscow?" because even the cleverest of spies is unable to read minds. But you may ask, "What did Tito *say* about Sadat's visit to Moscow?"

In the early planning stages of an espionage operation, there are what we call the "broad" targets. A whole country is certainly a "broad" target, and so is a large geographical area such as the Ukraine. For the planning of an espionage operation, even a ministry of war or an office within that ministry must be narrowed down. This is done by a "target study," which collects sufficient "operational data" to narrow down the target to such items as file cabinets, desks, closets, and even wastepaper baskets and to identify "subtargets"—i.e., places where the desired secret documents may be kept temporarily (e.g., desk tops, OUT baskets, messenger bags, etc.). An agent possessing the combination to the war minister's safe is of tremendous value. An agent (a charwoman, perhaps) whose duties include emptying the war minister's personal wastepaper basket * is ordinarily less valuable, but certainly preferable

---

* In all great governments, offices containing secret information have precise procedures for destroying "classified waste," and the employee of such an office who carelessly puts classified waste into ordinary baskets

to an agent whose only qualification is an ability to get into the defense-ministry building.

"OPERATIONAL DATA"

"Operational data" is information which the espionage special-ist accumulates for the purposes of planning his own opera-tions. It will include, first and most important, all that data that makes up the target study: location of the target and sub-targets, what is needed to get into the target and its sub-targets (e.g., safe combinations, special keys, etc.), all security devices protecting the target and subtargets, identities of per-sons with legal access to them, and security controls on these persons. It will also include a wide range of information that may suggest means of contacting and then influencing one or more of these persons. For example, lists of employees owing money to office credit unions can be very valuable. So can membership lists of various employee associations, in particu-lar those which are entirely social in nature. One Soviet case officer in London is known to have concentrated on bulletin boards in government offices. Even such simple items as an-nouncements of office parties, charity drives, and employee-union meetings give helpful hints about the off-hours behavior of the employees, and announcements such as "1970 Volks-wagen for sale" and "Passenger, sharing expenses, for car trip to Glasgow" sometimes constitutes a gold mine of possible contacts. There is an instance in which a Soviet case officer in

---

not clearly labeled DESTROY is punished. Punishing the minister himself, however, is awkward. Besides, the thinking of ministers is normally far above such mundane matters as wastepaper baskets. For this reason, it seems, the higher one goes in a bureaucratic hierarchy the more likely one is to find espionage gold mines in the form of personal wastepaper baskets. Since this fact is as well known to counterspies as it is to spies, top-ranking people in government services ordinarily have their waste-paper baskets, desk tops and drawers, closets, and old raincoats lying about checked by security officers specially assigned to the task. It thus becomes the task of the officer planning the penetration to recruit the security officer for his agent rather than a mere charwoman.

Washington, D.C., established contact with a prospective agent by having one of his principal agents answer a billboard notice advertising a car pool.

Any case officer worth his salt will at least have telephone directories of all offices on his list of assigned targets, whether unclassified, classified, or made up piecemeal from various probings; floor plans of those offices; the makes and locations of all principal safes and filing cabinets; copies of regulations pertaining to handling of classified documents; personnel tables; arrangements for physical upkeep of the buildings; and such details as how tea and coffee breaks are handled. He will also have conducted sufficient surveillances of a selected cross section of the employees to have a general idea of how they live outside of working hours and what off-hour security controls exist. If he is a really imaginative case officer, he will have established means for getting at the registers of all the principal hotels in his assigned country, the passenger lists of all airplanes entering and leaving the country, and even lists of automobile registrations.

Chronologically, at least, keeping the operational-data files up to date is the first duty of the station chief and his case officers, and some officers get so carried away with the duty that they are slow in getting around to using the files for their intended purpose, the spotting of desirable agents. For years a favorite topic of argument among intelligence officers of many nationalities was which service had the most interesting operational-data files. It was finally conceded that the French *Service de Documentation Extérieure et de Contre-espionnage* deserved the prize for an amassment of data which a disaffected employee used as a basis for the famous *Sinners' Guide* series. Most of the issues were withdrawn as the result of action either by the SDECE or by publishers facing libel suits, but *The Sinners' Guide to London*—containing, among other things, the addresses and descriptions of high-class brothels, massage parlors, homosexual rendezvous, group-sex clubs, opium dens, and witchcraft covens, together with gossipy little bits about their famous and wellborn patrons

—may still be bought under-the-counter in some London hotels for £100.

The aim of the target study is to establish that the documents you are seeking are located in a particular safe in a particular office, and that such-and-such a person, among all those who have access to the safe, is the one most likely to yield to temptation. Actually, the results of the ordinary target study are rarely that precise. Instead, it will turn up the fact that the documents sometimes move about during the day—from the hands of a confidential secretary to the desk of an officer, and sometimes in the satchel of a messenger to the desk of an officer in another office, then back again through the same route—and that they are kept not in one safe but in several, or possibly in locked filing cabinets split under a number of different headings. More often than not, it will establish that more than one person handles them in the course of a day—or *could* handle them, if properly instructed, without exciting suspicion.

Any one of these persons could be considered a prospective agent; to put it another way, a list of these persons will be your list of prospective agents. The list may be broken down as follows:

> *Primary prospects:* officers, confidential secretaries, security officers who are legally entitled to remove the documents from the files and handle them without exciting suspicions;
>
> *Secondary prospects:* file clerks, typists, messengers, and others who handle the documents in the course of their duties, but who cannot legally on their own initiative take the documents from the files (and who wouldn't normally have access to the files outside of working hours);
>
> *Tertiary prospects:* charwomen, electricians, plumbers, and others who have access to the offices in which the files are

located but no excuse to get at the documents—and no ability to do so except by chance.

Naturally, the case officer first concentrates on the primary prospects, descending to the other categories only after he has eliminated the primary categories as possibilities. We must recruit *somebody* to start with, possibly more than one person, if only to get at such operational data as will enable him to figure out means of working his way up to a prospective agent on the "primary" list.

Two kinds of prospective agents fit none of these categories. One is the official who is on overseas duty, but who may eventually be transferred to his home headquarters. Prospects such as this are comparatively easy to screen, approach, and train, and they can often be of value before they are transferred. A first secretary in the Soviet Embassy would be an interesting haul for either the CIA or the SIS, and a first secretary of the U.S. Embassy in Paris would be an interesting haul for the KGB. Contrary to what the diplomats may think, the American, British, and Soviet Embassies in Paris and other major capitals *do* handle large amounts of secret correspondence that would be of interest to each other's intelligence services, and they are in themselves worthwhile targets for espionage. Moreover, a diplomat recruited in a major capital normally stands a greater chance of getting a home assignment than does a diplomat in some backwater such as Conakry.

The second kind of prospective agent outside the main categories is the personal contact, especially female. Until recently, every major intelligence service drilled its personnel not to discuss even the most trivial official matters with their spouses; but this has changed. Today, the American, British, French, and Soviet diplomatic services regard wives as part of husband-and-wife teams, and all four countries have courses especially for wives. Although there is no way of compiling dependable statistics, I have heard more than one member of a major intelligence service speculate that about half of the agents in the world were recruited through their wives, and that a large number of agents *are* wives.

Although the day of the Mata Hari femme fatale is over, it is simply amazing what a generally discreet official will tell to some sweet, innocent-looking girl with whom he is infatuated. Upon hearing from a defector of the secrets a female Soviet agent had picked up from her lover in the State Department, the CIA's Allen Dulles remarked that he thought "It's being spread about that mistresses are no longer used as spies just to throw everybody off guard."

The same applies to household servants, especially house-keepers and maids. It has been established that, for whatever reason, people tend to trust their female servants much more than their male. Once a servant has been around so long as to become "a part of the family" it is hard to believe that she or he could be reporting to some foreign intelligence agency any secrets that might be dropped at the dinner table. Government officials, especially diplomats serving abroad, are warned not to discuss secret matters in their homes, even when they have been "swept" for hidden microphones, but anyone who has spent any time in the home of top American or British official knows that secret matters *are* discussed, and in the presence of servants.*

CIA and SIS case officers have learned that Soviet and Bloc officials are equally careless—although they know that some of their servants are planted there by their *own* security services, and that their conversational indiscretions might land them in serious troubles. A friend of mine who is a CIA "bug man" tells me that on a tape recording picked up from a microphone under the dinner table in the home of a Soviet diplomat, the

---

* A belief that one's servants are too stupid or short on English to understand confidential official discussions is one reason for this carelessness. It is insufficiently understood that espionage services have briefing and de-briefing techniques by which even a semiliterate agent knowing but little of the languages of the conversations he overhears can make himself tremendously valuable simply by being on the lookout for specific names and phrases.

diplomat's wife is heard chiding the diplomat for something indiscreet he had apparently said in the presence of a servant who had just left the room.

"Do you suppose she is an American spy?" asked the diplomat.

"God help us, let us *hope* so," answered the wife.

MAKING CONTACT WITH THE PROSPECTIVE AGENT

The target study gives us what we need to know in order to select our prospective agent, but there it ends. We are left with the really difficult problem of making contact. If the man is a foreign-ministry official who circulates freely in the *corps diplomatique*, the job is less complicated; many a normal diplomatic contact has led to one party's being turned into an agent by the other. More often, though, the prospective agent is a lowly clerk, while the case officer is an officer of a foreign embassy, and the enormous social gulf between them makes contact a severe problem.

Since the wise strategist starts at the goal and thinks his way back to the starting point, the effective case officer first selects the agent he wants, then chooses the principal agent with the best chances of recruiting him. An intelligence station will always have on tap a number of prospective principals who have proved themselves recruitable and who, collectively, have access to the milieus that prospective agents frequent. After selecting his prospective agent, the case officer will then check all the operational data he has accumulated on that prospective agent—his range of social contacts, clubs, hobbies (especially those which involve group activity), religious activities, and various personal services he employs, from his dentist to his milkman. Added up, all this information describes what is known as the prospective agent's "area of contact," and is represented graphically by a circle surrounding a dot which represents the prospective agent himself.

If we draw an "area of contact" circle around the case officer or his resident, we will probably find that it in no way overlaps the circle of the prospective agent. The trick then is to find someone with a circle which overlaps both that of the case officer and that of the prospective agent—or, failing that, someone whose circle overlaps that of the prospective agent and, at the same time, overlaps the circle of someone else whose circle, finally, overlaps that of the case officer or his resident. In the spirit of Archimedes' "Give me enough levers and I'll lift the world," imaginative espionage specialists believe it is possible for literally anyone, given enough contact circles, to get to anyone else—including the Queen of England or Howard Hughes. Linking a case officer, or his resident, to an agent is not nearly as difficult as it may first seem; no more than four rings are normally required—and these, usually, can be cut down to three after the operation is established.

SELECTING THE PRINCIPAL AGENT

The trick lies in finding the right principal agent. The principal is by definition someone who *can* meet a prospective agent. If he can't—and if you can't help him figure out some way of doing so—find another one.

In its early days, the CIA course in espionage included a lecture entitled "Selection and Recruitment of Principal Agents" —but officers returning from the field soon reported that there was nothing to be said in such a lecture which a halfway intelligent espionage specialist couldn't figure out for himself. A case officer spots some clerk in the defense ministry whom he would like to have as an agent; he has him followed to determine his profile. In the course of this surveillance the officer notes the man's contacts who lie within his own area of contact —or his resident's, or that of some other principal whom he already has on tap. Unless the prospective agent is a total hermit, who sees or speaks to no one outside his office, he is bound to have some points of contact with the outside world, one or more of which is within reach of the one or more of the case officer's prospective principals.

While the case officer is concentrating on his prospective agent, literally dozens of persons belonging to what espionage officers call "the fringe" will be presenting themselves, directly or indirectly. "The fringe," which exists in every capital, consists of those members of the indigenous population who gravitate toward the foreign community. They are travel agents, journalists, academicians in certain lines of study, artists, writers, and simply people who have studied in foreign universities. They are equally at home at diplomatic cocktail parties and at local gatherings. Local security agents will have been planted among the fringe, of course, but they tend to stand out like sore thumbs because their bosses, suspicious of genuine fringe members, generally choose for their agents persons who have no fringe characteristics, then give them inadequate expense accounts so that they are seen drinking beer when everyone else is on gin and tonic. Diplomats and newspapermen who frequent the Nile Hilton Hotel in Cairo will know what I mean.

The fringe is full of prospective principals—persons whose *dream* is to be in the employ of some well-paying foreign government. Fringes are most conspicuous in capitals of the so-called Third World, but they are also in evidence in Warsaw, Prague, and even Moscow. In Washington and London the Soviets can find in this group, numerous people who wouldn't actually spy, who would be delighted, for appropriate fees, to perform small services that would help a Soviet case officer line up his operations. To find such persons, all the Soviet case officer needs is an expert knowledge of American or British income-tax laws.

Moscow is supposedly the toughest nut for the American or British case officer to crack. But I know an SIS officer who organized several espionage operations in that city, right under the noses of the Soviet security authorities, by following a very simple rule. When he first arrived, he studied the "contact circles" of various clerks in the Foreign Ministry and other Government offices. Soon he had dozens of prospective principal agents whose areas of contact overlapped both his own and those of the few clerks he had decided to recruit as agents. They all lacked two requirements, however: they lived in mortal fear of their security services, and they were insufficiently senior to openly meet with foreigners except in crowds. So the SIS officer asked himself: Who in the U.S.S.R. are not afraid of the security authorities and are confident enough to publicly contact foreigners? Any member of the Communist Party! The officer thenceforth looked exclusively to the Communist Party for his principals, wondering why he hadn't thought of it before. I have been told by friends in the CIA that not mere members, but full-time Party workers make the best principals because they can stretch their areas of contact any way they want inside the Soviet Union.*

BEGINNING THE INVOLVEMENT

The difficulty is not in getting the principal to meet the prospective agent; it's in building on the original contact. Slowly, cautiously, without arousing suspicions, the principal must build a relationship with his prospect that will eventually lead him to the point at which he is "recruitable." During this time, known by case officers as the "development period," the principal must not give the slightest indication that he has an interest in the prospective agent's job or secrets. Even if the prospective agent brings up such matters himself, the principal should affect a lack of interest in them until he is certain the prospective agent is ripe.

In his first meeting with his prospective agent, the principal must remember "the opening part of a sales presentation is to

---

* A friend of mine in the CIA who is an Irish Catholic tells me that the Agency's espionage specialists who deal with the U.S.S.R. have found that Communist Party organizers are "ideologically Communist only in the sense that Jesuit priests are devoutly Catholic."

125

sell the presentation itself, not the product." He must devote himself to convincing the agent that there is something to be gained from the relationship itself, and that the "something worthwhile" will be in no way connected with the prospective agent's job interests. In dealing with a particularly sensitive prospect—for example, a spinster, who has undoubtedly been warned again and again to be on guard against men who pretend to want love and marriage—it is imperative that the principal hold out only attractions that have "Novocain"—suspicion deadeners—built into them.

The success of a principal in getting successfully through the development period seems to depend, first, on an ability to dig beneath appearances and get a *dependable* answer to the question "What, apart from his job, does the prospective agent want from life that he or she is not getting?" and second, on an ability to suggest to the prospect that the principal can be instrumental in getting it for him or her, adumbrating the suggestion both so effectively and so subtly that the prospective agent is prompted to take the initiative in maintaining the contact. If the prospect has a wife dying of cancer, the principal "once had an aunt who lingered for months before dying of cancer" and so is able to be keenly sympathetic to the problem and offer helpful suggestions. If the prospective agent is a spendthrift and chronically in debt, the principal sees this as the result of that commendable quality Thinking Big, and he knows some unusual way of arranging low-interest loans. (Later, he shows that he knows a thing or two about how the prospect had *better* solve the problem, or he will wind up losing his job.) If the prospective agent has a mistress, the principal has one too. The point is that while the principal shows *no* interest in the prospective agent's business life, he is increasingly sympathetic toward his personal problems.

In the CIA's course on "The Selection, Development and Recruitment of Agents," students are asked to suggest ways in which personal relationships may be developed for *any* ulterior purpose—whether it is selling a product, gaining influence for lobbying purposes, more sexual seduction, or espionage. There is never a shortage of ideas. In addition, in a review of specific agent recruitments, the students find that the variety of ways in which a personal relationship may be nurtured is so wide that no rules can be laid down. There are two pointers, however, which clearly emerge from the variety of cases. The first is that, at least in the beginning, the simplest and *least* personal yearnings of the prospective agent are the most easily played upon: for example, plain loneliness, feelings of inferiority, or a desire to have an occasional meal in a good restaurant which, on a civil servant's pay, would otherwise be out of reach. More personal yearnings can be identified later. The second general rule is to be sufficiently sensitive to realize when an apparently lonely person really *likes* being alone, so that the principal can entertain the prospect without annoying or patronizing him.

BROADENING THE "AREA OF CONSCIENCE"

Once a relationship has been established, and after the principal has become sure of the prospective agent's motivations and prejudices, the principal begins to introduce two new elements: dependence, and an interest in the prospect's job. The prospective agent must be so used to the principal's favors that he takes them for granted and doesn't even question the possible motives behind them. As a rule, it's not the size of the favors that counts; it's their regularity. The prospect must grow to *depend* on them to such an extent that he would miss them were they to be cut off.

Generally a person will more readily allow himself to become obligated to another if he is provided with an excuse relating to some cause he regards as worthy. A prospective agent who would not think of accepting straight gifts of money to pay off ordinary debts might happily allow some friend to pay the hospital bills of his ailing mother. Receiving such help is even more palatable if the friend is able to convince the prospective agent that he is not paying the bills himself, but is simply using his influence with the hospital to obtain a sub-

127

stantial reduction. The point is this: the principal must not only get the prospective agent into the habit of accepting his largesse; he must enable him to rationalize it so that it will not be a constant burden on his conscience.

This question of conscience comes up particularly when the time arrives for the principal to start showing an interest in the agent's job. Remember the case of "Emily." Foster didn't immediately tell Emily that he wanted to recruit her as an agent. Instead, he asked her for some favor which connected with her job and which involved a security violation so small that she didn't have the heart to refuse. After Emily had done a string of small favors, her conscience had learned to justify them—or, in the jargon of espionage specialists, her "area of conscience had been expanded." In taking the prospective agent up to the point of actual recruitment, the principal never asks him to do anything that lies beyond this "area."

Typically, the first task given a new agent is the theft of a classified telephone directory or any item which the principal can present a plausible reason for wanting, but which carries a low security classification. The agent wrestles with his conscience, then decides to do as the principal has asked. He removes the classified directory (or whatever) from his desk as he leaves his office at the end of the day, delivers it to the principal (who probably makes no use of it at all), spends a sleepless night imagining that at any moment his organization's security officials will be knocking at the door, gets the directory back from the principal in the morning, takes it back to the office, and breathes a long sigh of relief. It was easy! The next time it is easier. Finally, the agent removes simple documents of low classification without any worry or twinge of conscience whatever. At this time he is ready to be moved to more important missions.

Eventually, of course, he realizes that he is working for an espionage organization; but *it is not necessary that the agent know for which espionage service he is working.* If the principal is properly covered, he could be representing *any* espionage service, governmental or private. If the prospective agent hates Americans, the principal agent can tell him he is acting in behalf of the French—or the British, the Soviets, or some Senator or crusading newspaperman. The possibilities are infinite. I have a theory that *most* spies really don't know which espionage service they are working for. Their principals will have figured out which services their consciences are most likely to tolerate, and will have recruited them under these covers.

REGULARIZING THE OPERATION

There is a brief period, the first month or so after beginning his real work, when an agent is in a state of euphoria. He has overcome his initial fears of getting caught; he has realized the blessings of the easy extra money brought to him by his spying; his "area of conscience" has been "stretched" to such a point that what he does seems almost entirely justifiable. During this period it looks so easy that the agent is likely to become reckless. The principal must step in at this point and give the new agent what is known as the "bittersweet talk." It varies from service to service, but the thrust is always the same:

> "You have just undertaken a way of life that promises you well-being, security, and peace of mind in return for duties that will be very easy and require but little of your time. But there is one requirement: you must follow our instructions to the letter. They are very easy instructions; following them will put no strain on you, but you may occasionally fail to appreciate their importance, become impatient, and be tempted to ignore one or another of them. *This must not happen.* As long as you follow our rules we will give you all the backing and protection you need. But if you break any one of them, our obligation to you is over."

This is no mere pep talk; the principal means every word he says. He tells the new agent that his safety is more important than any information he might conceivably bring in—and he means it. This is one of the most important rules of agent management: the agent himself is always more important than his information. Maintaining such an attitude might occasionally mean passing up some item of tremendous importance, but in the long run it pays off because it keeps the agent feeling safe and happy and maintains his productivity over a long period of years.

Beginning with the "bittersweet talk," the principal commences a complete overhaul of his relationship with his recruit. From a friendship built on mutual interests and the sharing of personal confidences, it becomes one of employer to employee. The feelings of friendship, goodwill, and sympathy remain—it is necessary that the principal and his agent genuinely *like* each other—but the agent must be made to understand that he cannot take advantage of these feelings for purposes that are inconsistent with those of the principal. The constant meetings that were necessary during the development period must end. Once the agent is recruited, contact should be infrequent and irregular.

This new relationship must be carefully planned by the principal—with the help, of course, of his case officer or resident. The first step is to review the agent's daily routine. The purpose of the exercise is to answer the question: Exactly how would this person spend his waking hours were he *not* an agent? His life after becoming an agent must be, to all but anyone keeping him under *complete* surveillance, *identical* with what it was before—unless, of course, there are changes in it that can be justified without reference to his new duties.

Under the cover of normal behavior, the agent has three positive acts to perform: he must take documents from his target office, copy them, and return them to the target office; he must put the copies in some place where the principal or his cutout can get at them; he must occasionally meet with the principal merely to keep up the contact, or to discuss problems or receive new instructions. Regularizing the operation consists of arranging for the performance of these three acts without their making the barest ripple on the surface of the agent's day-to-day behavior.

The most dangerous act is the removal and return of the secret documents. The Minox camera—or, rather, a smaller version developed by a Japanese company especially for the purposes of industrial espionage—remains the favorite means of copying. With it, the agent photocopies the documents in his own office, and takes home the negatives in something as small as his cigarette lighter. To use any kind of ordinary camera, the agent would have to stay late in his office, lock the door, prop up the documents under an especially strong light, and make other suspicious movements. In most Communist governments it is a rare official who has enough privacy to accomplish this safely: the agent would excite suspicion merely by staying late, and if a guard found his office locked he would immediately trigger an investigation. Consequently, in these countries the Minox is indispensable.

There is another machine, a variant of the Diebold copier of the Fifties, that was used to good effect for a while by both Western and Bloc espionage operatives. This handy gadget, which looks like an ordinary notebook, takes pictures automatically as documents are slipped into it. Its use is so simple that an agent can take photocopies right at his desk, even with others in the room. The Soviets are now on to it, however, so that merely possessing it is incriminating. Its use has been all but discontinued except in countries where office employees are so unfamiliar with modern gadgetry that it can go unnoticed.

In some instances the agent may use the target office's own photocopying equipment—provided it has been established that any record of its use can be expunged. The Xerox photocopiers used by the CIA, for example, have been specially adjusted so that the number of copies made of any document is permanently recorded—you cannot, for example, set the control at "6" when it is ordinarily at "5" and then turn it back after you have run off an illicit extra copy. The Soviets, for their part, try to apply so many safeguards against illicit office copying that they overlook the electronic devices, and American and British agents working there have no trouble using office equipment. Soviet agents planted in the American and British governments, on the other hand, find it difficult to fool the security controls on office equipment, but seem to have little difficulty in getting the documents themselves out of their offices and doing their photocopying at home.

Then there is the old trick, used by stenographic agents, of making an extra carbon of everything they type. Or there is always that old standby, human memory—which can be trained to a high degree of precision.* Or an agent can take the actual documents, mark them for incineration, put dummies in the BURN baskets, and then take the originals home. There are numerous safe ways of getting copies of secret documents, or the documents themselves, out of a target office. The choice is not made casually. And since it is the first item in the principal's planning session with the agent, the principal will go to extra pains in examining all the possibilities just to impress the agent with how meticulously every move must be planned.

Next is the question of delivery. Once the agent has the documents out of his office, together with any written reports of what he has seen or heard, what does he do with them? Does he code them in secret ink, reduce them to microdots which can be disguised as punctuation marks in innocuous personal letters, or send summaries of their content by short-wave wireless? No. Except in the most primitive of operations, he puts the material some place *that he visits normally* so that

---

* Most manuals on the organization and management of espionage systems so emphasize the importance of acquiring original documents or perfect photocopies that some case officers try to dispense with agents' reports altogether. They soon learn, however, that there is no point in passing up the valuable information that their agents may get merely as the result of keeping their ears open, and they begin to accept written reports—and even to encourage them, as long as the agent doesn't begin to regard them as substitutes for the real thing. The really effective case officer takes the best he can get, whatever it happens to be.

the cutout or courier can get at them. Pay special attention to the phrase "that he visits normally": The space behind the mirror in the men's toilet of the Nile Hilton is an excellent "dead-letter drop" for some agents—but not for the agent who never goes to expensive hotels and who would look out of place there. Another spot would be under a rock in a wooded area—but not unless the agent was in the habit of taking walks in the woods before he became an agent. Similar consideration must be given to "brush" exchanges which can take place at concerts, football games, and visits to other crowded places. The exchange of shopping baskets in a supermarket as portrayed at one time in the comic strip *Buzz Sawyer* is a perfectly valid "brush" exchange. No matter what the site, the objective of the planner is to select a place that is easily accessible to the agent in the course of his normal movements and allows for a secret exchange.

Finally, there is the question of the now irregular meetings between the principal and the agent. It is usually better to have these meetings in the open, preferably with other people around. A sure way for an agent to come to the attention of his security officer is to be seen in some out-of-the-way place dining with one other person. It is a rare sort of social gathering or sports match at which two persons are unable to have all the conversation necessary. The principal will, of course, have a special "safe house" where he can meet the agent when serious, floor-pacing meetings are essential, but it will be used only rarely—and only after the agent has been thoroughly drilled in countersurveillance techniques and has been equipped with a standard cover story to explain his being out of circulation for the durations of these special meetings.

TRAINING OF THE ESPIONAGE AGENT

Contrary to popular opinion, the espionage agent gets very little training. There was a time when the great services drilled every agent in a wide range of spy techniques—but thanks to the Soviets' experiences, they have all learned that such training often does more harm than good.

After World War II, the Soviets found out to their cost that training of an agent either gives him professional mannerisms, which are undesirable, or scares him. One of their best agents, a Pentagon employee who otherwise might never have been caught, drew the attention of FBI agents who had him under routine surveillance because he practiced "countersurveillance techniques" every day as he went home from work. Had he innocently gone his way every evening, the FBI agents would have dropped him after a few days and moved on to a "spot" surveillance of some other employee.* But once his professional behavior drew their attention they regarded him as worthy of *intensive* surveillance—which, as the Soviets have learned from sad experience, *nobody* can escape.

On the other hand, training an agent might merely frighten him or activate his conscience; for that matter, so would any instructions that unduly dramatized to the agent the fact that he had become a spy. The whole technique of agent management is one of underplaying the job. Although the principal must constantly emphasize the necessity of the agent's sticking painstakingly to instructions, he must at the same time make the agent feel that his job is a simple one and pooh-pooh any misgivings that what he is doing might be harmful to his country's interests.†

---

* Every employee of the U.S. Government who has access to highly secret materials is at least occasionally put under "spot" surveillance which rarely lasts more than a day or two.
† In the days when the Soviets relied heavily on their Communist parties and before they got around to modern techniques of conventional espionage, they deliberately ingrained in their prospective agents the habit of thinking conspiratorially. One disaffected CP member told his FBI interrogators, "Even when there was no need for it, our cell leaders insisted on our taking indirect routes to meetings, which were in places that not only *were* secret but *looked* secret, and using cover names and all sorts of other devices just to keep us thinking in terms of secrecy." And later, a Soviet agent who turned himself in to the FBI as the result of a crisis of conscience said, "I really didn't worry until they began to give me all that training. Then I suddenly felt *dirty*."

In a properly organized espionage operation, the duties of the agent are so routine that he is able to carry them out with his ordinary skills and common sense. Training an agent is ordinarily no more than teaching him how to recognize traps that might have been planted by the security people, how to thwart spot checks that security officers might make of safes and filing cabinets from which the agent has removed documents, how to get to meeting places without being followed, and what to do in the event of emergency. If the operation requires any actions more complicated than these, then it should be so reorganized that the burden for such actions falls on the principal or another professional. In the ideal modern espionage operation, the agent does *not* use secret inks, radio sets, except for receiving, or special smuggling equipment. These are matters for the professionals. And obvious professionalism can be as undesirable in spies as it is in prostitutes.

COMMUNICATIONS, INTERNAL

Internal communications are those concerning all that happens to an agent's materials from the moment they leave the target office until they are ready to be transmitted outside the country. External communications are those incident to getting the materials out of the target country and into the hands of the espionage branch's processors at headquarters. If the taking-off point is an intelligence station in an embassy in the country where the agent operates, there is no problem of external communications: they are handled by diplomatic bag. More often than not, however, a station is concerned not with operations in the country where it is located but with operations in some neighboring country.

In speaking of communications, espionage specialists use the term "station" to indicate all points where the agent's materials and reports stop after delivery and before pickup, or merely change hands. (The term used in this sense should not, of course, be confused with the "station" in the diplomatic installation which houses the "station chief" and his staff.) The most-used station is the "dead-letter drop," and it is of three types: "city"—a "drop" located in some very public place, and hidden by the very fact that it is accessible to so many people; "country"—a "drop" in some secluded place rarely frequented by anyone; "moving"—a "drop" in a train, bus, subway, airplane, or delivery truck—unknown to the driver. Whichever type is used, it must be one that is accessible to the agent in the course of his *normal* movements.

The "city drop" is the most tempting: it is normally the most convenient, both to the agent and to the principal agent or courier; it allows for quick transmission; and it is generally quite safe. Once an operation is believed to have become suspect, though, the city drop is ruled out unless it can be virtually the same as a "brush contact." Typical city dead-letter drops are behind a mirror in a men's washroom in a filling station; under a seat in a movie house; in a rarely used reference book in a library; in a trash can that is not due to be emptied for some hours. All sorts of ingenious places have been thought of, but the planners must remember this: there is *no* place so ingenious that it will be overlooked in a search by even routinely competent security investigators. Once an agent has come under surveillance, a city drop can be used safely only when the material and documents are picked up within seconds of being dropped.

The "country drop" has almost the opposite advantages—and disadvantages. Once the agent can find the time and excuse for visiting such a place, it can take a whole army of security investigators to search the entire path that an agent might take in the course of a walk or horseback ride in the country. Consequently, the country drop is generally favored, particularly when the agent is a walk-in, or became operational under circumstances that left doubts in the mind of the case officer. Since Sub-Lieutenant Bingham and his wife were recruited as the result of Mrs. Bingham's having presented herself at the Soviet Embassy in London, the Soviet case officer *assumed* his use of them would be short-lived. But he apparently thought that before the British security authorities decided to wrap it up he might get at least a few documents from Mrs. Bingham. Realizing she was a poor risk, he insisted on a country drop, although it was extremely inconvenient for himself as well as for the Binghams.

A "moving drop" is often tempting, because it may serve the desirable purpose of enabling the agent and his principal (or courier) to be separated from each other by miles. The recent waves of hijackings have greatly lowered the popularity of airplanes as dead-letter drops, but the agent's materials and reports are, after all, usually paper and not metal, and as recently as January, 1973, a Soviet agent in a military installation in New England was known to have been "dropping" his reports in the paper-towel container in a lavatory of the Boston air shuttle. He was caught purely by accident: the container inexplicably flew open, spilling obviously official documents over the floor—to be retrieved by a steward who was an avid reader of spy stories.

Lavatories on trains and buses are often used for dead-letter drops in the same way as those in hotels and movie houses—with the added advantage of being mobile, and the added disadvantage of risks due to breakdowns or changes of schedule. There are many other possibilities—from that of the agent who got his materials and reports out of the target building by dropping them into the soiled-laundry chute to the use of a traveling lending library. Case officers generally frown on anything that smacks of *Mission: Impossible*. Before they agree to *any* element of an operational plan, communications or any other, they run it through their "slipup list"—a standard checklist of everything that could possibly go wrong. It is a rare moving drop that can survive such a checkout.

The ordinary courier is still very much in use in the business of espionage, and he can be anyone who has normal access to the agent plus a wide range of contacts which could include the principal. An ordinary postal letter carrier is, of course, the best possible courier; as recently as 1970, FBI agents keeping a suspect agent's house under surveillance reported that *no* one had made contact with it—only to have their superior remind them that the letter carrier had visited it daily. Milkmen and garbage men are also possibilities; so are repairmen of various kinds, provided that there is sufficient excuse for them to visit the agent with a fair degree of regularity.

Then there is a wide range of persons whom an agent may "brush" in the course of his off-hours activities. We have already mentioned the swap of shopping baskets in a crowded supermarket. There is also the swap of identical briefcases in a crowded subway or railroad station, or even a simple pickpocket operation in any crowded place. The dark of a movie house, despite the fact that it has by now become a cliché of spy films, remains an ideal place for the brush contact— though perhaps not quite ideal from the agent's standpoint unless the picture is one he's really willing to sit through, as he must, from beginning to end.

The main problem of the brush contact is that of setting it up, because it is often better for the contacts to be irregular. Even when it is agreed that there is no objection to a regular brush, such as one taking place on a crowded subway which the agent rides every day, arrangements must take into account the unexpected changes of movement that occur in even the most well-ordered lives. In order to set up brush contacts, or "quick exchanges" (i.e., drops in city "stations" for immediate pickup), the principal and the agent must agree on a set of simple coded messages. Double-talk is forbidden: it is easy to decipher, and even if a third party were unable to make out what it meant, the very fact that it was being used would cause suspicion. A simple, straightforward statement made according to a prearranged code, however, need not appear extraordinary—for example, a simple comment made over a telephone such as "Sorry, I seem to have dialed the wrong number" or a picture postcard saying "Having wonderful time" on it. The signals listed in Appendix C—all of them totally innocuous-sounding—were the *only* ones given an agent who functioned for fourteen years in a European capital without being detected although he was under intensive surveillance at least three times. The agent is given a blind telephone number and a neutral address; he is told to make his calls from a public phone and to mail his cards from a variety of much-used boxes, such as those in hotel lobbies.

For the principal, communications are more complicated. He must maintain a variety of "clean" telephone numbers and addresses at which to receive calls and written messages. A Soviet principal in London kept as many as twenty different telephone numbers receiving messages—among others, those of a "turf accountant" (a British shop where one places bets on horse races), a "dial-a-meal" catering shop, and an accommodation address and three or four that took messages on tape recorders. Some of these phones were totally under his control, receiving only messages related to his espionage operations, but many belonged to genuine commercial or private establishments of such a nature that it was possible for him to intercept his messages there securely.

There is little wrong with use of the open mails for the transmission of operational messages. In the United States, Britain, and many European countries, the security agencies must have very concrete evidence before they are allowed to tamper with a suspect's mail. Besides, there is no dependable way of determining the origin of a letter or postcard: the security police can't keep every mailbox in town under surveillance. It is the recipient who has to worry, and messages are mostly, at the rate of about five to one, from the agent to the principal rather than vice versa. An agent may be supplied with an assortment of postcards, all in the handwriting of someone out of the country, and when he wishes to send a certain message he simply chooses an appropriate card from his collection and drops it into a mailbox. The principal may reply by sending any one of *his* assortment of "trash"-mail advertisements. Novels by John Le Carré (whose real name is David Cornwell, and who was once a senior member of the British secret service) provide numerous authentic examples. In one of his stories, the principal informed the agent that he desired a special meeting by sending him a tract requesting a donation for some charity, and the agent found out when and where the meeting was to take place by picking up a ticket at a pre-designated theater booking office. The agent showed up at the performance for which the ticket was booked, took his assigned seat, and found the principal or a courier in the seat next to him. There, he received direct instructions where next to proceed. Although as a novelist Mr. Le Carré must lean somewhat toward the flamboyant, as a former espionage specialist he knows that the essence of successful espionage is simplicity.

In planning of espionage communications, unnecessary exposure of one member of a system to another must be avoided. It is essential that the agent and the principal know each other: the agent needs guidance and inspiration from the principal, and the principal needs to "feel the agent's pulse every now and again." But there is rarely any good reason why a cutout or a courier need know the identity of the agent or even of the principal. Ideally, he will have been recruited by someone who has since left the jurisdiction of the security authorities under whose noses he operates, and his day-to-day control is accomplished under cover. His job is the simple one of picking up messages from an unidentified and largely unidentifiable stranger and passing them on to another unidentified and largely unidentifiable stranger. Whether he is moving (a courier) or stationary (an ordinary cutout—such as a proprietor of a newsstand, or a washroom attendant), there are numerous ways in which he can be "insulated," as espionage specialists say.

COMMUNICATIONS, EXTERNAL

Obviously, the best way of getting an agent's materials and reports from the target country to the espionage branch's head-quarters is the diplomatic pouch. The American and British services normally run their operations on a "third country" basis, so a border crossing may first be necessary. This is sometimes accomplished by ordinary smuggling. Other times special provisions can be made so that a station chief receives materials from operations run in his country by his colleague in a neighboring country, while otherwise keeping himself dissociated from the actual operations. Or a station chief can make arrangements with a friendly foreign intelligence service for the use of its pouch—in which case he might allow the foreign service's station chief complete access to the intelligence (minus, of course, any information that might identify the agent and other operational personnel), or he might code it or "sterilize" it, and reward the foreign station chief in some other way.*

Ordinary written reports can be transmitted as innocuous letters, starting with "Dear Mary" and including enough personal references to make them look harmless, or they can be written in secret inks between the lines of purely personal messages and sent through the open mails. Original documents, on the other hand, written in the language of the target country on official government stationery and bearing SECRET stamps, can be sent out neither by nondiplomatic courier nor by ordinary mail.

Everyone has read about microdots (the dot on the "i" in the word "microdots" could conceal, in microcopy, a page of print the equivalent of the page you are reading now) and other sophisticated ways of reducing original documents so

---

* Even the most unscrupulous espionage branches like to pretend that the diplomatic bag is one item that is off limits. All the same, I know station chiefs who spend a high percentage of their waking hours trying to figure out ways of stealing diplomatic bags that they believe to be carrying materials of their opposites. And there is the case of the CIA and KGB station chiefs who swapped their embassies' bags long enough to allow each to photocopy the contents of the other. It was a real swap: each had good reasons to believe that the other was acting independently of his headquarters and that, therefore, the material in both bags was genuine, so their respective "hauls" gained them tremendous praise in their respective headquarters—until both headquarters saw through their fake explanations of how they had come by the bags. The KGB officer was never heard of again, but the CIA officer was merely fired.

that they can be smuggled in small objects. But these have one drawback: they are highly incriminating, and they can be recognized even by an ignorant house servant provided he has been told what to look for. As for secret compartments in luggage or briefcases, the worldwide attack on heroin smuggling has now grown to such proportions that it is impossible to use such means for getting original documents, or full-size photocopies, past customs.

The result is that when it comes to transporting actual documents or full-size copies, the case officer more often than not has to have his principal store them for long periods before an appropriate means of transmission can be devised.

The agent himself should never be allowed to keep anything incriminating in his possession—no sophisticated copiers, no radio-transmission sets, no secret inks. If risk is to be run it is the principal, or some expendable cutout, who must run it. Not only is the principal more expendable than the agent; he is better prepared to look after himself in case of his operation's being "blown."

Secret writing *is* effective. The major intelligence services have devised a method of using chemically treated pads that is virtually impossible to break. The principal agent writes an innocuous "cover" message—a love letter, a piece of normal business correspondence, or whatever—then between the lines writes his espionage message, either using a colorless ink or by writing it with an ordinary ball-point pen on a specially treated sheet. This sheet is then placed over the cover message, and the agent steams the letter to smooth out any traces of pressure caused by the pen. Afterward he mails it according to established rules. To intercept his letter in the first place, security agents would have to impound the mailbox within seconds after he mailed his letter, or go through thousands of letters in the central post office not really knowing what they were looking for. Even if they intercepted the letter, they would have to stumble onto the right developing agent at their first try, or risk destroying the secret writing so that even the right developing agent wouldn't work. If there is any danger to the use of the best modern forms of secret writing, it is that of the principal's being interrupted by some outsider as he is steaming his message or hanging it up to dry. There is nothing telltale about the materials he uses.

Clandestine radio is also safer than is commonly supposed. Even with the most modern detection equipment, frequencies used for espionage transmissions are hard to catch—and still harder to identify for what they are because the transmissions sound like ordinary coded messages used legitimately by diplomatic installations and commercial concerns. Even if they come under active suspicion, by the time the direction finders ("DF-ing equipment") are in place to seek the point of origin, the message is over. Naturally, the "DF-ers" listen for the next transmission, but it may be on a different frequency and originate from a different place. Modern security agencies claim that they have sophisticated equipment which will overcome these difficulties, but it simply isn't so. The airwaves are full of illicit transmissions—from China, from various parts of Russia, and from parts of the Third World. When the senders are caught it is usually as the result of tip-offs from suspicious neighbors rather than from successful DF-ing. DF-ing gets the security agents to the right general area, but that is about all.

Another point in favor of clandestine radio: the latest equipment is small, can be made to look like a simple transistor radio, and uses very little power. In fact, it can operate on batteries, and is consequently immune to the "grid" system by which the Gestapo caught Allied agents during World War II.* Until recently, security agents bursting in on someone sending a wireless message would find him wearing earphones, hunched over a sending key, and backed by a huge transmission set with aerial wires running out the window. Now,

---

* Knowing that a transmission was being sent from a certain general area, while listening in on their own radios Gestapo officials would cut off the electricity in that area sector by sector. When the transmission abruptly stopped they knew they had located the right sector, and the job of locating the transmitter was simplified to one of searching the buildings in that sector. Had the transmitter been operating on batteries it would have been immune from such a method of search.

enemy agents would find him lying quietly on his bed ostensibly listening to music, with no transmission equipment they could recognize except by taking apart every electrical appliance in his apartment. If the man is truly suspect, the security agents *will* take everything apart, but at least the sender is not liable to attract the attention of nosy neighbors or others who might for one reason or another gain a peep into his living quarters.

The "screech" is an ordinary tape recording so speeded up that it sounds like a high-pitched whine of the sort common to a bad telephone connection or a faulty radio transmission. The sender plays the tape in the background as he carries on an ordinary conversation or sends a harmless "ham" radio message, and unless security officials listening in are on the alert for it, it goes unnoticed. Meanwhile, a tape recorder at the other end picks up the whine at the same speed at which it was transmitted. When it is slowed down to the original recording speed, the vocal or code message can be heard. Recently engineers have shaved off high sound frequencies in international telephone lines so that "screeches" are usually unintelligible, and monitors have been trained to watch for them. They are still used to good effect on "ham" radio transmissions, and I understand that some modern services have "scrambling" devices which work at ordinary frequencies and make "screeches" that can be untangled at the receiving end from ordinary voice communications, yet remain undetected by monitors. The day is past, however, when a simple adjustment on a fair-quality tape recorder allowed a principal agent to squeeze ten minutes of "screech" into the background of a one-minute cover conversation—thereby saving money as well as accomplishing his communications objective.

Finally, there is the ordinary courier smuggling reports, as opposed to original documents or photocopies—sometimes in the clear and sometimes written in secret ink. Reports, being paper, get past all the masses of new special equipment used to detect hijackers or smugglers of drugs. Customs inspectors, being too busy to read ordinary written materials, generally let anything pass that doesn't have SECRET or CONFIDENTIAL prominently stamped on it in their own language. It seems safe to say that *most* espionage reports taken by couriers from one country to another are in the form of hand- or typewritten letters mixed up with quantities of neutral papers with similar outward appearance. Secret writing is also used, of course, but many principal agents are more afraid of getting caught in the act of writing secret messages than they are of the customs officials. Besides, preparing secret messages is a lot of trouble.*

The main drawback to communicating by courier is the expense: it would have to be a pretty valuable batch of espionage reports to justify the cost of an airplane ticket on an international airline—and espionage reports are rarely worth the cost of a coded telegram, much less that of moving a human body back and forth. Members of airline crews are often used as couriers—provided an adequate number can be found who are not already involved in some profitable fiddle or other—as are regular travelers of various kinds. There is only one problem: security officials of some countries *assume* that regular travelers are taken advantage of by a wide variety of persons and organizations who would smuggle goods or documents, and they keep a special lookout for them. Thus, a

---

* Penalties for involvement in espionage being what they are, the layman may find it difficult to believe that an agent, principal, or courier would take even the slightest chance. The bane of the case officer's existence, however, is that overconfidence which inevitably creeps into his operatives' attitudes, thereby endangering their lives as well as their operations. After some months in the business, it all looks so easy—and writing messages in secret ink is such a bore. A principal agent once told me, "I don't make a *habit* of sending messages in the clear, but sometimes I'm in a rush, and the chances of being searched are so infinitesimally small that I sometimes take a calculated risk." Well, his number eventually came up. His courier was searched from head to toe, and the papers he was carrying were examined word by word by a competent translator. His case officer told me that the "sometimes" had slowly become "often," and by the time the courier was caught the principal was sending almost all of his reports in the clear.

145

regular traveler may get away with smuggling for months, then one day be submitted to a surprise search thorough enough to uncover anything illicit he may be carrying.*

PAY AND INCENTIVES

Success in any espionage operation all comes down to motivation: the properly motivated agent, with adequate intelligence and a minimum of training, will generally figure out the right ways to do things and take all the necessary precautions. The most important question for the case officer is "Why do my spies do what they do?" Principal agents, couriers, and utility agents of various kinds are easy to understand because their motivations are normally supplied by their cover occupations. But the motivations of the most important member of the system, the ordinary agent, are a persisting mystery.

Why do spies become spies? I knew the original "Emily" very well; I knew the original "Mickey" to speak to, and he and I had many mutual friends; I knew at least three U.S. Government and two British Government employees who turned out to be "Mickeys"; I knew the most famous of them all, Kim Philby, better than anyone else, excepting two or three British intelligence officers. Shortly after I ran into Philby in Beirut in 1957, I was asked by friends in the FBI and the British MI-5 to keep an eye on him and to report signs that he might be spying for the Soviets. Without his being aware of it, I made a personal study of him. I have heard just about all the opinions worth having on what made Philby become a

---

* It should be noted that most couriers do not themselves know the true nature of the materials they are carrying. They are given batches of papers of which the espionage reports are only a small part, and the espionage reports are generally so written that they could be interpreted as normal commercial correspondence. After all, even the most unpolitical foreign representative of a commercial concern occasionally has to write his home office about political, military, and other matters that concern his business.

Soviet agent. I have also had in-depth interviews with a representative number of Soviet and Satellite defectors and former CIA and SIS agents who were recruited as they worked for official Soviet and Satellite agencies. Even so, I still have no firm views on what makes spies spy and defectors betray their countries.

And I don't think anyone else has. A review of the whole range of known spies and defectors shows that the ideologically motivated agent is a rare bird indeed. Most espionage agents don't themselves fully comprehend what they do, and in most cases the very simplicity of their motivations makes them hard to recognize.

I believe that experience comes frighteningly near to indicating that as many as one out of three government employees who have passed all the security clearances might become, provided the right circumstances, agents of a foreign power. A CIA case officer confronted with a target within, say, the Polish Government to which only three persons have access would be confident enough of penetrating it to *assume* success. Although we have no sure way of knowing, the converse is probably equally true. A CIA security officer once said, "Potential spies are at least as plentiful as potential alcoholics." I am inclined to agree.

Case officers *don't like* ideologically motivated agents. Oh, a little ideology—provided it is not inflexible—is sometimes good for salving the conscience; but case officers seem to be universally agreed that the best agent is motivated by purely personal considerations, that he "doesn't see any harm" in what he is doing, and that he gives little, if any, thought to what good he might be doing to others than himself.

How do we handle this ideal, non–ideologically motivated agent? There are certain very definite rules which sophisticated espionage branches follow:

1. Buy the man, not his information.

2. It's the regularity and dependability of the pay that matters, not the amount.

147

3. Supplement the agent's income from regular sources enough to ease his financial worries, but not enough to cause him to make basic alterations in his life-style.

4. Pay no bonuses in connection with specific acts. Give the agent only rewards that will make him think in terms of consistent performance rather than individual "coups."

The reasons for these rules should be obvious, but apparently they are not, because many services, notably the French, failed to recognize them until recently, and even experienced espionage specialists sometimes forget them. Until the great intelligence services arrived at their present positions of knowing about all they need to know concerning their respective "other sides," tempting possibilities kept turning up to shake even the most rulebound case officers. Before the CIA had its present knowledge of Soviet missile capabilities, the CIA agent who demanded a mere $100,000 for a demonstrably authentic TOP SECRET Soviet Defense Ministry document would probably have gotten it.

Now the scenario would be something like the following: The agent says, "I can get for you a document showing all the Soviet's missile capabilities, but I'll be wanting a hundred thousand dollars for it." The principal agent says, "You are getting paid a salary to produce anything you can get your hands on. If you hold back, you will not be fulfilling the terms of your employment." The agent says, "Yes, but this is out of the ordinary. At least I should get a bonus"—to which the principal replies, "As your efficiency and conscientiousness improve so will your pay, but we measure you not by the importance of the information you bring in but by the thoroughness and dependability you display in getting it." He goes on to explain that an inefficient agent who stumbles onto a major piece of information will not be rewarded so well as the efficient and conscientious agent who makes no coups but who convinces his principal that he has not missed anything. The agent grumbles and fusses, and is often a long time in getting the point, but when he finally does, he is a better agent.

Moreover, he resists the temptation to withhold important

items because of some notion that he can get a better "price" for them if he presents them at a favorable psychological moment. And he resists the temptation to fabricate information so as to please his principal agent. Once the agent has become convinced that his thoroughness and dependability are what is important, he will unashamedly inform his principal agent, "Nothing to report this week," if such is really the case, rather than feel that he has to concoct something just to hold on to his job.

How much should the agent be paid? An agent's salary is determined less by the value of his information than by the size of his overt income. For example, a CIA agent who is an official of the Egyptian Ministry of Defense and whose income, from "perks" as well as salary, is $500 per month might receive an agent's salary of $250 per month—half again his overt salary. Almost anyone having his income boosted by a certain percentage will gradually increase his living standard to absorb the additional amount, and will soon get so used to it that to lose it suddenly would cause grave hardship. An agent who is paid *too* much, however, or who is given large periodic bonuses, is likely to overspend and to draw suspicion to himself. In any case, an agent should not be so well rewarded that he is tempted to neglect his regular job. He must need *both* his overt and his covert salaries.

Considerations such as these must be taken into account, and not the true value of the agent, though once the case officer decides that he truly needs such-and-such an agent, he must resign himself to paying *whatever* that agent should be paid on top of his overt salary—$200 or so to the agent earning $400, or $2,000 or so to the agent earning $4,000 a month— in order to motivate him properly. Some of the best agents are paid $100 a month; some of the worst, $2,000 a month.

The payments are normally made in cash—though, when they are in large amounts and the agent is in a position to leave his country from time to time, they may be made to a Swiss or Lebanese bank account. Cash is preferable, because the agent should be motivated to *spend* it. When the principal sees his agent living exactly as he lived before going on his payroll, and saving *all* of his pay, he worries about the fact that the agent is not sufficiently *dependent* on his agent's pay. One day those Soviet agents in the United States who save up large amounts in Swiss banks will prove this point to the principal agents who manage them. We know of several cases of Soviet agents who saved up as much as they thought they needed for retirement, then resigned from their cover jobs— which, of course, meant resigning from their agent work.

Won't the Soviets cause trouble for those agents who refuse to continue? While we would like to think they are such treacherous scoundrels that anyone would be a fool to become an agent of theirs, the fact is that the KGB, like the CIA and the SIS, uses coercion only when there is a good chance of converting it into positive motivation. Once an agent is definitely in the employ of a modern intelligence service, he must be made to feel that the service won't let him down. If he is ever given reason to suspect that his superiors have betrayed some other agent, his own confidence will be shaken. For this reason, when an agent announces that he does not want to go on, even the Soviets must accept the loss with good grace— and assure the agent that they are doing so, so that he will not be driven by fear to defect.

This is not to say that coercion—intimidation, blackmail, holding loved ones hostage—is not used to good advantage. It is. But only to establish a hold on the agent. Afterward, a more positive motive must be developed. If a prospective agent is recruited by the threat of publishing pictures showing him in a homosexual act, the threat is administered by someone other than the principal who had developed him. The principal should play the role of a sympathetic confidant, one whose help can be counted on to get the agent out of trouble. Although the agent may not be so stupid or naive as truly to believe in this performance, the principal's persistence in it will enable the agent to rationalize a way out of his predicament. As quickly as possible, the principal must enable the agent to deceive himself into believing that he would have become an agent even had he not been caught with his pants down, and that what he is doing is justifiable on its own merits.

BLACKMAIL AND COERCION

One might think that in this so-called "permissive age" blackmail would no longer be an effective means of recruiting agents. Lord Lambton, the British peer who was photographed in bed with a pair of London prostitutes, scoffed at the idea that he might have been blackmailed, and intelligent citizens believed him. The fact is, however, that blackmail now plays a greater part in the world of "dirty tricks" than it ever did before. In a permissive age the temptation for a prospective agent to stray is great, but his fear of being found out remains roughly the same.

Lord Lambton may have been speaking the truth when he said he would have snorted at a common blackmailer such as a Soho pimp saying to him "Give me a thousand pounds or I'll send these photographs to your wife." Sophisticated pressure, however, is not applied in that way. Had the KGB been out to blackmail Lord Lambton, these are the steps they would have taken:

1. A KGB case officer would have approached Lord Lambton through a principal capable of meeting him on more or less equal social terms. Giving some plausible excuse for knowing about the compromising photographs, the principal would have offered to help effect their return, making it absolutely clear that his sympathies were entirely with Lord Lambton.

2. The principal would then have advised Lord Lambton in the strongest possible terms that he should refuse to pay one penny for the photographs, "even if it means public disgrace, the end of your career, and the loss of your family's love and respect." He would have assured Lambton that he would "somehow" obtain the photographs without paying anything for them, but that Lambton should on no account tell *anyone* else about the matter.

3. After a pretense of delicate negotiating, the principal would have delivered the photographs, complete with negatives, to Lord Lambton and assured him that there were no more copies and that he should consider the incident closed. (Some blackmailing case officers have their principals say, "I am *reasonably certain* there are no more copies, but this is unsubtle and rarely necessary. Even the most naive victim, whatever the assurances, will for the rest of his life suspect that the blackmailer will be holding on to the odd copy or so for a rainy day.) The principal would have adamantly refused any offer of reward.

4. After a suitable period passed, the principal would have begun to ask small favors—favors so small that Lord Lambton would have found it difficult to refuse. From then on, Lord Lambton would have been developed just as "Emily" was developed.

Those who know Lord Lambton doubt that even the subtlest approach would have ensnared him, but that's not the point. The skillful case officer settles for *whatever* he can get. Once he sees that the principal is not going to succeed in actually recruiting his victim, he withdraws and holds on to whatever position he has attained.

The value of having even a small toehold on a blackmail victim is exemplified by the story of two American Congressmen who got themselves into compromising circumstances in Cairo some years ago. During the months just before their visit, the Egyptian security authorities were known to have acquired blackmail materials on a number of foreign diplomats, and the Embassy security officer adopted a policy of warning all visiting VIPs of the dangers of Cairo night life. When the two Congressmen were told explicitly where to find call girls, they could not resist noting the names of one or two of the places.

Sure enough, the next morning the head of the Foreigners Section of the Ministry of Interior called the Embassy security officer to tell him that his two visiting VIPs had been picked up in a local nightclub by a pair of prostitutes, who had taken them to their room in a cheap hotel and had them photographed by a voyeur friend. The Egyptian official delivered the photographs to the security officer without comment. The negatives were included, and the incident was believed closed.

Two years later, the Egyptian Ambassador invited one of the Congressmen to lunch and pleaded with him to discontinue his consistently pro-Israel stand and to vote sympathetically on the Arab side on a bill that was about to be debated. Although there was probably no real threat in the Egyptian Ambassador's manner, the Congressman's guilty conscience made him suspect that a threat was implied. "Mr. Ambassador, are you thinking about an incident that happened in Cairo a couple of years ago?" he asked.

The Egyptian at first affected a blank look, then broke into a smile of pleased recollection. "Oh, *that!*" he said. "I had completely forgotten." He wagged his finger reprovingly. "You were a very naughty boy!" He then returned to his serious manner and, without mentioning the incident again, resumed his arguments. Days later, when the vote came up in Congress, the Congressman, who normally would have been vociferous in his support of the Israeli side, remained silent and absented himself when it came time to vote.

Espionage services use intelligent, emotionally stable women for a wide variety of purposes, including the seduction of prospective agents. They use prostitutes, male and female, only for the purpose of getting prospective agents into compromising positions—never to obtain information. The overly zealous prostitute who shows an interest in her clients' secrets would probably be cut out of the action by the case officer. Her job of compromising is quite enough. In the world of "dirty tricks," there are hundreds of such women, and they are very useful.

In the early days of the CIA, the espionage branch for a while helped the French SDECE maintain a high-grade brothel in Paris for the purpose of luring diplomats into compromising positions. It turned out, however, that the main customers were Middle Easterners, Americans, and Australians (in that order), with no Bloc diplomats at all, so the participation fizzled out—just at the time, incidentally, when the house was beginning to make huge profits. The CIA is now out of the brothel business. All the same, the CIA, the SIS, the KGB, and other modern intelligence services—and *all* security services, modern or not-so-modern—keep a close eye on brothels, call-girl agencies, massage parlors, shady nightclubs, and even mailing lists for pornographic literature and respondents to sex advertisements, in the hope of spotting the name of a person on whom they would like to have blackmail information, or on whom they would not want the opposition to have blackmail information. (Lambton, incidentally, had already been spotted by MI-5 some weeks before he was exposed.) For this reason, anyone whose career depends to any degree on a public "image" is a fool to yield to this type of temptation.

DEFECTORS AND "WALK-INS"

A defector is a citizen of any country who, because of personal troubles or disillusionment with that country, decides to go over to its enemies. "Defection" is the abandonment of loyalty. Kim Philby was not a defector: he did not one day decide that he would no longer be loyal to his country; he insists that by the time he skipped out of Beirut and went to Moscow his loyalty had been with the Soviets for thirty years. Such agents as "Emily" and the various "Willies" were not defectors: in their cases, the question of loyalty came up only incidentally if at all. The ordinary espionage agent convinces himself that he is "not really" being disloyal to his country and that what he is doing is in the long run *good* for it. The defector, on the other hand, believes that his country no longer has anything to offer him or that its environment is actively hostile to his well-being.

The "Mickey" is a type of espionage agent who is often mistaken for a defector. "Mickey," remember, had no particular interest in forsaking his country and going over to the Soviets. As he envisioned his future, he would serve the KGB well for a number of years, then take his earnings and retire to Mexico or some South Sea island—all the while remaining, inwardly as well as outwardly, a loyal American citizen. If, to you and to me, he was obviously *not* a loyal American citizen, that is because we haven't been through a process of rationalization as "Mickey" had.

"Mickey" was what is known to espionage specialists as a "walk-in" agent—an agent who offers his services to a foreign espionage service without being solicited. Walk-ins are of two categories: amateurs, whom the service generally presumes to have been "blown" before they are activated; and the few professionals who, like the original "Mickey," know how to make their approaches without detection.

If the approach is made by an amateur, the case officer's emphasis is on determining the walk-in's chances of having escaped detection. If it is made by a professional, the emphasis is on establishing control. With either kind, the case officer almost never exposes himself until certain basic questions have been answered. In fact, the walk-in is first seen by someone not only outside the espionage branch but outside any branch of the intelligence agency. Since almost all walk-in approaches are made to diplomatic missions, this someone is normally a member of the consular staff. If an employee of the U.S. Atomic Energy Commission wanting to become a Soviet spy "walks in" to the Soviet Embassy in Washington, D.C.—or, more likely, a Soviet embassy in some country where he is vacationing—and demands to see "whoever is in charge of intelligence," he will be directed to the consular officer whose duty it is to humor such visitors. The same is true if a member of the Soviet equivalent of the AEC wants to become an American spy. In either case, the applicant will not be allowed anywhere near any genuine intelligence officer * until he has been thoroughly "vetted."

---

* Under the title "I Spied for Britain," a London newspaper some time ago carried the story of a British journalist who had presented himself at the British Embassy in Beirut asking to see "the intelligence officer" and had subsequently been assigned a set of simple codes and given

The consular officer's part in the vetting consists of getting answers to three basic questions: Who is the walk-in and what are his credentials? What are his reasons for offering his services? Who, besides the walk-in himself, might know about the approach?

The walk-in who is not a professional intelligence officer may be expected to open with what is known as the "Doctor-I-have-a-friend-who-thinks-she-is-pregnant" line. Such walk-ins hem and haw, refuse to give their names (or give false names), ask such questions as "I don't really work for the Atomic Energy Commission, but suppose I *did* work for it—what use could you make of me and what would you do for me in return?" The properly trained "front" regards such an attitude as a good sign, because it sets the walk-in apart from the numerous cranks and phonies who come to the embassy demanding to see "the intelligence officer." * Usually the few clues obtained in the interview allow the case officers to figure out the true identity of the walk-in later on, but the "front's" first job is to find out all he can about who the walk-in is and what secrets he has access to.

He then has to discover as best he can what the walk-in's

---

various "secret missions." The story was so obviously fake that it was only laughed off by Beirut's intelligence community. But there have been cases in which similarly motivated journalists have developed sounder bases for stories of this kind because of an irresistible urge of some consular officers, bored with their work, to pretend that they are really intelligence officers under cover. "In Beirut," an SIS friend of mine used to say, "all the intelligence officers pretend to be clerks and all the clerks pretend to be intelligence officers. It sometimes makes life difficult."

* All American and British embassy personnel (and, probably, the personnel of most other diplomatic services) have been warned against adventurers of their own nationalities who wish, merely out of patriotism, to furnish information that they get as a result of their regular activities. There is a by now well-known trick of international crooks: they offer their respective embassies political, military, or economic information, some of it very good, and when they are caught at their crimes— smuggling gold, trafficking in drugs, fighting as mercenaries, or whatever—they "confess" that their illicit behavior was only cover for intelligence activity, and therefore was patriotically motivated.

reasons are for coming. As a matter of routine, he considers the possibility that the walk-in may have been sent by "the other side" either in an attempt at penetration or for purposes of provocation. Only an extremely unsophisticated espionage or counterespionage service would believe that a walk-in stands a chance of getting past the consular "front" until he really proves himself of worth. It is safe to say that 99.99 percent of those who present themselves at embassies as walk-ins are self-motivated, but the consular officer is still under strict instructions to handle each one as though he might be one of the .01 percent. He asks the questions; he answers none. If the walk-in persists in asking questions, he says, "I will report your visit to the proper authorities, but first I must have all the facts." If the walk-in insists, as many will, that "I will talk to no one but the head of intelligence himself," the front remains adamant—reminding the walk-in that just by making the approach he has probably already passed the point of no return, and had just as well go through with his decision. "You must help me before I can help you," he says. If the walk-in gets up and walks out there will still be means of identifying him and, at some later date, turning the approach around—a fact that should be made clear to the walk-in before he leaves.

The front should not expect to get a completely true story—especially with respect to the walk-in's reasons for coming. In many cases the walk-in himself won't fully understand what drove him to his decision. Even if need for money is what prompted him, by the time he reaches the front he will have done so much rationalizing that he will be unable to give a coherent explanation of his motives. This is unimportant. What is important is that the front get the walk-in's statement into some kind of record. Ordinarily, he will have been provided with a hidden microphone and a tape recorder. If he doesn't have one, he should take notes—making it absolutely clear to the walk-in that he is doing so. Following the set questionnaire provided him by the espionage branch, the front tries to learn the exact nature of the walk-in's financial difficulties, or financial needs that must be satisfied, and any grudges or emotional pressures that may have contributed to his move. He tries to get at least enough information to enable the case officer, should he decide to recruit the walk-in, to choose the best method of approach.

Only a small percentage of walk-ins are ever recruited, but the information obtained by the front is kept on file for possible future use in connection with other recruitments. The reason so few volunteers are finally recruited is that most fail to answer satisfactorily the front's third and most difficult set of questions. These queries relate to the walk-in's activities from the moment he decided to offer his services right up until the moment of the interview. The front wants to know if the walk-in discussed his decision with anyone else and whether any of his movements departed from the normal. If the walk-in brought documents to the meeting, how did he get them? Does he intend to return them? If so, how? What preparations did he make for the visit to the embassy? What excuse will he give later to anyone who might have seen the walk-in come to the embassy? Considering the surveillances that are maintained these days in all capitals of the world, the chances of a walk-in's escaping notice as he enters an embassy or the home of one of its employees are fairly slim. The result is that even if the case officer decides to employ a walk-in of this category, he will probably regard him as expendable.* In other words,

---

* Although many details of the case are still under the protection of the British Official Secrets Act, it can be reported that Mrs. Maureen Bingham, the wife of the Navy sub-lieutenant who entered the Soviet Embassy in London in 1970 to offer her husband's services to the Soviets, was spotted immediately by MI-5 officers, and that the Soviets assumed this to be the case. MI-5 let the case run for eighteen months before wrapping it up, thereby causing the Soviets to hope that Mrs. Bingham's original visit had escaped notice. But when the Soviet case officers learned of various indiscretions of Mrs. Bingham's that could not conceivably have been missed by MI-5, they realized for sure what they had been suspecting all along: that the information furnished to them by the Binghams was, unknown to the Binghams themselves, "disinformation." Having committed only expendable personnel and operational facilities to the venture, they quietly let it drop—and MI-5 moved in.

the officer will employ him in such a way that there is something to gain if the operation works out but nothing to lose if it fails.

The walk-in who is a member of an intelligence organization —or who, for some other reason, has expert knowledge of how to "walk in" without drawing the attention of his government's security forces—is given more respectful treatment. He knows enough to make his approach in some Third World capital, and he knows the only effective way to make a secure approach is to seek out a social occasion and make a "brush" contact with a well-chosen intelligence officer of the other side. He can drop a note on the officer, or simply state quickly that he is available—from then on leaving it to the other side to make the approach. This, of course, is how "Mickey" made his original contact. Afterward, the operation can be managed in a professional manner, comparatively safe from detection.

In dealing with a professional intelligence officer who knows exactly what he is doing and all of its implications, much of the "development" process can be skipped. All the same, the principal assigned to the case must do everything that is necessary to run the operation as if the walk-in had been recruited at the espionage branch's initiative. A walk-in of this category will do all he can to sell his information, not himself, but the principal must still initiate the concepts of agent management that have been found effective in controlling the man rather than his material.

5

COUNTERESPIONAGE

. . . and there are spies spying on spies.

THE ACT of espionage is unlike any other criminal act
in that it leaves no traces. Indeed, unless the agent is caught,
the government office that has been penetrated is usually unaware that any crime has taken place.

The actual detection of espionage is a very specialized task,
and the officers in a government's espionage branch responsible
for it are of conspicuously superior quality. Sir Dick White,
before becoming chief of the British SIS, made his reputation
in the handling of counterespionage cases. So did Tom Kara-
messenis, until early 1973 the CIA's "DDP" (Deputy Director,
Plans—the head of the agency's espionage branch).

Detection is but a small part of the business of countering
enemy espionage. There is "counterintelligence," the inclusive
term which intelligence and security officers use to indicate
activities ranging from the building of barbed-wire fences
around secret installations to the penetration of foreign espionage services. There is "security"—or "straight security," as it is
called by officers who wish to separate purely defensive measures from the more aggressive kind. There is "counterespionage," which, to the consternation of semantic purists, means
the penetration and manipulation of foreign espionage services.
And finally there is "counterintelligence" used in a more restricted sense to mean the investigation of what are erroneously

called "cases of espionage." Instructors in intelligence schools argue endlessly over these definitions, but since they guide the naming of espionage units, they will suffice for the purposes of this book.

SECURITY

The majority of the people in counterintelligence are involved in "straight security," or preventive counterintelligence. During World War II, whole battalions were assigned to police defense installations, to check the coming and going of the employees, and to drive armored vehicles carrying secret papers from one such installation to another.

In general, the duties of straight security forces may be classified as follows:

1. *Physical:* barriers; guard and alarm systems; closed-circuit-television surveillance; pass systems.
2. *Personnel:* investigation of backgrounds of employees; "vetting" (i.e., record checks); "father confessor" systems.
3. *Communication:* Administration of classification systems (RESTRICTED, CONFIDENTIAL, SECRET, and TOP SECRET); communication and storage of classified materials; administration of codes, cryptonym systems, devices for disguising communications, and receipt and recording systems.
4. *Checks:* After-hours checks to ensure that safes are locked, wastepaper baskets empty, typewriter ribbons and carbon papers removed; electronic "sweeps" in offices where microphones might have been planted; monitoring of telephone conversations for loose talk; periodic spot surveillances of employees; administration of lie-detector tests.
5. *Discipline:* prescribing security rules for employees, training of employees in security rules, and recommending punishment for employees breaking security rules.

This is a pretty dreary set of chores. They call for painstaking, humorless, cold-blooded application of a very special kind of talent. I remember once having a friend of mine in the CIA cafeteria say, jokingly, that he was so broke he was thinking of selling a few state secrets to the Russians in order to raise money to go to the Harvard–Yale football game. A hand coming from somewhere behind was clamped onto his shoulder, and a stern voice said, "Come with me." The security officer to whom the hand belonged found the remark no joking matter, and he kept my friend in his office for the better part of the afternoon questioning him. Finally satisfied that he didn't have a case of potential defection on his hands, he gave my friend a stern lecture on the need for a serious attitude toward security, placed ten demerits in his security scorecard, and curtly terminated the interview. In CIA, a total of thirty demerits will get an employee a week's suspension from work without pay, with proportionally stiffer penalties as for a higher score. The accumulation of fifty points in any one year, which could consist of a string of five-point offenses such as leaving a safe unlocked or dropping classified waste in the wrong basket, results in automatic discharge. The British have more relaxed procedures; the Soviets, stiffer.

A few days later, the same friend found himself cut in, via a crossed line, on a telephone conversation between two colleagues who were discussing extremely secret matters. Unable to resist the temptation, he disguised his voice and said, "This is a security monitor. You are guilty of a most serious security violation. You will both report to the Director of Security at four o'clock this afternoon to present oral reports of your indiscretion." The two offenders, frightened out of their wits, presented themselves at the Director's office at four that afternoon to find my friend already there, having been apprehended by a security monitor who was listening in on *his* conversation. The three were compelled to stay after work every day for two weeks to see films on security, and take written tests to prove that they understood the principles illustrated. My friend got ten more demerits.

Occasionally one gets the impression that security offices are not so much at war with spies as with their own people; but the fact is that security officials are extremely sympathetic to employees of their organizations who are wayward in security matters. The employee who lands in a scrape with security implications knows that he may safely report his troubles to the security office in accordance with what is known as the "father confessor" policy. An employee who has been caught in a police raid on a brothel, or whose wife has become a nyphomaniac, or who has in some other way become vulnerable to blackmail need not fear that by telling his "father confessor" he will unduly endanger his position; this would be far more the case if he kept silent.

The typical case coming to the attention of Security's "father confessor" is that of the senior government employee who has absentmindedly left a briefcase full of secret papers in his automobile, unlocked, in a public parking lot. He comes back an hour later to find the briefcase intact, but is terrified that enemy agents may have photocopied the documents. If he reports the incident to his security officer, it becomes the occasion for a thorough investigation—involving an interview with the parking-lot attendant, an inquiry into the ownership of other cars that might have been in the lot at the time, and so on—but the employee himself is only given a mild reprimand, and made to understand just how much trouble his slipup has caused. If he does *not* report the incident, he may discover later that it was not enemy agents who photographed his documents while they were left behind in the car but a member of his own security team who had the parking lot or the employee himself under surveillance. His punishment in such a case would be severe.

At least, the employees are made to think that this is the case. There is no way of knowing how many slipups of this kind go unreported, but anyone who has ever worked in a "hot" government office will tell you that belief in the omniscience of Security amounts almost to superstition, and that any employee who has *not* availed himself of the "father confessor's" friendly ear in circumstances of this kind is subject to an incredible number of sleepless nights.

It is my personal theory that it was the introduction of the lie-detector test, now used in most "hot" U.S. offices, which made security officials adopt more reasonable attitudes toward their employees. Initially there was tremendous objection to this security device on grounds of "invasion of privacy," but the philosophy, as stated by the CIA's top counterespionage expert, "the Fisherman," prevailed. "If you don't want to give up your right to smoke cigarettes," he said, "don't take a job in an explosives factory." When the general application of the lie detector flushed out serious security risks who would otherwise have gone undetected, its value was considered proved. Within one year of its installation, in some eight or ten offices including three branches of the CIA, it had identified over a hundred clear-cut security risks: practicing homosexuals, drug addicts (and at least one drug pusher), former Communists, and persons who admitted to having passed TOP SECRET information to Congressmen, newspapermen, businessmen seeking Government contracts, and other outsiders. There were no cases, to my knowledge, of actual spies for foreign governments having been uncovered, but we have subsequently learned from defectors that the principal espionage services of the world working against the United States had to drastically revise their policies.

The humanizing effect of the lie-detector test on security officials was remarkable. "Do you know that over ten percent of the unmarried men and *fifteen* percent of the married men in this Agency habitually masturbate?" a bemused security official told me some weeks after the installation of the CIA's lie-detector program. He went on to give similar percentages with respect to how many CIA officers, some of them persons of unquestioned integrity, patronized prostitutes, maintained illicit sexual liaisons, and were engaged in affairs with their secretaries or their colleagues' spouses.* "At last," Colonel

* Government-wide statistics compiled shortly after the introduction of the lie-detector test (in 1950) show surprising disparity in the kinds

"Sheff" Edwards, Chief of Security, once told a friend, "we now have a better understanding of what constitutes a normal human being."

There is plenty of evidence to indicate that he is right. Using highly reliable statistics on the sexual behavior of upper-middle-class America in conjunction with "confessions" from government employees covering a range of peccadilloes from stuffing a parking meter to having participated in group sex, security officials in Washington's hot offices can now define a "security risk" in fairly precise terms. Moreover, with the "father confessor" system they have been able to lower the percentage considerably.

I'll explain. What makes the difference in whether or not an employee is a security risk is the extent to which he feels shame about something in his past. If he is so ashamed that he would submit to blackmail rather than have it revealed, he is a security risk. Just after World War II, an employee might have submitted to blackmail over some comparatively trivial irregularity, since the consequences of his superior's finding out about it were more frightening than those of paying. With the advent of the "father confessor" system, however, an employee knows that he can expect sympathetic treatment. And he can therefore be counted on to report blackmail attempts to the security office. Before the introduction of the "father confessor" system he would have been a security risk; now he isn't.

This does not apply to sexual deviates and ex-Communists:

---

of human weaknesses found from agency to agency. CIA officers, for example, engage in a considerable amount of adultery but never pad expense accounts. (I am reliably informed that no case of a padded expense account has ever been uncovered at the CIA, despite really intensive periodic checks.) Scientists, on the other hand, appear to masturbate more than other government employees, and to engage in such odd transgressions as writing poison-pen letters about their colleagues. ("As many as a third of the anonymous tip-offs we get," a security official told me, "are proved to have come from members of our scientific staffs.") The only admission from the State Department's career diplomats produced by the lie detectors with any frequency is that of having entertained leftist sentiments while in college. Otherwise, our diplomats seem to be so free of sinful pasts "as to be incapable of understanding the rest of us," as Colonel Edwards used to say.

even though the employee would merely laugh at anyone threatening exposure, he is declared a security risk simply "to keep Caesar's wife above reproach," as Allen Dulles used to say, and to forestall Congressional witch-hunters. The same is true of former drug addicts and ex-alcoholics, since there is considerable evidence to indicate that they are more liable to crack than other people.* Almost every other kind of irregularity is dealt with as an ordinary human foible.

Straight security includes not only following employees about, hearing admissions of their transgressions, and keeping personal records which indicate their peculiarities and shortcomings; it includes investigating their backgrounds prior to employment, and afterward running regular spot investigations. The thoroughness with which all offices containing secret information are investigated is worth emphasizing in this context, if only to destroy the notion that an espionage service could penetrate one of these offices entirely from the outside. Given the background investigations to which all employees of hot offices must submit, penetration by such means is virtually impossible: anyway, near enough to impossible to make it not worth the risk. The way to penetrate a hot office is to find someone who is *already* employed in it, and for this reason the facts about each employee that would be of interest to a foreign espionage service are precisely the same as those sought by his own security investigators.

A "personnel investigation," as the investigation of a prospective employee is called, consists of tracing the prospective employee's life history from the time he was born up to the present, and ascertaining that the person applying for employment is without a doubt the one who has been investigated. Switches have been tried. The State Department once had a

---

* While the CIA and some other intelligence organizations will not employ ex-alcoholics, they are extraordinarily protective toward those employees who became alcoholics in the line of duty. Certain sections of the CIA, ones that deal only with unclassified materials, apparently have little purpose besides that of providing jobs for CIA personnel who cracked up in Vietnam, or in the "Battle of Washington" which accompanied it on the home front.

case of female identical twins who pulled a job switch whereby one, a chronic gossip, wound up in the Secretary of State's office and the other in the motor pool in a job requiring only minimal security clearance. The Atomic Energy Commission once employed an ex-alcoholic who had managed to assume the identity of a recently deceased brother with all the qualifications. Both cases were quickly uncovered, but there have been enough others to suggest that sometime, somewhere a successful switch *might* have been effected. In every known case, the person making the substitution fitted the same personal-history pattern as his opposite—with the exception of the one item that might have caused him to fail the security screening. It would be impossible for a complete stranger, especially one coming from abroad, to learn every detail there is to be known about an identity he hopes to adopt and to memorize it so thoroughly that he could pass a security investigation of the person to whom that identity belongs.

The lowest form of the personnel investigation is known in America as "the records check" and in Britain as "vetting." It consists merely of a review of all available public records that might contain information on the "subject," as well as certain nonpublic records such as those of credit agencies, banks, and schools. Ordinarily, the simple "records check" suffices for charwomen, janitors, maintenance personnel, and others employed by hot offices whose work does not authorize them to have access to classified materials. It will also suffice, sometimes, for the clearance of contract employees and for outsiders who, for one reason or another, are allowed temporary access to secret materials—for example, representatives of IBM, NCR, or another of the large computer companies who visit CIA offices to estimate what extensions in the Agency's computer systems are required. It is only the starting point, however, for all employees who have real access to classified materials. Such people are given "full security investigations."

The full security investigation, conducted mainly by interviews with friends, enemies, nursemaids, schoolteachers, relatives, playmates, schoolmates, neighbors, tradespeople, and others, involves not only the re-creation of a factual life history, from birth to the present, of the prospective employee, but the creation of a complete "character profile." Since security investigators are not necessarily expert judges of character, they are given stereotyped questionnaires to guide them. Psychologists in the security office then use the material in putting together "profiles" which are probably very accurate—certainly accurate enough to enable them to spot vulnerabilities which might be exploited by a foreign espionage service.

Although the personnel investigation is enormously expensive, results indicate that it is worth the financial outlay. On more than one occasion, J. Edgar Hoover argued convincingly to Congressional critics that had the FBI's simple personnel investigation been universally applied by the U.S. and British governments, every known case of Soviet espionage could have been prevented. What Mr. Hoover said is not entirely true: FBI-type investigation would probably have uncovered Burgess, Maclean, and Philby, but it *didn't* in fact uncover "Emily" and "Mickey." Still, he had a point. Such investigating, provided it is conducted discreetly and sympathetically, makes the job of foreign espionage services infinitely more difficult.

The goal of security is not the complete elimination of foreign espionage activity but, as the CIA's Sheff Edwards used to say, "giving our enemies higher walls to scale." This is particularly true of physical security—the construction of electrically charged barbed-wire fences, closed-circuit-television surveillance systems, and the like, plus pass and badge systems to exclude all but authorized persons from places containing classified information, and to prevent even those persons from removing classified materials they should not.

There are many jokes about the supposed ineffectiveness of all physical security. Although much of it is as elaborate as a James Bond movie set, unauthorized visitors often penetrate it. A salesman for the *Encyclopaedia Britannica* recently passed through guards, television "eyes," and all, and sold several sets of his encyclopedia before he was apprehended. I have myself, purely by the accident of getting off the elevator at the wrong floor, wandered into offices of the State Department that are forbidden to all but some twenty officers. I even glanced at TOP SECRET maps and charts before anyone discovered I was there. In another instance, the cast of a spy movie called *Scorpio*, having been allowed through the main gate at Langley, Virginia, had great fun getting into various sanctums sanctorum by presenting their American Express credit cards to guards harried during rush hour.

The foreign espionage operative who concludes from such stories that he may safely crash one or another of the U.S. Government's hot offices would be making a serious mistake. His chances of getting in are, let us say, one out of ten; his chances of getting out after completing his mission are no better than one of fifty—as indicated by checks made by security inspectors who, from time to time, try to get past their own pass systems just to test their effectiveness. The *Mission: Impossible* sort of raid on a hot government office is "not on," as our friends in the SIS would say.

If there is a criticism to make of the physical security defenses around U.S. Government installations, or those of other governments for that matter, it is that they are far more extensive than they need be. After World War II, intensive interrogations of German intelligence officers who had run agents in England and America disclosed that they knew of no case in which any of their agents had even tried to get past a physical Allied security barrier, and that had such barriers not existed it would not have affected their efforts one way or another. We have subsequently heard from Soviet defectors who were formerly concerned with espionage operations against American and British targets that it would never have occurred to them to try to send espionage operatives through our security barriers. I am told by friends in the CIA and the SIS that their attitude toward security defenses in Bloc countries is much the same, except for one thing: during recent years there have been several occasions when specially trained units of raiders, chosen from émigré organizations and internal resistance groups, have successfully struck at hot government offices and stolen secret documents much in the manner of bank robbers. But defenses against raids of this kind are usually the responsibility of military, not civilian, security offices.

Anyhow, it is the job of the security officer to ensure that even should an outsider gain entry to a hot office, whether by sneaking into it or by storming it, he won't know how to put his hands on anything of value. Even a CIA officer working in "Branch A" would have a hard time getting into a safe in "Branch B," or finding what he was looking for even should he succeed in getting in. One confidential secretary working at a desk right beside another confidential secretary might get lost in the other's desk or safe—as every intelligence executive knows who has had the problem of getting along with a substitute.

Hot offices are tightly compartmented; keeping them so is the job of the security office. We spoke earlier of the "need to know" principle which is enforced by Security from the encouragement of simple self-discipline by individual employees to the way documents are handled and stored. The government employee who asks another, "Are you cleared for TOP SECRET?" is showing that his security office hasn't briefed him properly. There is no such thing as a general TOP SECRET clearance. An employee in a hot office, unless he is one of a very few officers right at the top, is cleared for some TOP SECRET documents and materials but not others. Unless he has some rare across-the-board responsibility, there is no clearance which entitles him to look at any TOP SECRET document he chooses.

If he is in an office containing particularly hot material, merely getting to see a document is no assurance that he will be able to understand any more of it than he "needs to know." In the CIA and the SIS, for example, cryptonyms are used extensively to indicate persons, places, and projects. When I was acting as a consultant to the CIA on training techniques, I had the opportunity to examine dozens of operational reports, but since all names, countries, and targets were indicated by cryptonyms, I had no idea at all of their identities and could make only the vaguest guesses about what the Agency was up to. I suppose that if I had been allowed the time, I could eventually have "broken the code"; but only the officer who works full-time on each case has the time—and more often than not, he doesn't *want* to know. Richard Helms, when he was Director of Central Intelligence, refrained from learning the names of more than a handful of top agents whose cases were of such importance that he personally had to keep up with them. *

Despite the probable futility of an agent's getting inside a hot office, the security office devotes a considerable percentage of its attention to security checks both during working hours and after them. At CIA, a team of security checkers makes the rounds of all offices at least twice a night. They are looking to see if any safes have been left open or show signs of being tampered with and if any classified documents have been left out, or any "classified waste" left in ordinary wastebaskets. At the State Department and other hot buildings that receive outside visitors there is a nightly electronic sweep of all offices in a search for microphones and sending sets that some enterprising visitor might have planted.

The reason behind these precautions is not the thought that some agent might stumble on a target safe which has inadvertently been left open, but the belief that laxity can become habitual. "It's like ensuring complete hygiene in a hospital," says a lecturer in a security course. "Once you let a nurse get away with not washing her hands before an operation, you can assume that hygiene will slowly go to hell from then on."

COUNTERINTELLIGENCE INVESTIGATION

Apart from those officers whose job it is to terrorize and sympathize with personnel on security problems, the "straight se-

---

* During World War II, the OSS cryptonym for Germany was "Twelveland." The oft-repeated story of the tableful of German officers in a Dublin restaurant singing "Zwölfland über Alles" to annoy some OSS officers at the next table turned out, upon investigation, to have been apocryphal.

curity" people are at the bottom of the intelligence community's caste system. One notch above are the counterintelligence investigators. The U.S. Government has some half-dozen "CI" investigative agencies, from the FBI and the Army's Counter-Intelligence Corps (the CIC) to the special investigative units with the Postal Service, the Federal Communications Commission, the Civil Service Commission, and the Treasury, Commerce, and Interior departments. The British have two—the Special Branch of Scotland Yard and the so-called MI-5—and the Soviets one major agency, the KVD, plus an unknown number of specialized ones.

The counterintelligence investigative agency is responsible for "investigating cases of espionage." Strictly speaking, there is no such thing as a "case of espionage," at least not in the usual sense. There is no observable act of espionage; no one calls the FBI to say, "Come quickly! Someone has broken into my office and committed espionage." There may be some indication that the act has been committed, but such identifications correspond to actual espionage in the way bloodstains correspond to a murder. Even when highly secret documents are missing there can be no presumption of actual espionage. Even a half-trained spy does not remove documents for long enough to allow their absence to be noticed.

It may be quibbling somewhat to insist that "cases of espionage" are more properly referred to as "cases of *suspected* espionage," but grasping this point is essential to understanding the contest between spies and counterspies. What CI investigators investigate rarely has anything at all to do with true counterespionage—that is, action directly in conflict with the efforts of foreign espionage. Rather, it is concerned with the investigation of conditions that foreign espionage agencies might exploit.

The most frequent assignment for a CI investigator is the ordinary personnel investigation. It is conducted on behalf of the "straight security" people, and under their watchful supervision. It is good training for new investigators, though they later grow to hate this kind of investigation. When Frank

Kearns, the famous foreign correspondent, and I were doing personnel investigations for the Army CIC back in 1941 we used to make our inquiries by telephone, or fabricate them, then go to the ball park or the movies. Today there is so much investigating of investigators that this sort of thing is no longer possible.

The lowest-level "positive" type of counterintelligence investigation, ranking in importance just above the ordinary personnel check, is a category of cases designated by the word DISAFFECTION. These are cases of employees, reported directly or through the "suggestion box," who appear unduly upset over missing a promotion, who indicate their loyalties may have been shaken by some event, or who seem capable of rash action. They are deemed indicative of investigation by the nearest CI office both because their manifestation of discontent might have excited the interest of an espionage recruiter and because they may be thinking about offering their services to a foreign agency.

The "suggestion box" is a more valuable feature of the American security system than one would think. Not only does it produce genuine leads, but it also provides security offices with yet more "windows," as they are called, into the private lives of government employees. The prototype, in the Army Chief of Staff's office in the Pentagon, was quite literally a "suggestion box" such as you see in country-club locker rooms, airliners, and other places where comments of members, customers, or passengers are solicited. At local Army bases, along with instructions to GIVE US YOUR SUGGESTIONS FOR MAKING OURS A BETTER ARMY, there was an unmistakable hint that anyone suspecting a fellow soldier of having treasonable inclinations could get his suspicions off his chest by dropping a note signed or unsigned into the suggestion box.

The original practice was discontinued, along with the Army's so-called "CS" (Confidential Surveillance) system,* but in more sophisticated forms it is still in widespread use.

---

* During World War II, the Army's Counter-Intelligence Corps administered a confidential-informant system in which one out of every fifty

The forms vary from agency to agency, but every employee of every hot office in the U.S. Government is urged to voice any suspicions he may have of his fellow employees. He is given secure means of doing so, and his confidences are respected. The British Government won't admit that anything resembling a suggestion box exists, yet the facilities are there, and the British official is intelligent enough to figure out how to use them without being told. In the Soviet Government, and in the governments of most Bloc countries, the system is spelled out in detail—together with warnings that the government employee who does *not* report his suspicions is in serious trouble if they later turn out to have been correct.

Aside from providing an emotional outlet for scientists in hot offices, these suggestion boxes are of genuine value in providing leads to so-called "disaffection" cases. A typical case would be that of an employee who is overheard by a fellow employee making a series of telephone calls which indicate that he owes large gambling debts and is seriously worried about paying them. Frank Kearns and I had exactly this case in Washington, D.C., in 1941. An Army major, with access to highly secret code materials, was overheard by his secretary arguing with a gambler who was apparently threatening to beat him up. She reported the conversation, along with other indications she had noticed that he might be on the verge of doing something desperate, and Kearns and I were immediately assigned the job of keeping him under surveillance. After office hours that day, he jumped into his car and raced around Washington for an hour or so, stopping at various friends' houses (in attempts to borrow money from them, we later learned), then went back to his hotel near Union Station and shot himself. When we examined his room and his pockets, we found clear indications

---

soldiers was instructed to file periodic reports on the other forty-nine. According to orders, members of the "CS" system were supposed to report only indications of serious disaffection, but the temptation to report ordinary gossip, including the sins of their commanding officers, was irresistible, and after several embarrassing blowups resulting from instances of *trop de zèle*, the system was discontinued.

that he had been collecting secret material of value to the Germans and was investigating various way of getting in touch with German authorities. This was, of course, before we were at war with Germany.

A CIC investigator's "bouquet" * of disaffection cases, which might be three-fourths of those in his IN basket, would typically include: an employee who frequently makes unfavorable comparisons of his own country with the country of the enemy, an employee who declares he wants to "get even" with his organization because of some slight or injustice, an employee who seems overwhelmed by financial obligations, and an employee who has made disparaging remarks about the race or religion of whomever informed on him. There are more cases of this last kind than of any other.

Next to the suggestion box, the most prolific source of leads for counterintelligence investigators is the security system's surveillance of foreign embassies, residences of foreign diplomats, and other places where contact may routinely be made by an employee of a foreign espionage service. Surveillance of all embassies and diplomatic residences in Bloc countries is so strict that a citizen would be foolish to enter any one of them without first explaining the purpose of his visit to his own security authorities—unless, of course, he is prepared to stay. British and American embassies in such places have safe means for exporting defectors out of the country, but there is no safe means of reintroducing into the local society a person who has come into one of their embassies without prior clearance. Surveillance of Bloc diplomatic installations in Washington, New York, and London is not nearly so strict, but the chances are slight of anyone's getting in and out without having his name wind up in some security SUSPECT file.

---

* The United States got into the business of spies and counterspies only in 1941, remember, and like all people undertaking a new and fascinating line of work we had to invent a jargon, just to give ourselves that warm, professional feeling. Many of the words we used— "dead drop," "blown," "bouquet," etc.—didn't grow naturally out of the work but were inventions of OSS types who had been mystery writers.

Most American and British citizens who visit Bloc diplomatic installations do so for entirely innocent purposes. At parties the Soviet Embassy in Washington gives on national holidays one might see a large sprinkling of Congressmen and State Department and CIA personnel. FBI personnel, I understand, are there only as part of the catering staff. The number of ordinary citizens who go to Soviet consulates for touring visas is considerable. Nonetheless, anyone with a sinister purpose who thinks that he can disguise his visit to a Bloc diplomatic installation by crashing a party or asking for a visa is mistaken. In almost all Western cities where there are Bloc diplomatic and consular installations, a "light check" is made of all persons entering, and rarely will it fail to single out those visitors who have access to government secrets and whose disloyalty might have dangerous consequences. When they have been spotted, these visitors become the subject of intensive investigation.

Another type of case appears on the counterintelligence investigator's desk marked POSSIBLE COMPROMISE. In one week, in my CIC days, I had three such cases, all so seemingly trivial that they make terribly drab recounting but of such tremendous gravity to my bosses that I had to spend days on each.

One, as I remember, concerned a safe which, through a faulty mechanism rather than any fault of the responsible secretary, was discovered to have been left open for a week. Every night the secretary had locked the safe, signed the certificate saying that she had done so, and called her superior over to check after her. Late one Friday as she was closing the office she noticed that if she twisted the dial with some violence, even after the safe had been properly locked, the door would swing open. She called the security office, and was instructed to stand by. When I interviewed her the next morning, she told me that the night-duty security officer, a guard, and a mechanic appeared within moments and held her and her superior for almost two hours, examining the whole office as well as the safe itself, and getting statements from all employees who had not yet gone home. Since the mechanic estimated that the lock could have been faulty for as long as a week (it had been returned from an overhauling about a week earlier), I had to envisage every possible compromise that might have occurred, then make whatever investigations were necessary to prove with absolute certainty that they could not have.

Since there were three possibilities I found I could not rule out, Security went on record as recommending that the documents in the safe "be presumed to have been compromised," and the officer in charge of the office had to act in accordance with the recommendation or accept the responsibility for anything going wrong afterwards. Since he knew that some of the information could have been compromised in other ways —simply by loose talk by one or another of his employees, for example—he took the former course—at tremendous inconvenience to all concerned.

The "suspected leak" comes under this category of investigation. The most important kind is the one that is noticed as a result of some action of "the other side." We are told by Soviet defectors that hardly a week passes when some strategist in the Kremlin does not notice an action by the U.S. Government "that it would not have taken," says the strategist, "were it not in possession of some of our secret information." A frantic investigation takes place, a lot of people come under suspicion, and, sometimes, some poor innocent is led away to Siberia.

In many of these cases the Soviets are simply overestimating the cunning of our State and Defense departments: many of the actions our government takes that look so clever to the Soviets are arbitrary or whimsical. Egypt's President Nasser once told me, "The genius of you Americans is that you never make clear-cut stupid moves—only *complicated* stupid moves which make us wonder at the possibility that there may be something to them we are missing." Only in the rarest instances will the Soviets' suspicions be well founded. The American and British governments act overtly only on those leaks which have come about naturally—for example, a misplaced Soviet diplomatic bag that has fallen into our hands, or papers found on the body of a Polish diplomat who has been run over by a New York taxicab. Only when national security is at stake will either of our governments take any action on the basis of an agent's report or a continuing leak that would prompt "the other side" to seek out the agent or block the leak.

Bloc governments, however, are less scrupulous in the protection of their sources. Intelligence analysts of the American and British governments follow their moves in tremendous detail and, by means of "game" techniques, estimate the reasons for them. For a variety of reasons, motives behind the decisions of a totalitarian government such as the Soviets' are much easier to discern than those behind the decisions of democratic governments.* When a Bloc government takes some action that can be explained only by its being in possession of some secret of ours, our "game" techniques will be quick to spot it,† and a counterintelligence investigation will immediately be set in motion.

Finally, we come to that category of counterintelligence case which every CI investigator longs for—and which, once he gets it, inevitably becomes a matter for day-to-day dispute between his own investigative unit and that of the espionage branch's counterespionage specialists. As long as the investigation is of an incident, not a person, and as long as the person is only slightly suspect, the CI investigator can keep the case, with the counterespionage specialists' blessing. But the small

---

* In examining the behavior of a democratic government, an intelligence analyst must bear in mind that its leaders must play three games at the same time: the international, the domestic, and the personal. Also, he must remember that what is ostensibly a move in one of these games might be merely a reflection of some move in another. Motives behind the actions of truly democratic governments are therefore often difficult to untangle. Those of monolithic dictatorial governments, however, are usually fairly transparent, even when—*especially* when—there is some attempt to disguise them.

† As British MI-5 interrogators set out to nail the Soviet "atomic secrets spy" Klaus Fuchs, they had only one solid point against him: that a certain item of information known only to him and one or two others had somehow reached the Soviets.

10 percent that do not turn out to be false alarms immediately claim the interest of both units.

A "suspicious incident" is much more likely to result from some freakish set of circumstances than from an actual slipup. Spies don't jimmy safes; they have the combinations. They don't steal documents; they remove them in the normal course of their duties. If they take documents home in the evenings for photocopying, and if a midnight security check shows them to be missing, the professional agent not only will have a perfectly plausible reason for having taken them, but also will be able to demonstrate that he did "homework" on them. A good spy may be caught in a minor security violation, but the chances of his being blown are slim.

Just the same, spies *are* caught, and not entirely as the result of defectors' supplying their names. Sometimes the employing government betrays the fact that it has received secret information. Often decision makers will actually forget the initial source of their information. President Johnson used to startle his subordinates by blurting out some piece of TOP SECRET information at a press conference because he had forgotten that he had seen it in a TOP SECRET report and was under the impression that he had read it in that morning's newspaper.

Sometimes an agency may decide that some danger indicated by an agent's report is more important than his personal security. In Nasser's later years, a CIA agent close to him reported that a group of army officers were planning to "kick Nasser upstairs" and rule the country as a military junta. The CIA sent the report straight to the White House, and was directed not only to tell Nasser all about it, but in order to convince him of the authenticity of the report, to reveal the details of the plot and their source. In direct disobedience to the last part of this order, CIA case officers who controlled operations in Egypt reshaped the information in such a way that it would mislead Nasser with respect to the identity of the source. Nevertheless, when Nasser was told of the plot he instituted a spy hunt which frightened the CIA in Egypt out of its wits. At least one agent was among the many suspects rounded up—not because he had supplied any information on the plot but simply because he *conceivably could* have. Even though the CIA had saved its specific informant, the bureau lost others—and in a questionable cause.

Perhaps the most important source leading to the capture of spies is the trap. While he is inside a target, an agent is supposed never to do anything that can't be explained in terms of his normal job. If he walks into a trap—i.e., picks up a tempting "hot" paper which has been placed in his path—it should make no difference, since his explanation for having done so can be made in terms of his legitimate interests. No matter what instructions he has been given, if he one day stumbles on an extraordinarily significant document the temptation to depart from instructions "just this once" will be very strong. If the subject matter contained in the report is obviously outside his legitimate interests, he will have a difficult time explaining to those who laid the trap why he took it.

Traps may be planted even among those documents to which the agent has normal access. For this reason, agents are instructed never to lie about having taken a document home. If an agent takes a document home and later denies that he has done so, he may be asked to put his fingers under an ultraviolet light. If they glow, as the result of having picked up a fine powder sprinkled on the document by security officials, he is in trouble.

As a normal part of their training, agents are warned against all known traps that may be placed in their paths. But new ones are constantly devised. Once a security service suspects that a leak is coming from such-and-such an office, the variety and number of traps the experts will plant in it are such that the *only* way an agent can escape them is to behave *perfectly* in accordance with his training. Since no one is perfect—especially when the fact that he is under suspicion is unknown to him—the chances for a slipup are great. The effectiveness of a system of traps depends on this fact.

One more source of leads to spies is worth mentioning—not because it is of any lasting importance, but because it has on one or two occasions been used with spectacular success. In the mid-Sixties, a security officer in the Pentagon came up with the following: "We have definite information that one or more persons in the Purchasing Office have been furnishing secret information to outsiders, and that some of this information has been reaching not only contractors but agents of foreign powers. We also have information that indicates who the guilty persons might be. But we want a minimum of trouble; we only want to be assured that the leaks are stopped. If all those in this office who have given any outsiders any information at all, no matter how seemingly innocuous, will come forward and admit it, their confidences will be respected and no action will be taken against them."

Aside from the usual number of compulsive "confessors," * there were so many employees who took advantage of the offer of amnesty that Security had to let off more violators than the bit of hard information that the ploy produced was worth. No bona fide spies were drawn out, but it seemed that half the office had been in the habit of passing information to competing contractors, crusading journalists, and mere curious friends —including, in one instance, the commander of the division to which the purchasing unit belonged. Offer of amnesty notwithstanding, Security *had* to punish some of the guilty, so the ploy could never be used again in that office.

"TRICK OR TREAT"

By whatever means a foreign agent is discovered, Security must make one fundamental decision: do we use him or do we punish him? In totalitarian countries, the security authorities usually take the latter course. The Americans and the

---

* Compulsive "confessors" of espionage are as much a nuisance to CI officers as are confessors of other types of crimes to ordinary police, especially when they have had access to enough inside information to make their confessions sound genuine. Mrs. Bingham, mentioned earlier, is the only known case in recent years of a compulsive confessor who *really was* a spy, although not one taken seriously by her masters.

British, however, deal somewhat more delicately with the spies they capture. There are advantages every now and then to publicizing the capture of an agent, but there are also disadvantages. Sometimes a captured spy whose masters do not know he has been captured can be of great value.

The alternatives open to an American or British security service when it catches a spy are these: bring him to trial; dispose of him without bringing him to trial ("Mickey"); take his earnings away from him and turn him out to pasture ("Emily"); use him for the dissemination of "disinformation."

Counterespionage specialists lean to the last three of these alternatives, while the security authorities prefer the first. If the spy is caught only after lengthy surveillance, and is "broken" only after a long period of investigation, his potential usefulness will have been dissipated, and in all probability the fact of his capture will have leaked out to the press. In such cases, all alternatives except the first are inoperative. If the case was originally handled by the publicity-conscious FBI officials, there will be pressure for a trial in any case. When the FBI catches a spy, its Director likes to advertise the fact in large headlines.

Security officials of the State Department, the Department of Defense, the CIA, the Atomic Energy Commission, and other "hot" organizations look at the capture of a spy somewhat differently. They feel the less said about it the better. If they can make use of him for "disinformation" purposes, they will demand, with a better-than-even chance of success, that he not be brought to trial. Even if there is no real use for him, they would prefer having him "die of the measles," as wags at the CIA put it, than be punished by legal means. If there is no convenient way of administering the "measles," they may even favor simply letting him go.

This is particularly true of the counterespionage specialists of the CIA—and, of course, of those of the British SIS. These specialists are members of organizations which themselves recruit and manage spies: they can hardly be horrified at a discovery that "the other side" has done the same. I am of the opinion that had Kim Philby * been at all cooperative at the time of his near capture in Beirut, he would have been brought back to England, interrogated for a month or so, then given a small pension on which to live out his life on some Channel Isle. Of course, he would have had to endure the day-by-day possibility that some senior SIS official in London might sometime decide that a case of "measles" was in order; but even with that fear, life on, say, Jersey would be infinitely preferable to what he now has in Moscow.

Upon capture of a spy, it is important to get a confession out of him within hours. His interrogators will say, "You're going to confess eventually, so why not talk now while you have something to offer?" The confession must be complete. As long as the agent claims any degree of innocence it is to his advantage to withhold information, but once he has made a full confession he will want to tell everything he knows, in order to ingratiate himself with his captors.

Unless the case has been initiated openly by the FBI or the police, the arrest should be done in absolute secrecy. The agent should simply disappear—and at a time when he will not be missed. Unless he confesses and agrees to cooperate within a period during which he will not be missed, and can be reintroduced into his normal life without arousing suspicion, he will probably have to be turned over to the FBI and brought to trial. The FBI, handicapped as it is by all the rules of evidence, is powerless to deal with him in any other way.

A typical scenario might be the following:

---

* For Philby's benefit, should a copy of this book get to him, I would like to express a reasonably expert opinion that even now he could probably make a satisfactory deal with his old friends at the SIS. But Philby doesn't need me to tell him that such a thought will have crossed the minds of his present masters, and that they will be on the lookout for signs that it might have crossed his as well. Anyhow, the hint is worth dropping, because an old pro like Philby will know enough not to attempt the break himself, but merely to pass word that he is ready. Even were he under constant surveillance (and he apparently isn't), there would be dozens of ways for him to do so securely.

1. The Soviets suddenly cancel plans for moving their fleet through the Bosporus into the Mediterranean, and they do this after making preparations and commitments that can be abandoned only with considerable loss of face in the Arab countries.

2. The CIA's Kremlin-watchers can figure out only one possible explanation: the Soviets have learned of the U.S. Government's TOP SECRET plans for turning the Soviet move to embarrassing disadvantage. They conclude, therefore, that there must be a Soviet agent in one of the State, Defense, National Security Agency, or CIA offices who knew of the TOP SECRET plans.

3. An investigation is launched by the security offices of these four organizations, and a review is made of the documents containing the TOP SECRET plans, the safes they are kept in, and the handling they receive in the course of a day's work. Upon examining the documents themselves, the investigators quickly perceive that they are incomprehensible to anyone who is not familiar with the plans and who is without certain technical qualifications—in fact, anyone lacking such background knowledge and qualifications wouldn't even realize that the documents were important enough to steal. This narrows down the investigation to four or five persons.

4. The four or five suspects are put under intensive surveillance, and the investigators on the case are told that concealing their presence is more important that losing the suspect.* The surveillances are so thorough, however, that they succeed in monitoring all the moves of the "subjects" without the subjects' realizing that they are under surveillance.

---

* Upon being assigned a surveillance job, the investigator's first question must be "Which is more important—not to lose the subject or not to let him know he's being followed?" To conduct a surveillance that will be sure of keeping the subject 100 percent under observation *and* not be blown, requires many investigators. In following Judy Coplon about New York City, the FBI at times had as many as sixty officers on the job. It took this many just to carry out the surveillance tricks that can be pulled on a New York subway—like those of the Frenchman in *The French Connection.*

5. The surveillances—and the accompanying investigations —narrow down the suspect list to one person. As the surveillance on this individual is intensified, enough evidence is usually produced to indicate that he is indeed a Soviet agent. (I use the word "evidence" loosely here, because it inevitably contains items acquired by illegal means which not only couldn't be used in court, but would make prosecution difficult.) Some young and inexperienced member of the security office making the discovery asks, "Shouldn't we tell the FBI about this?" His older colleagues take him aside and explain the facts of life to him, and if he is slow in grasping them he is the very next day transferred to an Army base in Goose Bay, Labrador.

6. The security office to which the suspect belongs informs the head of the organization: in cases such as this, only the top official himself can make the essential decisions. The instincts of this official will be those of self-preservation—the good of his agency and, forgivably, of himself. Before taking drastic action, he will want to "give old John the benefit of the doubt" and to have a frank talk with him. Upon reflection, he may decide that he doesn't know "old John" well enough to get the truth out of him, so he decides that the "frank talk" should be conducted by an employee in whom he has particular confidence, and who is known to be a close friend of the suspect's.

In either case, this procedure has the approval of most security authorities—not only because they realize that many heads of agencies will resort to it whether their security experts like it or not, but because it really does make sense. Consequently, when the top official makes his wishes known, his security experts give him advice on how to handle the interview, and they make arrangements to hear the whole conversation from the adjoining room and to record it on tape. They make sure that the interview takes place at a time of day when a summons to the boss's office, or to that of the suspect's friend, would not be out of the ordinary. They have investigators posted outside the doors and windows whose job it is to apprehend the suspect should he decide to make a run for it.

7. As the FBI authorities piously point out, the agency head who decides to confront the suspect without first clearing with the FBI is "in for a penny, in for a pound." If the suspect confesses, all well and good. But if he storms out in high dudgeon, there can be all hell to pay. If the security people are convinced that the suspect is guilty, they have no choice but to pick him up and do whatever is necessary to get at the truth—even if it means spoiling any chances of later bringing him to trial. So if a hot suspect refuses to talk, they pick him up, take him to a room in the basement, and "try to *reason* with him," as a sober-faced friend of mine in the CIA puts it.

8. Let us suppose, for our purposes, that the head of the agency, in consultation with his security officers, decides that neither he nor any other person will be able to question the suspect effectively. The security officers will then continue their surveillance until they can pick him up without anyone's noticing either "the snatch," as an illegal arrest is called, or the fact of his absence. There are theoretically many possibilities, but in four out of five cases they settle on that magic time of day, four o'clock in the morning—when the suspect's blood-sugar count is low, and when the neighbors are sleeping deeply. The suspect is not arrested Gestapo style, but simply "called to the office for an emergency." If there is the slightest reason to suspect that his wife is in on his spying activities, she is taken along. If not, she is told by her husband, who is as anxious as his investigators to conceal the fact that he is in serious trouble, that everything is all right, and that after he deals with the emergency he will return home.

9. Although I do not wish to give a detailed description here of the methods of interrogation used in instances of this kind, the reader may safely assume that they work. If they don't work in time for the agent to return to his normal routine without having excited suspicion, the investigating authorities must decide whether the eventual confession is legally "clean" enough for the FBI or whether the agency

must dispose of the case in its own way. If the confession is clean, the chief must then decide whether it will better suit the purposes of the agency to turn the agent over to trial, with all the attendant newspaper publicity, or to dispose of him quietly.

For purposes of this scenario, let us say that the methods of interrogation *do* work, and that the agent confesses immediately, agrees to cooperate, and may be returned to his distraught wife in time to wash and shave, eat breakfast, and depart for work at the usual time. From this point onward, we have a so-called "pure" counterespionage case, a kind that is handled in America exclusively by CE specialists in the CIA's espionage branch, and in Britain by the SIS's "Section V."

"PURE" COUNTERESPIONAGE

The discovery, beyond a reasonable doubt, of an enemy spy in some sensitive government office is a highly dramatic affair. In these days of modern intelligence when spies are fewer in number and espionage has "come closer to home," as a friend of mine in MI-5 puts it, the spy's captors are likely to be his friends. "Emily's" superior tells me that he was physically sick at learning that an employee he had trusted for many years was, in fact, a traitor; the security officer who handled her interrogation, and who had known her for years, took the revelation almost as badly, although, of course, his professionalism saw him through the affair the way a surgeon's professionalism steadies his hand even when he is operating on a friend. "Mickey's" case was similar: the CE specialists who confronted him and interrogated him had been *directly* associated with him, both professionally and socially.

So was the Philby case, with which I was associated personally. When I went to Beirut in 1957 to set up a consulting firm, I was told by both CIA officers and SIS officers that Philby was still suspect, although he had been formally cleared of any connection with Burgess and Maclean, and that I would be doing a great service to my country were I to keep an eye on him. I did, as did other British and American laymen who were friends of his. Like all the others, I didn't have the slightest suspicion that he was a Soviet agent and, in fact, wouldn't believe it until he surfaced in Moscow and sent us all postcards. Believe me, it was a terrible shock.*

Philby got away, of course. But I am convinced that had he been caught, as he almost was, the handling of his case would have been almost a family affair. As it was, even after we all knew he was a Soviet spy, the leading families of the Anglo-American community in Beirut—diplomats, newspapermen, businessmen, whatever—rallied around Philby's family the same way they would have rallied around had he been killed in a traffic accident. The same with other cases I have known about. The few secretaries in "Emily's" office who had been told of her situation promptly went to the aid of her mother, who had had a heart attack upon having learned, through some slipup, of her daughter's crime. And when "Mickey" died. of a "heart attack"—or "measles," or whatever—his colleagues and their families were as kind and helpful to his bereaved family as they would have been to the family of any other colleague. This is not to say that the actions which the counter-espionage specialists take in such cases are not cold-bloodedly professional. They unquestionably are. I am only saying that the drama and emotional circumstances attached to appre-hending a friend, and in such a despicable act as treason, are considerably greater than those involved in apprehending an ordinary criminal with whom one has not mixed socially, and that there are advantages as well as disadvantages to this fact.

Today, in contrast to the situation with the espionage cases of the Fifties, the captured agent can be handled in an atmo-

---

* When I reported to my CIA contact that Philby had committed none of the acts on the checklist of those I was to regard as suspicious, he replied, "Aha! That is *very* suspicious. Any ordinary person, just out of innocence, is bound to stumble into at least *one* suspicious act. But Philby is studiously avoiding them all!"

sphere of great intimacy. Although there is no sympathy for the culprit because of friendship—there may, indeed, be considerable bitterness *—there will be empathy of a sort that could never exist between a detective and a bank robber. Not only do the CE specialists know *how* to break their captive; they know how best to prime him for possible use later.

The agent himself is of only limited use. Philby-type agents may be exceptional, because they were recruited and managed in the lax old day of espionage "networks," but agents of the "Emily" and "Mickey" types can supply little more than leads to elements of the espionage system that are *really* important. Once the agent is broken, he must be handled so that he can join his ex-friends, the CE specialists, as part of a team devoted to tracking down the principal agent and, to whatever extent possible, drawing him and *his* superiors into a worthwhile counterespionage operation.

Remember this: the principal *wants* to believe in his agent; to report to the case officer that his agent has been captured or turned is to report a failure—*his* failure. It is the same with the case officer, and even the station chief. When a station has a seemingly productive espionage operation under way, all the officers concerned with it may simply refuse to believe that it is not 100 percent perfect. When the CE specialists get

---

* In Philby's case, there was *considerable* bitterness on the part of his old colleagues, since they felt that he had betrayed them personally. After all, some of them had put their necks on the block in sticking by him when he was suspected of being the "third man" at the time when Burgess and Maclean fled to Russia. But note the attitude of Graham Greene and other such romantics who go out of their way to speak affectionately of Philby. And Philby's own attitude is interesting. When his wife, Eleanor, was in Moscow, my wife wrote her, "It is painful to think that during the years we all loved Kim and had him constantly in our homes, he was all the while laughing at us." When the reply came from Eleanor, it contained a postscript in Kim's fine handwriting: "My dear Lorraine: I hope you never have to learn, as I have, that one lives one's life in several planes, and when there is conflict between the plane of one's ideals and that of one's friends it is, believe me, no laughing matter. Please accept, for whatever they are worth, my assurances that I will always have only the fondest thoughts for you and my other friends in Beirut."

their hands on a cooperative enemy agent, they launch a campaign to lead the principal, the case officer, the station chief, and even those in the line of command back at the espionage branch itself into committing themselves to an operation that is fake. Surprisingly, the approach often works. During World War II, the British succeeded in recruiting as an agent the head of a major section of the Abwehr, the German army espionage service, simply by confronting him with the fact that his prize espionage network had for some months been under their control and that the information he had received from it—and had passed to his superiors—was "disinformation." They blackmailed him. They agreed not to ruin his career by blowing the operation, provided he would furnish complete details of *all* his section's operations and continue to disseminate all the "disinformation" they sent through the operation.

This is not the only way to recruit an agent within a foreign espionage branch, of course. There is the standard method of spotting, development, and recruitment described in Chapter 4, on Conventional Espionage. There are two differences, however. First, the CE specialists can offer their prospective agents not only money but tempting career advantages. The disinformation furnished the Abwehr officer by the SIS officers who recruited him was so much more impressive than what his operations could otherwise have produced that it earned him the Iron Cross. Second, since the member of the enemy espionage branch already knows the ropes, many shortcuts can be taken in his recruitment. It is with some justification that CE specialists claim that they are nothing more than especially astute espionage specialists. When X-2, the OSS's old counterespionage branch, combined with its espionage branch to handle both types of cases, the X-2 boys got all the key jobs.

The end result of counterespionage, of course, is to control the enemy's espionage operations—first against one's own government, second against friendly governments, and finally against other governments. Some of the CIA's most interesting CE operations have been penetrations of the Soviet KGB's penetrations of Czech, Polish, and Hungarian government offices, including the espionage branch of the Polish intelligence service. For the CE specialist, control is enough. During World War II, literally the whole German espionage system operating in Britain was under the control of British intelligence and security services, and no one suggested that the spies should be arrested and tried. Such an attitude brings the CE specialists into conflict with the straight security people, who cannot bear the thought that traitors should go unpunished. Sometimes they can be convinced that it is more profitable to keep the enemy agent happy, but when they can't, the CE boys hold on to their trapped spies anyhow. There is an old CIA saying, which undoubtedly has its parallel in other intelligence communities, "What the FBI doesn't know won't hurt it."

It is often enough just to keep the enemy's spy operations harmless. But once a sufficient number of his operations have been brought under control, outright "Deception" (note the capital "D") may be practiced on them. This fascinating field of CE was probably invented in Biblical times, but it was developed into a high science only in recent years.* From hoodwinking individual agents on an ad hoc basis ("disinformation"), Deception specialists have moved on to the business of so coordinating all "disinforming" as to deceive whole services.

Little is known about the Soviets' Deception, except that they practice it. In America and Britain, however, it can be reported that committees of military strategists, diplomats, economists, and scientists "game out" the intentions of various governments of the world and determine what picture of American and British policies and capabilities they would like those governments to have. Then the intelligence services estimate what, in the light of what they know of intelligence already in their hands, those governments will and will not swallow—their "credulity threshold," in other words. Some-

---

* See *The Double-Cross System,* by Sir John Masterman (Yale University, 1972), for an account of the "XX," or "Twenty Committee."

times a government is known to have so much intelligence already that only slight manipulations of its picture can be made. At other times, whole fictions can be foisted on it.

The difference between disinformation and Deception is not its importance or whether or not it involves the use of "controlled" espionage chains, but whether it is tactical—designed to delude one segment of an espionage organization—or strategic—designed to delude a whole government. Once, when I was trying to convince the Egyptian Government that it should reform its treatment of foreign oil companies operating in the country, I gave report after report to the appropriate ministry, setting forth my case. Nobody paid any attention, and whenever I talked to President Nasser about my recommendations he indicated that he had not seen them. Then I took the same recommendations, shaped them up as a report to the American Embassy, stamped them TOP SECRET, and left them in my hotel room, where they would certainly be found and photocopied by the local security police. Immediately, there was evidence that my recommendations had been read by half the senior members of the Government, including President Nasser. The ruse could quite rightly be called Deception, even thought it was simple and did not involve the use of agents.

During the Suez crisis of 1956, one of the more imaginative members of Secretary Dulles' "Middle East Policy Planning Committee" suggested a Deception operation which would convince the Arab governments that the Americans and the British were about to make a breakthrough on the energy front which "would be to atomic energy what atomic energy is to dynamite." By means of a Deception operation, we would convince the Arabs that we shortly would overcome our dependence on their oil and that they could no longer count on us to court them. They would thenceforth, we believed, be considerably less troublesome.

The operation, known as "Operation Rainbow," began with a huge dummy plant to be built at a secluded Western site and camouflaged so that under aerial reconnaissance it would appear to be an ultrasophisticated experimental power plant. Since the CIA's counterespionage specialists controlled the Soviets' network of "sneakies" in the chosen area, there would be no need to go to the expense of pumping out the fumes and vapors which the plant, if genuine, would emit: these could be put directly into the sneakies in convenient laboratories. There would be elaborate security systems, complete with klieg lights and guard dogs in the manner of one of those plants you see in James Bond movies, and visits by scientists of assorted disciplines would be arranged.

At the same time, we would arrange for leaks—items which, in themselves, were nonsecret but which would contribute to the jigsaw puzzle we intended for the Soviet intelligence analysts to piece together.

Finally, there would be a worldwide search for certain rare minerals—a *genuine* search, combined with transfers of funds such as would be necessary to effect their purchase. The whole operation, even after stringent economies which the CIA's "watchdog" committee insisted upon, would have come to something like $60 million. But had it worked, it would have eliminated a factor in the "game of nations" that was costing us tens of times that amount.

It was in the making of arrangements for the international transfers of funds that the operation came to a crashing halt. When we discussed the plan with officials of the Chase Manhattan Bank, we were shown a study prepared by its energy experts which proved that even the most optimistic plans for new sources of energy would be unable to meet American needs in the future.

The Deception planners already knew this, but they were unaware until then that Chase and, therefore, others outside of Government must know it as well. The project came to an ignominious halt—but it is still an example of the *kind* of operation a Deception group might launch. It also illustrates another point: while CE specialists figure prominently in the supervision of Deception operations, their controlled agents provide only about 5 percent of the information—the same percentage as any ordinary intelligence service. It just happens that the espionage 5 percent is usually the decisive part of the overall intelligence turnover as far as Deception is concerned. Were we to try Operation Rainbow now in the 1970's, we would probably dispense with the $60 million worth of plant and concentrate on the dissemination of espionage information that would subtly alter the picture produced by the enemy's jigsaw puzzle.

This is another way of saying that modern-day Deception is almost entirely a matter of straight counterespionage—passing information through controlled enemy agents * or our own agents inside enemy espionage services. With the scope and ambition narrowed down to this comparatively small segment of intelligence, the following principles guiding its use have recently emerged:

1. The objective of Deception is not to create entirely false pictures, but to make alterations or shifts of emphasis in the existing pictures that will result in the modification of policies affecting our interests. We are reconciled to the fact that enemy nations will have policies which adversely affect our interests; that is why they are called "enemy" nations. But we can often, through Deception, take the urgency out of them or decrease their effectiveness. No one would think of launching "Project Rainbow" today, but we have succeeded in convincing the Soviets (and the Arabs) that we have considerably more flexibility in meeting our energy requirements than is in fact the case. The truth has only recently begun to

---

* In *The Double-Cross System*, Sir John Masterman keeps referring to "double agents" as the channels for XX material. His book was originally written at the end of World War II, although it was published only recently. But even before the end of World War II the term "double agent" was discontinued in favor of "controlled enemy agent" in speaking of an agent who was entirely under our own control, capable of reporting to his original masters only as we allowed, so that he was entirely "single" in his performance, and by no means "double."

leak out, *after* the Soviets missed their chance to gain really decisive influence in the Arab world.

2. The objective of Deception is often to convey some truth that cannot be passed along by public announcements or the newspapers (because it wouldn't be believed) or by straight diplomatic communication (because of diplomatic complications that would certainly arise). When the Soviets stepped up their experiments in biological warfare a few years ago, and we were publicly claiming to be discontinuing ours, it was to our advantage to have the Soviets know the full truth: that the U.S. and British governments have *not* discontinued their experiments in the field of biological warfare, and although the stores of biological weaponry were publicly destroyed, our two governments have the capacity to rebuild them in a matter of weeks. With such new techniques as we have developed, we could remove the entire livestock population—or, for that matter, the human population—of the U.S.S.R., China, or any other country in a short period. Moreover, there is nothing the Soviets' scientists could discover in the next few years that American and British scientists haven't discovered long ago. We are way ahead of them, and they had best expend their energies crusading against the whole idea of biological warfare—which suits our purposes very well. We can't depend on the Soviets' learning this sobering fact of life from some modern-day Klaus Fuchs; but a controlled "Emily" whose principal and case officer have been brought under control is another matter.

3. Deception will not work—and indeed, shouldn't even be tried—until top policymakers are convinced of its necessity and have agreed to delegate day-to-day operations to a committee whose members have the time to keep entirely au courant of the project. During World War II, American participation in Double-Cross operations was held up for months —and at one point, it looked as though the British effort would be sabotaged—because some idiot of an Air Force colonel couldn't be made to understand that our controlled

agents had to send *correct* weather reports to their masters on the German side. All he could understand was that correct weather reports would help Luftwaffe bombers. He couldn't grasp the fact that if our controlled agents didn't send correct information, then the Germans would get it through other means and simply replace the enemy agents we had taken so much trouble to control. At the time, the British were in the position of controlling *all* German espionage operations in Britain, and had the idiot colonel won his argument, this happy state of affairs could have been brought to an end. But he didn't. After hearing twenty minutes of explanation, General Eisenhower overrode him.

4. Top-level coordination is necessary also for positive reasons—not just such negative reasons as dealing with unimaginative colonels. Governments do not act on single pieces of information; in fact, they don't even act on complete intelligence reports. Instead, they act on *conclusions* which they have arrived at after reading all the intelligence reports. To be effective, Deception operations must be launched with this fact in mind. In other words, Deception planners should concentrate on the probable *effect* of their materials rather than the content. This is possible only on the basis of an understanding of the processes by which the enemy's decision makers apply what they know to what they do—an understanding that is arrived at by "gaming," * accompanied by ordinary espionage penetration of the enemy's inner decision-making circles. The purpose of gaming as it is used in Deception is to predict enemy actions by the following means: (1) learning what intelligence the enemy has that might affect his judgments; (2) learning what personality factors will affect the manner in which he interprets the information and decides to act upon it; (3) altering his intake of information so as to form intelligence that is likely to alter his behavior in our favor; (4) monitoring the whole process, so that we might make such changes as prove necessary.

---

* See Chapter 9.

So, you see, CE specialists have responsibilities all the way up the line, from dealing with the detected spy to participating in an elaborate Deception operation. No wonder that the CE specialists, in any espionage service, constitute an elite.

THIRD WORLD OPERATIONS

And spies have a part in "the struggle for the Third World."

WE NOW come to an area of espionage activity which, for want of a better term, Western intelligence services call "Third World operations." The category includes all operations run in the so-called Third World other than those of the great powers directly against each other's diplomatic installations. A penetration by the CIA's espionage branch of the Lebanese Foreign Ministry would be a "Third World operation"; a penetration of the Soviet Embassy would not.

Almost all the heated criticism of the great intelligence services has been directed not at their espionage operations in the Third World, but at their supposed "clandestine warfare"— that whole field of activity by which an intelligence agency secretly influences events in another country. Clandestine warfare normally has no *direct* connection with espionage activity: obviously, the same facilities cannot be used for spying on a government and for working against it. But since a primary purpose of Third World espionage operations is to provide information to guide clandestine warfare operations, we had better pay it some attention. Here are some examples of the kinds of operations that constitute this controversial field of activity.

—Providing *secret* support to the government of a Third World country to enable its security forces to deal with its enemies, internal and external;

—Providing secret support to a dissident group in its attempts to take over a government by force;

—Rigging an election, or secretly sabotaging the attempts of others to rig the election, or in any way providing such secret support to chosen candidates as will ensure their winning, fairly or unfairly;

—Provoking a government into taking some desired action—for example, staging and publicizing fake insurgency raids so as to goad the government into escalating its counterinsurgency efforts;

—"Black propaganda"—i.e., the dissemination of information, true or false, which purports to come from sources other than the real ones;

—Discrediting of inimical persons, political groups, and other organizations (by poison-pen letters, by production of forged documents that may be attributed to them, by revelation of embarrassing personal information, etc.);

—Assassination, sabotage, terrorism, and other such actions which might further some national objective, either offensive or defensive.

The common element is secrecy—both in the conduct of the operations and in attribution. The landing of U.S. Marines in the Dominican Republic in 1965 was by no means clandestine warfare; the infamous "Bay of Pigs" operation in 1961 against the Castro regime in Cuba was *supposed* to be a clandestine operation, but in the middle of its execution it became an overt one; the U.S. Government's intervention in Guatemalan affairs in 1954 was half clandestine and half overt. The assassination of Palestinian terrorists in European capitals in 1972, so conducted that their assassins were unknown or were believed to be other Palestinians, were examples of Israeli clandestine warfare; the Israeli attack on Palestinian guerrilla leaders in Beirut in April, 1973, was not.

True clandestine warfare operations are the ones you never hear about: references to them do not appear in popular exposés of the CIA. With one or two exceptions (for example, the overthrow of the Mossadegh regime in Iran in 1953 and, perhaps, the CIA's role in Guatemala, which later was officially admitted), a clandestine warfare operation that has come to light is regarded as a failure. Since the CIA—and its British, Soviet, Israeli, and Egyptian equivalents—couldn't have more failures than successes and still stay in business, one must believe that despite all the exposés, the main body of the clandestine warfare is unknown to all but a few people in the inner sancta of the various governments.

The particular "Cold War" * in which modern clandestine warfare of the sort we are discussing became prominent began after 1945. Europe was facing economic collapse; the U.S. Government announced its intention to give European governments what aid they needed to recover; the Soviet Government announced it would "bend every effort in order that [American economic aid—the "Marshall Plan"] be doomed to failure"; and President Truman announced that the U.S. Government would "support free peoples who are resisting attempted subjugation by armed minorities or by outside pressures." The Cold War was on.

By the time of Winston Churchill's famous "Iron Curtain" speech in March, 1946, the Soviets had practically annexed half of Europe, and had made it explicitly clear that they were embarked on a program of expansion and proselytizing. As Churchill said, "From Stettin in the Baltic to Trieste in the Adriatic, an iron curtain [has] descended across the Continent." East Germany, Poland, Czechoslovakia, Hungary, Ru-

---

* The term "Cold War" seems to have originated with Walter Lippmann, who used it first in a column and later in a book of that title, in 1947. There were, of course, "cold wars" throughout the nineteenth century—particularly in the latter part, when the French, the British, and the Russians were intriguing against each other in the Balkans, in India, and in the Middle East. For an extremely interesting and illuminating account of the present-day Cold War, I highly recommend Louis J. Halle's *The Cold War as History* (Harper & Row, 1967)—in which, incidentally, he makes not a single reference to the CIA or any other intelligence agency.

mania, Yugoslavia, Bulgaria, and Albania became what we now call the "Soviet Bloc" and were subject not only to mere Soviet influence, but to outright domination. Soviet ascendancy was on the move, and our own efforts to halt it to date were futile.

The efforts, of course, were old-time diplomacy. We received promises from the Soviets to hold free elections in Bulgaria and Rumania, and the Soviets broke the promises, threw the leaders of non-Communist elements in jail, and installed Communist governments. When these actions resulted in the breakdown of the postwar London Conference of 1945, at which outstanding postwar problems were to be settled, the Soviets proceeded to do the same in the other countries. Secretary of State Byrnes protested, President Truman protested, the U.S. and British governments jointly protested, diplomatic notes were sent, and President Truman made a speech, described as "firm and forceful" by the press, in which he affirmed his "determination" that the countries of Eastern Europe should be "free to decide their own destiny."

Elsewhere, more forceful positions were paying off. When the Soviets tried to move into Turkey, hoping to take over the province of Khars and to gain a share in the administration of the Dardanelles, the Secretary of State informed the Soviets that this was not to be, and that we would forcefully resist even at the risk of World War III. A few months later when the Soviets announced that they would not discontinue their occupation of northern Iran, as they had agreed to do in a treaty of 1942, the Secretary of State sent the Soviets more or less the same message. In both instances the Soviets backed down, and when the United States sent military and aid missions to Turkey and Iran the Soviets' ambitions towards these countries were thwarted at least temporarily. Winston Churchill's remark that "there is nothing they [the Soviets] admire so much as strength" had apparently proved correct.

The State Department was now convinced that the Soviets had taken over Europe because we had not stood up to them, and that they had not moved into Turkey and Iran because we had. At the same time the British were disengaging themselves from their colonies, where nationalist movements were in danger of falling under Communist influence, and were discontinuing their aid to Greece and Turkey. If we did not move into the "power vacuum," the Soviets would.

Or so the leaders of the U.S. and British governments believed. In 1947, President Truman received Congressional support for such use of American military power as might be necessary to put down "violent revolution" in the Third World. In an address before a joint session of Congress on March 22, 1947, the President said, "We cannot allow changes in the status quo by such methods as coercion, or by such subterfuges as political infiltration." The rest of his address made it clear that he was speaking exclusively of *Communist* violence, revolution, coercion, and political infiltration. He also made it clear that the countermeasures he had in mind were to be overt, not covert. He had in mind "military advisory groups," material aid to indigenous military and police forces, and economic aid, all to be given to "our friends," as Allen Dulles was to call anti-Communist Third World governments, and left to them to use as they saw fit.

It did not take long for the White House to realize that overt aid had serious shortcomings. It often corrupted the recipient governments, creating revolutionary movements which could be put down only with increased aid. Moreover, it gave some recipient governments independence of a sort we preferred them not to have—an independence, for example, to play us off against the Soviets. So while the value of economic aid for humanitarian purposes was never questioned, the U.S. Government shifted its emphasis away from helping governments openly and toward fighting our enemies secretly.

This is where the CIA came in. A few background facts should be kept in mind:

1. Long before we shifted away from overt aid, the Soviets were already in the business of clandestine warfare, and were presenting threats—in the Philippines, Malaya, Burma, Indo-

nesia, and elsewhere—that could be countered only by means appropriate to that kind of warfare. Certainly, countering the Soviets with clandestine warfare of our own entailed less risk of setting off World War III than would open warfare.

2. The decision for the CIA to develop a clandestine-warfare capability was made by an elected official, President Truman, and was in no way arrogated by the CIA itself. President Truman's successors have, without exception, supported that decision.

3. The CIA went into these operations without enthusiasm, and refused to allow its espionage branch, then its only unit with clandestine capabilities, to have anything to do with these requirements other than to provide some of the operational data needed for their planning and execution.

4. Since its entry into the business of clandestine warfare, the CIA's activities in this field have been scrutinized in detail, either by officials reporting directly to the President (and, in important cases, by the President himself) or by some Congressional "watchdog committee" or by both. The accusation that the Agency is able to pull the wool over the eyes of its watchdog is not valid, although the Government's reason for insisting the opposite reflects no particular credit on its chiefs. Essentially neither Congress nor the White House wishes to face an outraged public if one of the operations is exposed.

There was a considerable interval between the time when President Truman decided that we were involved in a "war of subversion," whether we liked it or not, and the time the CIA became active. As far as I have been able to determine, the first out-and-out clandestine operation of the U.S. Government was the overthrow of the Quwatli Government in Syria, in which I was personally involved. As an ordinary embassy political attaché, I helped an ordinary military attaché advise the Army chief-of-staff, Colonel Husni Za'im, on how to conduct a coup d'état. As an ordinary diplomat, our Minister (there was a legation in those days, not an embassy) kept Washington informed. The Assistant Secretary of State for the Near East and Africa, not wanting to be kept informed in any particular detail, wrote to the Minister a letter hinting that his superiors would not be too unhappy were they to read in their newspapers one fine morning that President Quwatli, who would not make peace with Israel, had been replaced by a military dictator who would.* The CIA had nothing to do with it.

In fact, the CIA hadn't even been activated. The CIA had been formed in 1947, but at the time of the Za'im operation—March, 1949—it was still grappling with basic problems of organization, and its only branch authorized to conduct clandestine operations ("FI," it was called, not necessarily standing for "Foreign Intelligence") was preoccupied with the task of converting the wartime assets of the Office of Strategic Services into the basis of a peacetime espionage service. It was not until June, 1949, that the CIA was directed by an order of the National Security Council to create a capability for various kinds of covert warfare—including, of course, the overthrow or manipulation of governments in the Third World. It was not until almost two years later that the branch which was to carry on the warfare, the Office of Policy Coordination, had opened shop and announced itself ready for business.

The title Office of Policy Coordination, or simply OPC, was the invention of its first Chief, Frank Wisner, and is typical of the cover names the CIA uses to designate those of its branches which deal with highly secret matters. Wisner set up offices in Temporary Building "K" near the Lincoln Memorial in Washington, D.C., and began to recruit personnel. He was told by the Director of the CIA that he was not to proselytize among OSO officers, so he went outside the Agency to recruit what Stewart Alsop † has called "Bold Easterners" and what others have called "Ivy League dilettantes" or "rich game players." Before long, the "Bold Easterners" were engaged in a

---

* This is all recounted in detail in *The Game of Nations*, Simon and Schuster, 1970.
† See *The Center* (Harper & Row, 1968), which contains a particularly illuminating chapter on the people who have run the CIA's clandestine branches in recent years.

tremendous internal struggle with what Stewart Alsop called "the Prudent Professionals"—an assortment of former OSS counterespionage specialists, former officers of the Army's Counter-Intelligence Corps, and former FBI officers who were fugitives from J. Edgar Hoover. With Allen Dulles as Director of the CIA (he took over from General Bedell Smith in 1952, after serving as his deputy for almost a year), it is not difficult to guess at the outcome.

By early 1953, when the OPC was really ready to swing into action, its Bold Easterners such as Kermit Roosevelt, Tracy Barnes, Desmond Fitzgerald, and Richard Bissell were wearing a path to the Director's office to discuss all sorts of adventurous clandestine operations, while the OSO people were writing policy papers to one another. "Since really effective espionage operations are uneventful," said a plaintive OSO planning officer, "nothing ever comes up to talk to higher authority about." By the time the OPC and the OSO were brought under the direction of a single executive, the DDP (standing, arbitrarily, for "Deputy Director, Plans"), the top OPC people were well known to the "front office" on a first-name basis, while the OSO people remained in the background—except, of course, for a few masters of bureaucratic politics like Richard Helms, a few old OSS-ers who were Bold Easterners at heart, and a few irrepressible geniuses like Mother, the Kingfish, and Jojo.

Much has happened since the creation of the DDP and the entry of the CIA into the struggle for influence in the Third World. As far as the CIA's espionage specialists are concerned, the Agency's real mission in the clandestine field is the penetration of Chinese, Soviet, and Bloc targets, and the Third World is of only secondary importance. In 1955, the planning staffs of the espionage branch of the CIA recommended to the DDP that all stations in the Third World be closed except those which were convenient bases for the penetration of Soviet and Bloc diplomatic establishments. The recommendation wasn't acted upon, but the espionage branch thereafter tended to send only its second-best officers to Third World posts. The Agency's specialists in clandestine warfare, however, concentrated on the Third World—not only on Vietnam, but on the Arab–Israel conflict, the India–Pakistan conflict, racial strife in Africa, and the growth of Maoist influence in parts of South America. Similar changes of emphasis have taken place in branches of the British, French, and Soviet intelligence organizations that handle clandestine operations—all of which, incidentally, have adopted policies similar to those of the DDP in coordinating their espionage branches with their branches handling "dirty tricks."

The CIA's "department of dirty tricks," as some call that part of the "DDP complex" which was formerly known as the OPC, had a history of only ten years, dating from its first major successful, and consequently secret, operation in 1952 to the Bay of Pigs fiasco in April, 1961. In July, 1961, what was left of the clandestine branch, after most of its top officers had been fired or transferred to the espionage branch, was converted into a "support" branch which has four functions. First, it recruits specialist personnel—mercenaries skilled at guerrilla warfare, saboteurs, safecrackers, black propagandists, assassins, or whatever—upon the specific request of military commanders or, in certain rare cases, chiefs of diplomatic missions. Second, it trains them, giving them the best schooling known in these specialized subjects—better than that supplied by any other nation in the world. Third, it provides the trainees with whatever equipment and documentation they need. Fourth, it provides "backup" administration—e.g., depositing of pay in Swiss or Lebanese bank accounts, caring for dependents in case of accident, and the like. That is *all* the department does. It does not control the actions of its specialists. Their actions are entirely under the control of the commanders to whom they are assigned, and these commanders are in no way under the direction of the CIA. If there are CIA officers assigned to a commander to provide expert know-how in the use of these personnel, their capacities are advisory only and they are strictly under the orders of that commander. The commander is "line"; the CIA advisers are "staff."

The beauty of the weapon which the CIA puts into the

hands of a military commander or an ambassador is that he can take responsibility for it or wash his hands of it, as he likes. If it fulfills its mission quietly and successfully, he grabs the credit. If it flops—or becomes exposed to the glare of public scrutiny—he disowns it, and joins in the chorus against the CIA and its "freewheeling methods." Meanwhile, the CIA follows its policy: "Neither confirm nor deny."

ESPIONAGE STATIONS IN THE THIRD WORLD

The CIA has sixty-odd stations in various parts of the Third World employing some three hundred "generalists," espionage-branch case officers, and specialists of various kinds. Because of limitations in space and the number of "cover slots" allowed by the various U.S. embassies, clandestine operations and espionage operations are supervised by the same station chief, but the operations themselves are kept entirely separate. Since the number and size of clandestine operations throughout the world has in recent years been drastically reduced, the stations are in reality ordinary espionage stations.

It must be admitted that many of them are, for all practical purposes, useless, yet the U.S. Government maintains them for reasons that are sometimes quite incredible. Take the case of one country that was recently admitted to the United Nations. Its government's first act was to proclaim that the CIA was "supporting capitalist, pro-imperialist elements" in the country and encouraging them to overthrow or subvert the government. When U.S. Government representatives finally convinced leaders of the new government that such was not the case, and that the small staff of the newly opened U.S. Embassy could not conceivably be "CIA agents," the prime minister was insulted at the implication that his government was beneath our notice. As the result of an exchange of cables between Washington and the U.S. Embassy in his capital, a junior CIA officer was dispatched with instructions to "do something, anything," to convince the country that it was indeed taken seriously by the U.S. Government—seriously enough to be intrigued against.

An incident occurring in Egypt is only slightly less ludicrous. Until the time of the Egyptians' arms deal with the Soviets in 1965, the U.S. Government regarded President Nasser as sufficiently influential to merit most of the U.S. aid that he desired. One form of assistance was managerial advice in constructing a modern intelligence service. Accordingly, a straight liaison arrangement was set up between a CIA officer assigned to the U.S. Embassy and the Egyptian Mukhabarat el-Aam, and through this arrangement equipment and training material were channeled, excluding that required for espionage. In fact, the CIA officer thought one principal result of the training was to convince Egyptian intelligence officers that, in their case, espionage was useless and that properly used "alternative means" would amply service their purposes.

It was at least partly thanks to CIA assistance that the Egyptians built up one of the finest intelligence services in the world. Whether necessary or not, it was unthinkable that espionage should have only a minor role in any Egyptian intelligence service. "To us Egyptians," an official once said to me only half jokingly, "spying, tailing politicians, tapping telephones, and planting microphones is a way of life." It was also unthinkable to the Egyptians that the CIA's high praise for "alternative means" was not merely a smoke screen for the CIA's real interest, the planting of spies in Nasser's government. So, when the U.S. Government withdrew its CIA station from Egypt during the Six-Day War in 1967, the Egyptians concluded that the CIA had gone underground in their country.

From then on, responsibility for *all* liaison with the Egyptian Government was entrusted to a career diplomat named Donald Burgus. Burgus' extraordinary ability for acquiring information through entirely legal means was impaired by the Egyptians' suspicions that the "real" intelligence mission of the U.S. Government in Egypt was being achieved by means outside

208

Burgus' control. Tensions were eased when a "red herring" intelligence officer was assigned to Burgus' staff and told to organize just enough "operations" to keep Egyptian counterintelligence services happy. He got caught red-handed several times—once when he was overheard trying to convince an Egyptian pilot he should fly his MIG-21 to Greece and once when the Egyptians taped his secretary trying to tease secrets out of a Greek taxicab driver. When he departed at the end of his tour, the Deputy Director of the Mukhabarat entertained him with a farewell dinner.

These examples of Third World operations can hardly be called "typical." There are no typical examples, but the espionage branches of the American and British—and probably the Soviet—intelligence services spend an inordinately large part of their budgets on operations that are necessary for one obscure reason or another, but are only incidentally related to normal intelligence interests.

There are a number of CIA stations in the Third World which are more or less serious in purpose. Since their espionage operations are closely related to the U.S. Government's various clandestine-warfare programs, the station chiefs tend to fit a description coined in the old OPC days: "OSO officers who are OPC-oriented"—in other words, espionage specialists with a flair for clandestine warfare. In recent years, the quality of station chiefs in all but the most minor Third World countries has vastly improved. I don't know the present station chiefs in Teheran, Santiago, and Lagos (for example), but I am sure they are first-class senior officers who command the respect of Embassy colleagues and the local security officials with whom they conduct liaison. If not, they wouldn't have been assigned to those places.

The most important function of an espionage station in the Third World does not come under our definition of the "Third World operation." It is the penetration of "the opposition's" diplomatic installations. The other functions of a CIA station would be as follows:

—Penetrations of the local government and local political parties for the purpose of gaining information on pressures exerted by the Soviets, the Chinese, and other Communist countries.

—Dealing with informants (not necessarily true "agents") in the local "paper market."

—Dealing with any high-level government officials, political leaders, or respected members of the community who require secret financial aid or other kinds of support or who, for any reason, wish to have a relationship with the U.S. Government and to keep it secret. This is done only at the request of the government.

—Espionage and counterespionage operations incident to our Government's counterterrorist activity.

—Liaison with the appropriate local authorities.

The first of these tasks, penetrating the local government and political groups, is deceptively easy. "Everybody in the government wants to be our agent," a CIA station chief told a team of headquarters inspectors. "The problem is how to fight 'em off." The idea of "government," remember, does not command the awe of Third World peoples as it does our own. For centuries, the governments of these peoples have been imposed by foreigners. "I have always regarded screwing the government as an act of patriotism," a Syrian nationalist once told me, and he did not have in mind only the Turkish and the French administrations. He had the same attitude toward the governments of Syria after that country had become independent, because he assumed that before quitting the country the occupying authorities had managed to install puppets. In many countries of the Third World, Syria included, such an assumption is valid.

Whatever his motives, a typical Third World official who gains possession of secret Communist information has struck gold. He knows that if he does not capitalize on it someone else will, and, he will run, not walk, to the nearest American diplomat whom he can approach discreetly. "One hundred per cent of our local agents are walk-ins," a CIA officer in an African country told me, and there is no reason to doubt him. His only complaint was that a particularly astute local official, one who had been selling his office's documents for years, might "walk in" to half a dozen other embassies as well. A CIA officer in a nearby country told me that the reports of one Syrian agent were so fuzzy that they were obviously eighth- or ninth-level carbons, the others presumably going to better-paying embassies. It took considerable persuasion, together with a boost in salary, to get copies that the officer could read.

It is with perfectly good reason that the Egyptian, Libyan, Iraqi, and other governments forbid their officials to fraternize with foreign diplomats except in groups. The Libyans, having had important leaks even from their "Revolutionary Command Council," which is presumably composed of top patriots, have gone so far as to insist that Arabic-speaking Americans and Europeans who have been in the country long enough to have friends among the local officials leave the country.

Such measures discourage only the unresourceful, and Libyans who are would-be CIA agents, like their counterparts in other countries with stringent restrictions on contact with foreigners, manage to get through. In recruiting an agent in a Bloc ministry the problem is to find an employee who might eventually be induced to become an agent. In most Third World countries the problem is almost entirely that of making contact, and most Third World governments have come to accept their inability to keep secrets, and to make their plans accordingly.*

---

* One occasionally reads in the press that "months of planning" preceded some Arab terrorist raid (e.g., the Munich Olympic Games massacre), coup d'état, or other important action. Such claims are almost entirely false. The essence of Arab planning is to shorten as much as possible the length of time between the decision to act and the act itself. "Decide, then do" is the motto of Black September leaders. Every successful coup d'état attempt in the Middle East has been planned only hours before its execution. This included the coup by which Nasser, with General Mohammed Naguib as front, seized power in Egypt in 1952. It may be true that he took "years" to line up his capabilities, and that during the waiting period there were various feints and fake

In Egypt, once the late President Nasser realized that one in every ten of his officials would play Judas, he began to exploit the fact rather than fight it. He used to "generate secrets," according to the CIA station chief in Cairo, just for the purpose of leaking them to the U.S. Embassy. His main purpose was to scare the Embassy with reports of prospective Soviet aid, in the hope that the United States would respond by trying to outbid the Soviets. On one occasion, he *directed* a prominent Egyptian to secretly contact the U.S. Embassy and then had the "double agent" arrested as a CIA spy to embarrass the Americans.

The guile with which leaders of some Third World countries approach the problem of their Judases is one factor contributing to the existence of "paper markets" in their various capitals. In Beirut, where the Government doesn't bother to keep secrets, CIA and SIS files indicate that there are more than five hundred people in the information business—journalists, newspaper stringers, writers of "confidential newsletters," and simple peddlers of information—all quite apart from diplomats, researchers, and official information gatherers. The information generated by these people constitutes a "paper market" which the major intelligence services have no choice but to take seriously. Even in Cairo, Tripoli, Damascus, and Baghdad, where the local authorities maintain a tight surveillance and impose severe penalties on "those who spread rumors damaging to the revolution," paper markets exist—in forms, some think, that are made all the more virulent by the attempts to smother them.

Keeping abreast of the main currents in the local paper market is a task that falls to the CIA, SIS and KGB station chiefs in their respective embassies—not only because no one else is prepared to take it on, but because it might be disadvantageous to overlook it. Petty informants sidle up to diplomats of great-power countries, or come right into their embassies, even in Tripoli, and they must be taken seriously because

---

starts. But the coup itself took place less than twenty-four hours after he decided to act.

they just *might* have something of importance to say. There is hardly a Western diplomat who doesn't reflect every now and then on the Palestinian informant, a seedy, dishonest-looking little man, who did his best in March, 1973, to tell the American Embassy in the Sudan that "Black September" was planning to kill the American Ambassador. He could find no one willing to listen to him. "These creeps waste a lot of time," said the CIA station chief in a U.S. Embassy in the Middle East, "but think how I'd feel if I kicked one of them out and then learned later that he was going to report information which could have saved the life of one of my colleagues."

In a more positive way, an espionage station must take an interest in the local papers to stay on top of current trends. Much of the information is true or is based on fact; much of it is fabricated—but even fabricated information must have what intelligence analysts call "cultural validity" or it wouldn't remain in circulation; and much of it provides clues to the motives behind the more overt propaganda. It is true that some items of fabricated information gain currency simply because they appeal to the popular imagination, but these are quickly recognized by the professionals, so no harm is done.*

Needless to say, the station chief does not expose himself directly to any petty informant, nor does he allow his regular case officers to identify themselves. Instead, he ordinarily assigns a native member of the embassy staff to the job. The so-called "indigenous employee" performs various functions for the U.S. and British governments and certainly warrants our attention.

Third World espionage officials should take particular note

---

* *Ordinarily* no harm is done, that is. When I was in Syria back in 1947–1950, the amounts of money that the SIS was supposed to be handing out to its spies reached legendary proportions, until the SIS station chief in Damascus, with his meager budget, complained that he was having a hard time recruiting real agents. "If you can afford to give Husni Barazi fifty thousand pounds," the prospective recruit would say, "you can certainly afford to give me one thousand pounds a month"—an amount roughly twenty times what the SIS was in fact paying even its best agents.

of the following facts concerning citizens of their countries who are employees of U.S. and British embassies:

1. Embassy security officers *assume* that these employees, if questioned by their own governments, will tell them anything they want to know. It is the practice of both the Americans and the British to employ only native persons who are loyal to their own countries, and they expect from them only secondary loyalty—i.e., the kind that a private employer expects.

2. Having made such an assumption, our security officers have set up arrangements that make it virtually impossible for a native employee to acquire secret information of any importance. He can get personality information, and bits and pieces which might be of operational value to a sophisticated service, but that is all.

3. Knowing that many local security officials are too stupid to believe that an embassy's secrets are out of reach to a trusted native employee, embassy officers assume that the local security agency will attempt to recruit agents among the embassy's native staff. Standing instructions to the native staff are "Go ahead! Tell them anything they want to know. If you can't tell them enough to please them, come back and see us. We'll cook up enough to keep them happy. But for your own protection, you mustn't report to them that we're helping you."

4. In spite of such instructions, a high percentage of the native employees working for U.S. and British embassies will flatly refuse to report any information they learn about their employers, even when their employers give them permission to do so. From my own experience, I would say that well over 50 percent of these employees are loyal to this extent; that perhaps another 40 percent are loyal to the extent of reporting to the local security authorities as asked, but informing their embassy superiors that they have done so; and that the remaining 10 percent, out of fear or for some other understandable reason, will report to the local authorities whatever they want to know, even if they have to fabricate it.

In short, it is my impression that Third World security authorities underestimate the character of their own people.

The more patriotic and reputable the employee, the more likely he is to be contemptuous of these security authorities. If the embassies are allowed to employ only personnel actually *chosen* by the security authorities, you can be sure that there will be a high percentage of tricky types among them who will be only too glad to work their position both ways—to the ultimate advantage of the side that has the most to offer: i.e., ours.

The native employee who handles paper-market informants is often someone who is acceptable both to the station and to the local security service: in fact, he may be someone mutually agreed upon to handle day-to-day liaison. The information he acquires from these contacts is available both to the local government and to the station—but since the station pays his salary, and any expenses he might incur, the station usually has more control over the employee and primary benefit of his information. Furthermore, it is as an employee of the U.S. or British Embassy that the person in this role enjoys his prestige. Being an "Oriental secretary," as he may be called, gives him a position of awesome respect in the community—so much so that many of those in the local paper market prefer to deal with him rather than one of the American or British diplomats.

Whether these informants are seen by an "Oriental secretary," by an expendable case officer, or by some "straight" embassy official, station officers keep entirely behind the scenes in various capacities.

CONVERSION OF THE DIPLOMATIC CONTACT

Sometimes the embassy's high-level contacts are turned over to the station chief. Naturally, if some high-ranking official such as a foreign minister or a chief of police is willing to give important information to an embassy, he will usually want to deal with the ambassador or the deputy chief of mission, the DCM. Sometimes this is not so. In many stations, the OSO—or SIS or KGB—chief will be better known in the community because of his length of service and will have gained a reputation for competence and discretion. But regardless of whether a high-level contact gives information to the ambassador or to the station chief, the station tries to develop him as a "straight" embassy contact. If he is truly in a position of authority, he can impart even the most secret information about his government without being guilty of breaking his country's espionage laws. For a whole range of reasons, which apply to the station chief as well as to the "straight" officials of the embassy, it is better to exploit an information-bearing local official *as* an official.

A personal element often creeps in. In most countries of the Third World, the politicians are extremely insecure. They often have exaggerated notions about the extent to which great powers intrigue into their politics; they imagine that one of their rivals is backed by the Soviets, another by the British, and another by the French; they feel that if they are to hold their own they must get something more than tea and sympathy from the U.S. Ambassador. Such a politician will want a definite, continuing arrangement with the U.S. Embassy— sometimes involving no more than financial support to an election campaign, but more often including money for personal use and, sometimes, deposits to a Swiss bank "escape fund" to be used in the event of political catastrophe.

After the CIA's record in the Fifties and Sixties, it would now be difficult to convince a sophisticated reader that the CIA station chief would not leap to the assistance of such a politician just for the purpose of getting involved in local elections—or in local power contests, if the government is totalitarian. The fact is that the New Look in American policy is to assist friendly nations, by well-conceived aid projects, so as to help create an environment in which these countries stand a chance of winning their own battles. If we give clandestine aid at all, we do it not by helping "our friends" but by damaging their enemies—for example, by helping to expose the extent to which their enemies get illicit backing.

If for example the Foreign Minister of Lower Slobovia tells the U.S. Ambassador or the CIA station chief that he would like to put his confidential exchanges on a more permanent and "less official" basis, he is much more likely to find himself on an OSO payroll than on an OPC payroll. In any case, the moment money is passed to him, or an element creeps into the relationship suggesting that he may be in violation of his country's espionage laws, the "straight" part of the Embassy washes its hands of him, and he becomes the concern of the CIA station chief.

There is also the case of the high-level official of a Third World country who simply gets fed up, needs money, or wants "safe-haven" arrangements or security in general. There are many such cases; even military dictators, presidents, and prime ministers have approached U.S. ambassadors requesting personal financial assistance and the promise of a U.S. visa. Only rarely is the answer "no." The ambassador acquiesces if only to avoid offending the supplicant. But when the CIA station takes him over, it is almost always under an arrangement by which he is to supply information, not to behave to our liking politically. Whether he ever actually supplies any information is another matter, but at least that is the basis of the arrangement.

If there are any special techniques for dealing with "agents" of this category, they are the same as those of conventional espionage *after* recruitment, except that all sorts of euphemisms are used to enable the agent to delude himself into thinking he is *not* an agent while at the same time having no delusions about the controls under which he operates. Provided such an agent can be made to understand his proper role, and that it is assisted by his appearing to be *anti*-American, an arrangement of this kind can progress satisfactorily for years, with the CIA getting information of tremendous value, both to the embassy and to policymakers in Washington. More often than not the agent will persist in trying to make us believe that he is earning his pay merely by being "pro-American." Since being "pro-American" in many countries of the Third World means only showing that one is less anti-American than circumstances dictate, it is the belief of most station chiefs that "pro-American" agents are worse than useless. Since "termination with extreme prejudice" is not authorized in such cases, the station chief has to employ subtler disposal methods.

COUNTERTERRORISM

Espionage stations everywhere in the world are currently concerned with the problem of counterterrorism. Terrorist movements, most conspicuously the Palestinians' "Black September" but also various Maoist groups, have learned that they can improve the effectiveness of their operations geometrically by internationalizing them. If an anti-American terrorist group can't blow up the White House, it can attack the U.S. Embassy in London. If the British security authorities get tougher—as they have, along with the security authorities of every other European country—they can attack the U.S. Embassy in Sudan, or in any other place where there are only primitive local security facilities. Dangers to U.S. citizens and American interests increase dramatically the farther they are from the advanced nations—in other words, the deeper they get into the Third World.

Until recently, the CIA's counterterrorist effort was concentrated in Vietnam, where it was under the control of the U.S. military using specialists recruited, trained, and administratively supported by the CIA. Although the Vietnam operation "Phoenix" was in a sense an espionage operation, it was "tactical espionage" and too closely related to "clandestine operations" (e.g., assassinations) to be properly the responsibility of the espionage branch.* Phoenix has now been disbanded, and

---

* "Phoenix" was an operation in South Vietnam whose purpose was to increase the accuracy of the methods by which the South Vietnamese were spotting and "neutralizing" members of the Viet Cong. Under a unit known as "CORDS" (Civil Operations and Rural Development Support), which reported directly to the commanding general, in 1969 alone some 20,000 Viet Cong members were identified and 6,000-odd killed. Not surprisingly, "Phoenix" and its director, Ambassador William Colby, now Director of the CIA, have come under virulent attack from the American left-wing press. Despite all the information that has been dragged out by inquiring newspapermen, however, plus that given by

the CIA has since continued to "maintain a low profile," as the Agency's new Director, William Colby, says, in the counter-subversive business. Counterterrorism is now an interagency affair, with State, Defense, the FBI, and the Treasury Department all having their parts to play.

In the Third World, however, it is a different story. It is the responsibility of the OSO to build an espionage capability in these countries with pervasiveness and strength in inverse proportion to the capabilities of the local security forces. In Zaire, for example, where the counterterrorist capability of the local authorities is virtually nil, it is the responsibility of the CIA station to build the capability—while encouraging the Zaire Government to build its own.

In the field of counterterrorism, the role of the CIA is entirely that of information, and since terrorism is presumed to be a concern of most governments, it swaps information in such a way that it becomes the common property of all cooperating governments. Following the Israeli raid on the Palestinian Liberation Organization headquarters in Lebanon in April, 1973, various Arab governments charged that the Israeli raiders had planned their attack partly on information supplied by the CIA; some even charged that "CIA agents" had assisted the Israeli raiders operationally. Both charges are patently false. The CIA would never give the Israelis information to guide them to "Arab" targets *—any more than it would give an Arab government information to guide it to targets inside Israel. It would "pool" its information on terrorists by a multi-

---

Mr. Colby himself in testimony before the Senate Foreign Relations Committee, the whole truth about this remarkable operation has as yet been hidden from the public. It can at least be said for "Phoenix," however, that its surgical precision cost fewer lives than the shotgun methods used by the South Vietnamese police and security authorities before "Phoenix" got into the picture—and with obviously greater effect.
* Incidentally, one proof that the Israelis were not acting on CIA counterterrorist information—or, for that matter, on their own—is the fact that the Palestinians they killed were not terrorist leaders. It served Israeli purposes to say that they were, but the real purpose of the raid was not to kill terrorist leaders but to force the Lebanese Government to take action.

lateral exchange from which *all* governments desiring to counter terrorism, including the Lebanese, the Jordanian, and the Egyptian, would profit.

The charge that "CIA agents" assisted the Israeli raiders is even farther afield. The whole thrust of U.S. Government policy is to get local governments to accept their own security responsibilities, and it is therefore in total disagreement with the *apparent* policy of the Israeli Government—to wit, to take over from a sovereign country the task of dealing with terrorists taking refuge within its borders. Instead, it is in sympathy with the *real* Israeli policy, which is to goad the local government into taking its own action, although it chooses to accomplish this end by means rather different from those available to the Israelis.*

LIAISON

Rather than "goading," CIA stations prefer to think they aid and abet local governments in doing what they are already at least halfway inclined to do. In the case of the Palestinian terrorists, most Arab governments make excuses for their actions and refuse to disapprove of them openly, but there are only two whose sympathies are actually what they publicly claim them to be: the Libyan Government and the South Yemeni

---

* In considering the question of how an espionage agency can goad the government of another country into taking some action it wants that government to take, it is well to consider a technique that terrorist organizations themselves use. My friends in British security services tell me that in Northern Ireland, both sides in the war of terrorists have units whose duty is to attack their *own* sides—either to punish those who are thought lacking in zeal or to arouse widespread indignation. For example, there is at least one case of a priest's having been killed by Catholic terrorists in such a way as to make the Catholic population think the Protestants had done it. It is well known that Viet Cong "discipline" has been behind as many atrocities among Viet Cong followers as have the South Vietnamese, and in the Arab–Israel struggle the number of Arabs killed by Palestinians is something like three times the number of Palestinians killed by Israelis, and eleven times the number of Israelis killed by Palestinians.

Government. They actively aid the terrorists. The rest wage secret war on these terrorists while pretending to help them. The Syrian Government, the most two-faced of them all, has gone so far as to provoke Palestinian units into making raids into Israel, and then to tip off the Israelis. The Algerian Government donated a number of blank passports to al-Fatah for "Black September," then told the French security authorities how to identify the secret markings they put on them. And several Arab governments, while loudly refusing to contribute to the international "counterterrorist information pool," have turned their backs while Western agents slipped into their offices at night to photocopy their SUSPECT files.

Liaison between a great-power intelligence service and the security authorities of a Third World country is often much closer than the public is allowed to know. This is true of SIS liaison with the security authorities in the Republic of Ireland, Cyprus, South Africa, and even Rhodesia; it is true of the French SDECE liaison with Algeria, Guinea, and half a dozen other countries that are openly less than friendly to the French; it is true of the CIA in most Arab countries, most Asian countries, and countries all over the world whose leaders have loudly decried our Indochina policies while whispering, "Go to it!" offstage. Naturally, conducting "discreet liaison," as it is euphemistically called, requires the considerable skill of the OSO.

When the OSO first started pushing liaison as a means of fulfilling its requirements in the Third World, its representatives tended to speak of two overlapping circles. "This circle represents your interests," the OSO representative would say, "and this one represents ours." The resulting graph would show three areas—one indicating the local security agency's interests which the OSO did not share (including, of course, actions *against* American interests), second indicating American interests which the local agency did not share, and a third in the middle, where the two circles overlapped, indicating interests that were mutual. "This oval," the OSO representative would say, "represents an area in which we should cooperate."

A history of the CIA's liaison arrangements with Third World governments, if such could be written, would show that the area of mutual interest has in almost all cases proved to be far greater than the local security agencies initially realized. In many cases, an OSO representative is being absolutely truthful when he looks the chief of a Third World agency in the eye and says: "If we could help you to become so effective that you get one hundred percent of the information your government needs to keep itself secure, it would be to our advantage as well as to yours. You can count on our sincere support." But it is a rare Third World government that is willing to believe this. The conduct of liaison involves continuing intrigue, intrigues within intrigues, and counterintrigues in the style of the third Rome, all in aid of keeping the local agency from outsmarting itself—to its own disadvantage as well as to ours.

The CIA's honeymoon with the security authorities of Nasser's Egypt is a case in point. In the U.S.-Egyptian intelligence-liaison arrangement of 1953–1956, experts supplied by the CIA made it possible for the Egyptian Mukhabarat, and Nasser personally, to acquire literally all the foreign intelligence the Government needed to successfully conduct its international affairs and to maintain internal security. But its senior officers, and Nasser himself, persisted in believing that the CIA was misleading them for some sinister ulterior motive. Their refusal to credit what they learned through their CIA liaison caused the U.S. Government considerable inconvenience, and it brought down a series of out-and-out catastrophes onto Egyptian leadership.

The standard way in which the CIA establishes a liaison arrangement in a Third World country is to send someone from the Langley headquarters who is so senior that he doesn't have to worry about being exposed as a CIA official. He is allowed the hospitality of the local security authorities for a few days; gives his sales talk, complete with overlapping circles; and then brings out his catalogue of police, security, and intelligence goodies—everything from police billies and riot-control gas to a few "sneakies" of middle-level security classification.* He also gives samples, orally or in writing, of information produced by the CIA which the local government could not obtain despite the fact that it is of direct interest. If the local officials are impressed, the CIA official begins to talk in concrete terms. If the terms are acceptable—and there is always considerable haggling on both sides—the talks proceed until an agreement is reached.

A liaison agreement between the CIA and the security service of a Third World country is never allowed to become out-and-out public knowledge; enough secrecy is always maintained to allow either side to deny its existence in the event of adverse public reaction. Still, some of the Agency's arrangements come close to being common knowledge. These liaisons are always under the supervision of the American ambassador or, in the case of Vietnam, the senior military commander, and subject to the disciplines that control all aid programs in the country. When there is a greater pretense of secrecy, the liaison arrangement can allow for a considerable amount of "where there's smoke, there's fire" gossip, but ensure that people suspect a much smaller degree of liaison than is actually the case—for example, by allowing the public to suspect that someone in the Embassy generally thought to be "the CIA man" is contacting a local security official or ministry of interior official, but concealing the quantity of information and equipment that is actually changing hands.

Sometimes all or part of the liaison arrangement is conducted through a third country. In one case that I know of, the chief of state of a Third World country didn't want an intelligence arrangement connected to the kind of diplomatic relationship

---

* Figuring prominently on the list of "sneakies" that are made available to Third World security services are a number of items more interesting as playthings than as apparatus of practical value. They make wonderful gifts to cooperative but unbribable security chiefs—boutonnieres concealing miniature sending sets, cigarette lighters concealing miniature cameras, etc. The practice of using these items as presents was discontinued when a number of them were embarrassingly conspicuous at a convention of Afro-Asian security officials in Cairo in the mid-Fifties.

he envisaged between his government and the U.S. Government. He requested that we achieve our purposes by supporting a liaison arrangement between his security services and those of a European country with which he thought the CIA to be friendly.* The agreement was made—and in such a way that it not only boosted the CIA's capabilities with respect to that country, but improved the relationship with the European service.

At other times, the liaison arrangement *can* be kept entirely secret. In such cases, all the procedures for secret meetings, communications, cutouts, and other features of conventional espionage are put into practice. Needless to say, a high percentage of the liaison arrangements that are really secret wind up as conventional espionage operations—with the chief of the local security service on the OSO payroll as a career agent.

The question of training comes up frequently in liaison arrangements, and the OSO blows hot and cold on the subject. In an arrangement I set up myself back in 1950 with a Syrian chief of staff, the prime request was that the CIA train key intelligence and security officials. The requirement was enthusiastically received by the CIA, with the thought that CIA training not only would improve the efficiency of security services with which it hoped to cooperate but would provide a chance to win some of the trainees as "friends." Unfortunately, the possibility also occurred to the Syrian Chief of Staff, Adib

---

* It should be noted that even when the chief of state or the chief of security wants his relationship with the CIA to be direct, it is not necessary that the CIA send out staff personnel to conduct the various functions incident to the liaison arrangement—technicians, trainers, organization experts, etc. The CIA has a large stable of specialist personnel of a wide variety of nationalities, and they are controlled entirely by the CIA and not by governments of those countries whose passports they carry. Particularly useful for the purpose have been former Nazi intelligence officers whose records were not quite bad enough to make them worth chasing as war criminals and whose rank and appearance are such as to make a favorable impression on the local services. Better still, they are so out of date in their know-how, which was third-rate to start with, that there is no danger of their creating any Frankenstein monsters in the countries to which they are assigned.

Shishakli, although somewhat belatedly. When he eventually took over the country to become its dictator, he sent "our friends" to such posts as Deir ez-Zor, Qamishliyeh, and various oases in the Syrian desert. He remained as enthusiastic as ever for CIA training, but he used it exclusively for purposes of palace politics.

Stateside training of Third World intelligence and security personnel presents several problems. For one thing, the teaching is not always effective. "Even if you brought in a lot of African pygmies," an instructor at the CIA's "Good Neighbor" school in Florida told me, "for the first two weeks we would tell them but the second two weeks *they* would be telling *us* how it's done." This happens partly because those few CIA officers who are adept at the difficult art of "culture jumping" cannot be spared for the Training Division, and partly because the training programs are designed more to dazzle Third World officials with our superior competence than to make them truly effective when they return home. Often a ranking member of the group of trainees winds up his trip by requesting a long list of items that have caught his eye but that cannot be released. Upon being told that he can't have them, he goes home to report to his superiors that the CIA is furnishing only second-rate stuff and that only second-rate cooperation should be given until the CIA upgrades its generosity.

In this chapter I have spoken mainly of the CIA's espionage branch, but the lessons, I believe, are generally applicable. With a reputation for fantastic discretion and playing fair, the SIS manages to hold its own in the Anglo-American cooperation for liaison arrangements, despite the fact that it is unable to offer as much in the way of technical and material aid. I have even been told that there are SIS officers who sweeten their favorite liaison arrangements by coaching the local security chiefs in how to put the squeeze on their CIA colleagues; but I am sure that none of the SIS officers I know would stoop to such a practice. The Soviets, it appears, are just learning. Having come late into the liaison business in the Third World, they are making all the mistakes the CIA used to make. And since many of the security services with which they are now trying to build liaison have had years of experience at screwing the British, the French, and the Americans, the Soviets' job is much harder than ours was.

7

"SPECIAL PROJECTS"

*Also, there are secret intelligence operations
that only an espionage branch can handle.*

ANY ESPIONAGE organization that tries to cover the world soon learns that it cannot divide the management of its operations into neatly delineated geographical boundaries. The Africa Division of the OSO, through its station in Accra, recruits as agent a first secretary of the Soviet Embassy in that country; the first secretary is then transferred successively to Paris, to the United Nations in New York, and to Moscow. Should his management be transferred from area division to area division, or should it be left to an extraterritorial division which can manage him throughout?

Another example: The OSO is ordered to provide information on missile sites in Kazakhstan; on-the-ground observation is required in that area to supplement what can be seen by means of satellites. Should the job be given to the Middle East Division, to be carried out by the Teheran and Ankara stations, each of which will be so absorbed in national problems that the job may be neglected, or should it be assigned to a division which specializes in "denied areas" and which can use any and all field stations for the furtherance of its mission?

Another: The OSO's planning staff sees an opportunity to make use of some international student or labor organization, or some religious movement, to cover targets in many countries. Should the responsibility for exploiting the opportunity be divided among the area divisions covering those countries or, in accordance with sound management practice, be assigned to a single division equipped to cross national boundaries?

The problem of how to handle operations that didn't fit logically into any single area division came up early in the OSO's history—as, indeed, it had already come up in older espionage services. But it was the "sucker operation," as OSO planners called it, that forced the establishment of the OSO's "Special Projects Division." * When I took a look at this Division in the course of a bit of management consulting I did for the Agency in 1956, its Chief told me, "We have a lot of projects simply because they don't make sense in any area division, and many of these don't belong in the CIA at all. But somebody had to take them on, and we are 'it.'"

THE OSO AND ITS "SUCKER OPERATIONS"

On an average of perhaps once every two months, between 1949 and the middle of 1967, some imaginative U.S. Government official—from the State Department, the Department of Labor, or even the White House—would come to the Director of Central Intelligence with some unusual requirement. The example described below was actually brought to the agency prior to the Olympic Games of 1952 by a Congressman on behalf of an influential constituent. The Congressman pushed the following line:

1. A true capitalist government confines itself to functions that are not properly provided by private individuals and companies—running the fire department; providing police protection, sanitation, and basic public services; and defending the country. Consequently, capitalist countries usually lag behind socialist countries in activities that are neither profitable nor in the nature of a public service.

---

* I call it the "Special Projects Division" for purposes of this book, but the Division was long ago given another, and more nondescript, title.

2. Take the Olympic Games athletes, for example. American entrants are genuine amateurs, who either pay their own expenses or get grants from philanthropic organizations; many topflight amateurs can't afford the expenses, or have no basis to qualify for grants; many of the best "go professional." Bloc entrants, however, are chosen competitively at the age of seven and, at government expense, are trained for the whole of their competing lives. Bloc countries send to the Olympics only athletes in whom maximum potential has been realized. While they are technically amateurs, they are in the truest sense professional.

3. Thus, in international athletic contests our amateurs compete with Bloc professionals, and in certain sports they show quite poorly. This is intolerable; our national "image" suffers, particularly since the Communist press has effectively used this seeming weakness to argue that "the capitalist nations are become soft and effete."

4. For this reason, our Government must subsidize athletes of certain categories. Doing so is as defensible an activity as any of the other programs we regard as worthwhile and legitimate under our "information" programs.

5. But it must be done secretly: unlike socialist countries, we have no way of subsidizing athletes without clearly transforming them into professionals. This poses a problem, because the U.S. Government is without the means to provide secret subsidies of the kind required in this instance.

6. But there is the Central Intelligence Agency with its masses of secret funds. With all that money to throw around, let the Agency spend some of it constructively for a change. After all, the amounts will be small.

So the Agency—and, in turn, the OSO—gets stuck for a scheme to subsidize Olympic Games athletes. By the time of the so-called "student-grant scandals" of 1967, the CIA was supporting athletes, ballet troupes,* highbrow magazines, stu-

---

* One such group danced its way through Europe entirely nude except for flimsy American flags draped over the dancers' private parts. In Paris, they were billed as *les nues patriotiques.*

dent associations, university research centers, labor and cultural organizations, and a wide variety of one-shot schemes. The CIA became an easy touch: first, because some of the schemes—indeed, some of the most lunatic ones—were suggested by influential Congressmen who were always the first to howl when the Agency made a mistake and the first to appear outraged when the "scandals" occurred; second, because the Agency feared that if it said no, some other agency would take on the job, get permission to receive and dispense secret funds, and become a rival. "If they've got to be done," the Chief, Special Projects Division, told me "we'd rather do them than have someone else do them."

There have been many changes in this special division since it first began to function, in 1951, as "PPPM" for "Psychological Political and Para-Military." The original Chief, brought into the Agency by Allen Dulles, was one Thomas Braden, a brilliant man in his early thirties who had no interest in commanding an operation junk heap and who set about creating a special division to give covert support to international trade associations, student movements, and publications that were left-of-center but anti-Communist. His programs grew until they were exposed in 1967 by a national magazine. Following the resulting public outcry,* the division was cut down to a few paper shufflers. Many of its features, however, were worth saving and these were given to the Special Projects Division. These features were (1) a capability for acquiring masses of worthwhile information through student, labor, religious, educational, and émigré group channels and doing so in a way that would not offend the so-called "public conscience"; (2) a means for providing "unofficial cover" on an international scale; (3) a means for conceiving, planning, organizing, launch-

---

* In February, 1967, the left-wing *Ramparts* magazine disclosed the details of the CIA's financing of the National Student Association's overseas programs. The result, after a long Congressional hassle which was fully aired in the press, was a Presidential decision that "no Federal Agency shall provide any covert financial assistance or support, direct or indirect, to any of the nation's educational or private voluntary organizations."

ing, and providing continuing management for operations into "denied areas" from multiple bases and involving movements across area division lines; (4) a means for coordinating certain operations that may require instant worldwide coordination— e.g., the various defection programs, Soviet, Bloc, Chinese, and Cuban. As presently constituted, the Special Projects Division is a combination of Staffs B-III and B-IV and the Denied Areas Division as shown on the chart in Appendix A.

"HITCHHIKING"—USE OF STUDENT, LABOR, AND OTHER KINDS OF GROUPS

The "PPPM" Division was a hybrid affair, engaged in operations designed to influence ("clandestine activity"), operations designed only to get information ("espionage"), and the out-and-out "sucker operations" mentioned earlier. Since the student-subsidy scandal of 1967, however, the PPPM's successor has been concerned exclusively with espionage and activities incidental to espionage. It maintains contact with a wide range of groups, but makes no attempt to influence them. In fact, aside from concern over the possibility of more scandals, the Special Projects Division has been moved by a growing realization that these organizations are better sources of information if they are left to operate on their own and are simply monitored from without. A few members of these organizations are given special training, of course, and are in a sense "agents," but they are not employed by the SPD *as* members but as individuals who see no conflict in loyalties. Even though it has a few "agents" in these groups, it is the policy of the SPD to make use of the groups *as* groups and to do so only on a basis of friendly liaison.

The exploitation of an informational channel that the Agency cannot control is known as "hitchhiking." By hitchhiking on a student group or labor union, the SPD does not expect to gain espionage information of the sort produced by the area divisions, but it can acquire masses of data that will enable the

SPD to organize operations which are not banned by the Presidential order of 1967. The ban explicitly applies to "the nation's" educational or private voluntary organizations, and makes no mention of organizations that are located outside the United States and are in no way identified as "American." With the help of information coming from educational and private voluntary organizations based in the United States, the SPD has been able to penetrate hostile groups abroad so as to keep tabs on what they are doing and their sources of support.

Even in dealing with groups that are entirely foreign, the SPD operates under certain restrictions, some of which come from outside the Agency and some that it imposes upon itself.

The SPD will not support an existing group, or create a new group, that cannot plausibly seem to be self-sufficient. The Soviets and the Chinese support many groups that are suspect in the eyes of native populations because they obviously could not exist without outside support; the SPD does not. Partly because of sensitivities triggered in 1967 and partly because of sound operational practice, the SPD has been so conscientious in adhering to this restriction that not a single native group receiving SPD support has come under serious attack for being what it is.

The SPD may not encourage a group that is not *already* engaged in illegal activities to engage in such activities. It has no obligation, however, to clean up the morals of a group it supports, and it can even take advantage of the group's illegal or immoral actions as long as (a) no American or British personnel are involved, and (b) the laws broken by the group are not American laws. For example, the SPD may support a group that is engaged in smuggling across the Turco-Soviet border, or that owns bars selling alcoholic beverages in "dry" Libya, but it may not in any way involve itself in the international narcotics trade.

It may not create groups that might go into commercial competition with American business organizations, or in any way undermine the effectiveness of American business, cultural, or philanthropic enterprises. Before it can help an émigré group to start a shipping business, for example, it must consider the question of whether or not it would eventually take contracts away from an American firm.

These restrictions are not particularly crippling, as it happens; besides, they contain numerous loopholes, and occasional exceptions may easily be made. At present, the SPD gives aid to some thirty student associations in Africa, Asia, and South America.

In addition, the SPD, through one or another of its cover mechanisms, now gives financial support to student associations of other nations; grants scholarships to individual students, whether chosen by some panel of American educators or by the educational authorities of the students' own countries; furnishes books to libraries; subsidizes student publications; and gives other kinds of aid all designed to make better citizens out of the student populations and teach them enough about our country to lessen the likelihood that they will become our enemies. But although the SPD is now strictly a division of the CIA's *espionage* branch, it recruits few espionage agents from among the student beneficiaries. The purpose of "student development," as this kind of activity is called, is chiefly long-range.

Since this program got under way only a few years ago, it has hardly had time to show results. But there are already some successes. An operation that grew out of student development has become perhaps the best continuing source of information on the Palestinians' "Black September." Another group of students in Europe got information from older relatives, which they passed on to an SPD "front," enabling the U.S. Government to head off a right-wing military coup d'état that would have played right into the hands of the Communists. Other intelligence successes resulting from the SPD's activities among students have been less noteworthy, but the Division's planners believe that, in time, selected students will be in key positions in both left-wing and right-wing governments of the Third World, and in such numbers that "there won't be a closed door in any one of them," as the present SPD Chief puts it.

Through young SPD case officers directing native principals who are students in their early twenties, the SPD has recruited Maoist students in a variety of places ranging from Egypt to Great Britain. It has had similar success with labor movements—or rather, more success, since there is no reluctance to make agents of adults. In Egypt, SPD agents have followed Communist-inspired student and labor troubles since they began shortly after Nasser's death, and it was information from SPD sources, rather than information from the Egyptians' own sources, which persuaded President Anwar el-Sadat that the Soviets were a dangerous ally and that he would do well to slow down his plans for increased cultural exchanges with Communist China.

For a short period, the CIA's Special Projects Division had similar success in Britain—student movements and labor unions, incidentally, being the elements of British society in which it had a particular interest.* There were off-the-record protests to the CIA, however, not through SIS–CIA liaison channels but on higher Government-to-Government levels, and that ended the matter. There is a firm understanding between the intelligence services of the two countries that neither will conduct clandestine operations in the other, and relations between them are close. Still, it would seem logical that the British services would blink at the CIA's operating in areas on which information is desperately needed, but in which they cannot operate freely themselves.

Penetration of labor unions in the United States for the purpose of sniffing out Communist influences is entirely the job of the FBI, and the FBI is not nearly so tolerant as the

---

* It is well known that some of Britain's most influential labor leaders are Communist Party members whose objective is not so much to better the lot of workers as to bring down the system, but the nature of British Government is such that it is unable to accept this fact of life as a basis for policy.

234

British services in allowing other agencies to trespass in its fields of responsibility. As recently as 1960, our top military strategists feared that in the event we found ourselves in an armed conflict with any Communist nation we would suddenly see our ports, shipping, and critical industries freeze up as a result of strikes by Communist-led unions. It is thanks to the FBI that this is no longer the case: in the event of a showdown, non-Communist labor-union leaders, representing a vast majority of the members of even the most militant unions, would come out on top and the effectiveness of Communist agitators would be quickly neutralized. It is thanks to the SPD, however, that the same can be said of those countries of the Third World where energy and mineral resources vital to our national security are located. The contacts maintained by the SPD for purposes of developing a capability in the Third World represent one of the rare cases in which there is a certain amount of cooperation between the FBI and the CIA— which, incidentally, is gradually being widened to include cooperation with the British intelligence and security services for operations in Great Britain.

Oddly, it was labor-union operations of the SPD's predecessor organization, PPPM, that got it into "hitchhiking" on international criminal organizations, notably the Mafia and the Corsican underground, and into deep conflict with the FBI, the Bureau of Narcotics, and other law-enforcement agencies. It was the OSS's "Wild Bill" Donovan who conceived the idea of getting "Lucky" Luciano and other Mafia criminals out of jail, to use them not only to save Italy from the Fascists but to supply a corps of skilled safecrackers, housebreakers, and assassins who might be put to constructive purposes in wartime. It was not until the OSS became the CIA and the Mafia was used to save Italy from the Communists rather than from the Fascists that the impropriety of working with criminal elements began to occur to some Congressmen and the press.

The switch from resisting the Fascists to resisting the Communists was begun in 1945, when the Communists came very near to gaining control of labor unions, first in Sicily, then in

all Italy and southern France. At that time, cooperation between the OSS and the Mafia was successful in stemming the
tide. No serious historian, left or right, who is familiar with
the situation at that time can deny that had it not been for the
Mafia the Communists would by now be in control of Italy,
and the world balance of power would be decisively in favor
of the Soviets.

During the following two years, contacts with the Mafia
were broken, and when the newly created CIA opened its
doors for business in 1947 it was without assets to deal with
the recurring problem. It turned to the American Federation
of Labor, with its formidable array of contacts in Europe, and
in November, 1947, it sent a team composed of three OSS
veterans and three AFL representatives * to Paris, Marseille,
Rome, and Palermo with instructions from the CIA's Admiral
Hillenkoetter to do "something, *anything.*"

It took exactly two weeks, with three and four days spent
in each of the cities, for the AFL representatives to declare the
situation hopeless and to recommend to their OSS colleagues
that they save the situation in any way they could. On the day
the team arrived in Paris, an announcement by the political
committee of the French Communist Party calling for an all-
out struggle against the "American Party" brought rioting
crowds into the streets and caused the fall of the Ramadier
Government. On the day the team arrived in Marseille, the red
flag was hoisted over the Palais de Justice, and Communist
mobs were in control of the city, overturning and burning
automobiles and buses and breaking shop windows. Similar
receptions greeted the team in Rome and Palermo. It was in
Palermo that the CIA's OSS veterans decided they had no

---

* Quite on its own, the International Ladies' Garment Workers' Union
had attempted to promote non-Communist unions in France, but gave up
the attempt because of a shortage of funds. The three AFL representatives who accompanied the OSS-ers to Europe in November, 1947, had
no connection with the ILGWU—although they profited by the advice
of two ILGWU representatives, Jay Lovestone and Irving Brown.

choice but to turn to the Mafia. In the spirit of the defunct OSS rather than that of the newly born CIA, they did so without first requesting guidance from headquarters.

Within weeks, the Mafia and the Corsican underground, which the OSS officers contacted at the same time, had the situation in hand. Their methods were rough, but so were the methods of the Communists. Fortunately, the OSS-ers' campaign, as mapped out by their AFL friends the evening before they returned to the States, was run so economically that they achieved a maximum of results with a minimum of brutality. All the same, it did give the Mafia and the Corsicans a new lease on life, and when the trio returned triumphant to Washington they were promptly fired.

A policy was subsequently established that the Agency would under no circumstances associate itself with organizations engaged in crime; but the policy was modified when it was brought to the Director's attention that there were already simple penetrations of various worldwide criminal organizations run by other U.S. Government agencies—for example, the Narcotics Bureau had an agent planted by Luciano's side as henchman *—and that they were producing political as well as criminal information. It thus became CIA policy to allow penetration of criminal organizations under the same restrictions that bind the police and on condition that the SPD release to the appropriate criminal-investigative agency any leads on crime its penetrations pick up. At present, the SPD has penetrations of practically every international criminal organization of any importance. It has from time to time been accused of withholding criminal information—an understandable temptation, because the criminal-investigative agency might act on the information in such a way as to bring the SPD's penetration to an end—but following allegations made in 1972 and 1973 that the Agency was aiding and abetting narcotics smugglers, spokesmen for both the FBI and the Nar-

---

* S. Vizzini, now Chief of Police, South Miami, Florida.

cotics Bureau went out of their way to assure indignant Congressmen that the Agency was "as cooperative as could be expected" in passing on information about crime.

The CIA won't, on the other hand, attempt to reform persons engaged in criminal activity, particularly in foreign countries. If some division of the CIA is getting cooperation from the Government of West Patagonia in operations into East Patagonia, and if it happens that the West Patagonians smuggle heroin as a way of life, the Agency is not going to undertake the task of stopping them. Nor is it going to expand or divert its cooperation in such a way as to increase the take of criminal information at any possible cost to the take of political information. Any criminal information it comes across, however, in the normal course of the penetration will be passed on to the Narcotics Bureau—and promptly, too—provided the Narcotics Bureau agrees not to act on the information in such a way as to blow the CIA operation. The Narcotics Bureau will in almost all cases agree to this condition, because even in its own operations it sometimes forgoes arrests to maintain its sources. Still, in any case where there is a clear-cut issue of whether to wrap up a heroin ring that smuggles into the United States or to save espionage sources that produce political information, the former gets priority—unless it can be shown that the information is truly vital to our national security, and this is rarely the case.

The SPD's connections with international religious groups for purposes of aiding or supplementing espionage operations is almost as touchy an issue as its association with criminal rings. To start with, Jewish and Catholic organizations are out. If it were learned that a case officer had lined up a Jewish or a Catholic organization for espionage purposes, half the Agency would walk out. Contrary to some opinion, the CIA is definitely not a "WASP" organization; except for the units that deal with Middle East affairs, in which the Agency's Jews prefer not to work, its percentages of Jews and Catholics are considerably higher than the national percentages. Organizations stemming from other religions are fair game, however—

or they *were* fair game until, one by one, many of them turned out to have fanatical adherents in the Agency. For a while, Moral Re-Armament was believed to be a potentially valuable SPD asset. Then, just as the SPD was establishing contacts with Moral Re-Armament representatives it was learned that a deputy chief of one of the area divisions was a Moral Re-Armer and would proceed to his Congressman, also a Moral Re-Armer, and blow the operation sky-high should it ever get off the ground. The same for Seventh-Day Adventists, Jehovah's Witnesses, and half a dozen other religions with international followings. "Before we tie into a religious group," an SPD officer told me some time ago, "it's got to be so offbeat that anyone in the Agency who belongs to it may be fired as a security risk—and that does not include the Holy Rollers."

In the Middle East and the Far East there are dozens of offbeat religions which are virtually secret societies and which, entirely for their own purposes, collect huge amounts of information of startling quality on chiefs of state, cabinet ministers, military commanders, and other prominent persons. One esoteric sect, which happens to provide three-quarters of the servant class in a certain Middle Eastern capital, provided the local CIA station with most of the operational data needed for its espionage operations, besides a lot of tidbits picked up in family conversations. The local security service finally caught on to this fact, and consequently forced government employees with access to secrets to replace any servants of this sect with members of the country's prevalent religion. The quality of the food and service in civil servants' homes went down and the thieving went up, but the leak of secrets was brought to a stop—except, of course, those leaks which went to the security service itself.

Perhaps the largest category of interdivisional operations handled by the SPD are those making use of the émigré groups resident in the United States, various South American countries, and parts of Europe. Shortly after the war, aging émigrés from Czarist Russia, joined by a smaller number of disillusioned Soviet Communists, formed a near-fanatical secret organization known to the American OSO and the British SIS as "Nightingale." Although there was mutual loathing between the Czarists on the one hand and the ex-Communists on the other, both sides saw the advantages of sticking together in dealing with the various U.S. Government agencies that took an interest in them. Their cohesiveness was greatly enhanced by the financial support they got from a multimillionaire American who was involved in a one-man crusade against "the evils of Communism."

The American and British clandestine services had already developed a healthy dislike of émigré groups as such, and regarded them as no more than reservoirs where individual recruits might be found. With few exceptions, however, members of "Nightingale" held together as tightly as a labor union and provided the Defense Department, the State Department, and the CIA with floods of information on a take-it-or-leave-it basis—which, needless to say, was generally unreliable paper-mill stuff.

For all the propaganda the information contained, it soon became apparent to CIA evaluators that *some* of it was genuine and that it could have been acquired only from deep inside the Soviet Union. Prolonged discussion with the somewhat arrogant leaders of "Nightingale" failed to produce operational details, but it did convince the CIA officers who met with the leaders that "Nightingale" was indeed getting some of its members into and out of the U.S.S.R. OSO officers were assigned to find out just how "Nightingale" operated and how it could be turned into a trustworthy espionage asset.

The investigation, as one OSO officer put it, was "like pulling teeth." By cajolery, threats, and enticements of various kinds, the OSO finally got "Nightingale" leaders to agree, with the approval of their millionaire patron, to submit to a degree of operational direction from the OSO, to conform to OSO reporting practices (although not to reveal sources inside the U.S.S.R.), and to undergo OSO training—but not to allow its members to work for OSO as individuals or to receive pay except through the "Nightingale" bursar. Eventually, "Nightingale" agreed to set up operational bases in various European countries bordering on the Soviet Bloc.

Since all of the bases that were first set up were in Western Europe, the "Nightingale nightmare," as OSO officers had begun to call it, became the property of the OSO's Western Division. It soon became apparent, that under the WED's station chiefs the "Nightingale" bases would get only unenthusiastic handling, since a station with high-quality operations of its own is not likely to have much patience with operations over which it has only partial control. In addition, numerous problems soon arose that required the direct attention of Langley. So when "Nightingale" bases were set up in Turkey and Greece, countries that were the province of the Near East and Southern Europe divisions respectively the SPD was assigned responsibility for the entire setup.

For all its headaches, the "Nightingale" program became a model for the management of fanatical émigré groups—an especially apt model for the OPC, the CIA's clandestine-activities branch, in the days before the PPPM was taken over by the SPD. The OPC saw there were obvious advantages—in morale, security, and general motivation—in allowing the émigrés to work as groups rather than as individuals. For one thing, their disciplines and no-nonsense handling of the occasional traitors who turned up in their midst could not have been allowed in the OPC itself. By the time the SPD was a going concern, despite the fact that its interest was confined to espionage, it continued to handle "Nightingale" in the pattern that had been established. As it took on other émigré groups, the same rules applied.

The pattern has been improved by now so that the SPD's control is sufficiently tight to ensure high-quality operations but sufficiently loose so that it can overlook the excesses of this group or that when necessary. Naturally, it has by now penetrated all the groups and otherwise devised means of secretly monitoring their plottings. There is the occasional nasty scene as one or another of the groups discovers an SPD penetration and deals with it just as harshly as it would deal

with any other kind of penetration, but on the whole the relationship between the SPD and the various groups is har-
monious.

DENIED AREAS

The main value of émigré groups is their contribution to "denied area" operations. The OSO maintains stations in Moscow
and all Bloc capitals, but these are concerned entirely with
aspects of conventional espionage operations run against major
governmental targets in the capital cities. Those vast areas of
the U.S.S.R. and China to which even Soviet and Chinese citizens cannot freely travel must be covered by drops and border-
crossing operations which are very similar to those into Occupied Europe during World War II.

Emigré groups are not the only means of penetrating denied
areas, although some of these groups have by now so greased
the channels into their homelands that couriers move back
and forth with the greatest of ease, and with such confidence
as to make them careless. In late 1968, a "Nightingale" agent
was caught during a sojourn in the Georgian S.S.R. under
circumstances that demonstrated both the deterioration in
"Nightingale's" security and what a line crosser could get away
with in the way of carelessness and bravado. Fortunately, he
was so loaded down with smuggled articles, and so badly
briefed on his intelligence mission, that the Soviet authorities
decided he was a smuggler rather than an espionage agent,
and his contacts in the country were therefore not wrapped up.
But the SPD learned its lesson. From that time on, its denied-
areas operations depended on émigré groups only for operational data needed to guide operations that were entirely
under Divisional control.

Already, individual operators had shown what could be
accomplished in moving about the U.S.S.R. despite the tight
security controls that were supposed to bind the entire population. In 1956, Colonel Stephen Meade, whose CIA nickname

was "the Whistler," was parachuted into Azerbaijan in an effort to rescue a "hot" American scientist whose plane had crash-landed across the Soviet-Iranian border. Meade found the scientist and his fellow passengers, got them safely across the Iranian border, and then, "just for the hell of it," as he later told his superiors, decided to take a jaunt all the way around the Caspian Sea—from Astara up the coast past Baku to Astrakhan, then eastward through the Ukraine and down through Crimea to Sebastopol. At Sebastopol, with apparently no difficulty, he secured transportation across the Black Sea to an SPD "support" station on the Turkish coast. His superiors were furious, of course, but their indignation cooled when he presented a detailed account of his movements, complete with photographic illustrations taken openly with a tourist-sized camera. It was virtually a textbook for "tourism espionage," as Meade called it, and it opened up a category of denied-area operations which they had until then thought impossible. Before his retirement a few years later, Meade made three more such excursions into denied Soviet areas— one of which enabled him to photograph hidden rocket sites in Kazakhstan that were totally unsuspected at the time—and another deep into China.* What is remarkable is that although he speaks only a few of the languages needed in the places through which he traveled, he moved about openly, making friends wherever he went. Essentially, he broke every known rule for secret operations, except the rule that secret agents should avoid acting like secret agents.

As photographic and detection equipment on satellites has improved over the past few years, the need for operations into denied areas has been greatly cut back. The SPD's operations are now sharply pinpointed, and there is no attempt to make anything like a blanket coverage of the U.S.S.R. and China.

---

* "The Whistler" had earlier engineered the coup d'état that ousted the government of President Shukri Quwatli in Syria in 1948 and had carried out several other "political action" missions for the OSO's Near East Division—as reported in my book *The Game of Nations*. The character "Steve Wilmot" in the television series *The Game Players* is based on him.

CIA "requirements" will direct the SPD to pick up a sample of the water downstream from a secret plant, to confirm the presence of some hidden missile site that was inadequately photographed by a satellite, or to penetrate the camouflage around secret installations intended to mislead photographic interpreters. The SPD does have a small technical unit which, in cooperation with the National Security Agency, installs and maintains "sneakies" throughout the U.S.S.R. and Communist China—but increasingly, denied areas are surveyed more simply.

As I said earlier, the CIA has a branch, completely separated from its espionage branch, that interviews American citizens and others upon their return from trips to the Soviet Union, China, and other places of intelligence interest, but it only rarely interviews these travelers *before* they take their trips. One reason is that in most Communist countries, a person who has been briefed by an intelligence agency prior to his visit is automatically a spy—even though he sees no more than what any ordinary tourist would see. Consequently, anyone about to visit the U.S.S.R. or China who has the scientific knowledge and powers of observation to make him worth the risk of a briefing must be trained rather than merely briefed. Most visitors to Communist countries who are so briefed and trained are persons of other nationalities.

THE DEFECTION PROGRAM

Early in the history of the OSO, inducing Soviet and satellite diplomats to defect was a top-priority task of its field stations. One defector could bring in more valuable information than an agent, in those days, could produce in a year. Through the Fifties and into the Sixties, the OSO justified its existence by its successful defection operations rather than by its ordinary espionage operations. By the mid-Sixties, however, enthusiasm for defectors was beginning to wane.

One reason was the improved quality of ordinary agents. A defector would show up on the doorstep of the U.S. Embassy in Paris with stacks of secret papers and his embassys' codes, only to find that the CIA already had both the documents and the codes. In this instance his proffered gift would be a nuisance, since after the defection the Soviets would assume the CIA had the materials and would alter their behavior accordingly.

Toward the end of the Sixties, defectors' convictions that they should bring with them a code book almost destroyed the NSA's capability for deciphering "book" codes currently in use.

The trend was reversed in 1968, when the SPD was asked to devise a worldwide, tightly coordinated "defection inducement program," which would take the primary responsibility away from the various individual field stations. The first step was to get word to all would-be defectors (i.e., all Soviet and satellite government employees) that they would not *necessarily* be welcome should they present themselves at our embassies with their families in the middle of the night. The message, sent in ordinary "blind" memoranda, was so subtly worded that only those Soviet and satellite officials who were intelligent enough to be interesting as defectors would understand its full implications. Although the authenticity of the memoranda was beyond question, they were without headings, signatures, or identifying marks that would enable the Soviets to complain either to the U.S. Government or to the local authorities. Besides, the Soviets would hardly want to admit that their employees were all *that* vulnerable to defection inducements.

A would-be defector should not take the U.S. Embassy by surprise, but should simply pass the word, in any of a dozen ways, that he is ready to make the break. He must then make no further effort to contact the Americans, but wait for the Americans to contact him. When the contact is finally made, the cutout who makes it, probably not an American, may point out to him that in his present state he doesn't have enough to offer to make his defection worth the difficulties involved and that he should stay where he is until he has had time to prove himself. For a while he should furnish those documents which the cutout explicitly requests, and he should do so in a way that will minimize the likelihood of their being missed.

Naturally, there are exceptions. There are many Soviet and satellite diplomats, military officials, and scientists who would be accepted without a moment's hesitation—and they know it. But most would-be defectors are handled as ordinary "walk-in" agents, and they may become high-quality assets of considerably more value than they could ever be as ordinary defectors. A skillful case officer can calm the fears and anxieties of the would-be defector that led him to consider making the jump— or even coach him on how to circumvent the dangers that threaten him. He can build up an entirely new set of motivations—including assurances that in case of real danger the would-be defector and his family will be forewarned and whisked way to a comfortable haven. He can show him how, while continuing to furnish explicitly requested secret documents on a continuing basis, he can actually improve his standing within his own embassy, government office, or laboratory. More than one defector-turned-agent has built a successful career in the service he has betrayed by taking the sound advice of his CIA case officer.

An ordinary station officer should be able to handle most aspects of a defector case without outside help, although from the moment he sends his first cable to headquarters he is likely to be overwhelmed by advice from a wide variety of kibitzers. But there are some aspects that can best be handled, or can be handled *only*, by SPD officers who specialized in defectors. Remember, most defections are induced, and experience has shown that inducements are most effective when offered on a worldwide scale. Like the blind memoranda referred to earlier, such inducements are never sent in a way that seems directed at any one person or any one embassy. In addition, profitable use is made of connections between diplomats serving in different countries; diplomatic correspondence;* and even radio broadcasts and newspapers that reach countries beyond those in which they originate.

The inducements offered by the SPD's defection specialists are extremely subtle, but here are some examples illustrating how their program works. A Soviet diplomat who has defected to the CIA will write letters to officials and friends he left behind—not to those who are prospective defectors, but to others who are likely for one good reason or another to show the letters to prospective defectors. Normally, letters coming to a Soviet embassy from a defector, or from anyone outside the Soviet orbit, are snatched away by the security officer before the addressees have a chance to see them, but a letter may contain references that make it necessary for the security officer to show a letter to the prospective defector, if not to the addressee. The letter will drop hints that life is especially rosy on the Western side for Soviet defectors of certain categories. A news broadcast sent out over Radio Free Europe will drop hints that Soviet citizens of certain ethnic minorities might shortly be in for a bit of discrimination. The suggestion is passed out, in official communications and by ordinary rumor, that there have been security leaks which will cause investigation of those sections where the prospective defectors work. By the process of "Twenty Questions," vague rumors can be so loaded onto the Soviet and Bloc diplomatic services that they begin to center in on categories of desirable prospective defectors. Naturally, only a few of them may be expected to react to this process of "shaking the tree," but a few are enough. As long as these few have seen the blanket "blind" instructions telling them *how* to defect, they may come to the SPD's attention in such a way that proper use can be made of them.†

---

* While stealing another country's diplomatic pouch remains a difficult job, getting genuine-looking material *into* one is comparatively easy.
† All this may be news to the reader, but it is old stuff to the Soviet security services—so I am not giving *them* anything they don't already know.

The importance of the SPD specialist, in comparison with an ordinary competent area division officer, is that he will have a keen grasp of what pressures have been put on categories of potential Soviet defectors in general, and will probably know something of the internal conditions surrounding the defector, his family, and his work associates. In exploiting the defector, either by accepting him *as* a defector or by converting him into a "walk-in," the SPD specialist knows how to relate his case to numerous others, past and future. In addition, the SPD specialist is usually multilingual. These facts, plus the fact that the SPD officer deals also with émigré groups, denied-area operations, and other matters which make him eat, drink, sleep, talk, and think Soviet and Bloc affairs, puts him far ahead of the area division officers—who, after all, are concerned mainly with the countries to which they are assigned. Thus, in the OSO the Special Projects Division is virtually a Soviet Bloc Division, except that it does not control the station in Moscow, which is in the Eastern Europe Division.

"UNOFFICIAL COVER"

At first because there was no other place to put it and later because it turned out to make sense, the task of building "unofficial cover" was assigned to the OSO's Special Projects Division.

At times, during the first few years of the OSO's existence, the task proved so difficult that it was often set aside, with the OSO itself, as well as the State and Defense departments, becoming temporarily resigned to the necessity of depending almost entirely on official cover. Then there would be some great embarrassment such as a principal's getting arrested and "confessing" that he was being paid by "the CIA," naming some case officer under embassy cover as his contact—and the issue would resurface. Once again, there would be the ever-recurring pronouncement: "The espionage organization, if we must have such a thing, should be entirely outside the diplomatic establishment, run independently of our embassies and consulates, and so managed that our diplomatic representatives can honestly disclaim responsibility for them"—to quote an Assistant Secretary of State complaining to the then CIA's Director, Richard Helms, following a particularly acute embarrassment.

It all seems so simple to anyone who hasn't dug into the problem. At first glance, cover possibilities seem to abound—oil companies, airlines, news services, and a host of others. There are always enough apparent possibilities to justify an all-out search, so drive after drive is launched to "move the spies outdoors," as Undersecretary of State Nicholas Katzenbach said.

The outcome should be easy to imagine. The officials conducting the drive decide tentatively that the simplest yet most convincing kind of cover is a philanthropic organization; but just as they are about to take off for the Ford Foundation, the Rockefeller Foundation, or some other such organization, they remember the President's interdiction. Organizations such as these are out of bounds—not only the genuine ones, but ones the CIA might set up specifically for cover purposes. Ford, Rockefeller, and the others can spot a phony foundation even in remote Zambia and will complain to the White House, with irresistible persuasiveness, that phony foundations are likely to bring suspicion on *all* foundations.

As for international news services, journalist cover is bad even for individual residents and case officers, because real journalists are even cleverer than foundation representatives in spotting those of their colleagues whose real jobs and interests are other than what they claim. Reporters habitually read one another's stories, compare word counts, and watch movements —the competition in this field being what it is. Should the agency try to cover a whole espionage system by a news service, the entire community of foreign correspondents would deliberately blow it. And one could hardly blame the correspondents. They already have a hard enough time with the local security authorities.

So the officials turn to the most logical-appearing cover possibility of all, the international oil company. A major oil company has offices in or near most of the target areas; it is large enough to "hide" individual employees in such a way that their work and movements are not apparent to the outside world or even to other members of the company; it has its own communications, which are almost as secure as diplomatic communications; it has a legitimate interest in the politics, economics, and social conditions of the countries in which it operates; it pays high enough salaries to keep CIA officers at standards of living to which they have become accustomed. For cover, the major oil company is just about perfect.

But there is one thing wrong. No oil-company manager in his right mind would risk billions of dollars of investment, and jeopardize valuable concessions that he is holding on to only with difficulty, in order to aid some espionage operation, whose value he is bound to doubt. There is no use arguing "your patriotic duty" to the management of a major oil company. Oil company people not only don't like espionage; they don't like those who deal in it, and no amount of urging will change this. In fact, no amount of arguing will convince an oil company executive that a former member of the CIA is not *still* a member of the CIA—as those who quit the CIA to find jobs in the outside world learn to their sorrow.

Other international corporations—airlines, international banks, General Motors, General Electric, IBM—present other problems. These organizations expect a certain amount of work out of their employees—a whole day's work every day, in fact —and it is generally known that an employee who does less is soon fired. Since these companies, unlike the oil companies, do not maintain political departments or "government relations" departments, there is no way to "cover" a CIA station chief or case officer in any of them so that nonperformance of duties won't be spotted. It is obviously unrealistic to expect a CIA officer to do a full day's work to preserve his cover, especially when it is bound to be a particularly demanding sort of work, and then put in a good amount of time on his CIA duties.

Even should he be willing to try, he would quickly learn that anyone with his cover job in a foreign community will have a social life to lead. An IBM employee must act like an IBM employee off the job as well as on it: his friends must be those an IBM employee would normally have; his sports and social activities must also fit in; everything he does on the job and off it is for the good of IBM. This is just as true of the other big international companies. Working for any of them in a position that would be suitable cover would be a twenty-four-hour job. And being an intelligence officer already is a twenty-four hour job.

As for smaller companies with international interests, they sometimes are tempted by offers from CIA to give them representation abroad which they might not otherwise be able to afford. The XYZ Tool Company has no office in Cairo, and no immediate plans for opening one, so why not take advantage of the CIA's offer to send to Cairo, at CIA expense, an intelligent young man who speaks Arabic, who has a flair for making contacts and getting to know people, and who just might spend a few hours a week on company (i.e., "cover") business? What is there to lose?

Well, nothing, if the XYZ Tool Company is only window shopping with respect to international business. The CIA man using XYZ cover will soon learn, if he bothers to take his cover work seriously at all, that the XYZ company couldn't possibly compete with the ABC company, which is in the same line of business but with a *real* international setup, and that there is no point in trying. He digs in on his CIA work, and it soon becomes evident to one and all that he is not doing enough business for the XYZ company to justify his being kept there. "In a community like Cairo," a friend in the former U.S. Embassy in that city once said to me, "we live in each other's houses." Everybody knows what everybody else is doing. If you avoid the American community, that alone is enough to make you suspect. And if you mix in the way everybody else does, it soon becomes clear that you are not what you say you are.

Unless you really make business for XYZ. This sort of thing does happen every now and then. There are several small and middle-sized American corporations which have had tremendous success in Africa and Asia because, back in the late Forties and early Fifties, they agreed to furnish cover to CIA case officers. But look at it from the point of view of the CIA. In all of these cases the CIA officers worked hard at their cover jobs, as they were instructed to do, and made good at them. Before long they were more interested in their cover jobs than in the CIA, either because they were more challenging and interesting or because they offered higher pay, better working conditions, and better future prospects. I know quite a number of CIA officers who took cover assignments in Africa, Asia, and South America during the early Fifties and who are now senior executives of fast-growing companies—or owners of their own companies which grew out of the ones that originally provided them with cover. "The number of 'Dear John' letters I got back in the Sixties was beyond belief," the chief of the CIA's Near East Division told me.

Consequently, the SPD has had to organize its own companies—companies that carry on a sufficient volume of profitable business to justify their existence yet do not compete with other American companies, and still provide adequate cover reasons for OSO personnel to be where they have to be, travel as they have to travel, and make the contacts they have to make. Since the mid-Fifties, the SPD has built up four airlines entirely of its own; supported a number of foreign airlines in such a way that they can safely be used as cover by principals and cutouts; established a worldwide network of travel agencies; gone into and out of the shipping business and back in again; and established dozens of detective and credit agencies. The cover establishments are not highly profitable, but they at least *appear* to be profitable, and they operate in areas, functional and geographic, where genuine business enterprises wouldn't go because of risk.

THE FUTURE OF "SPECIAL PROJECTS"

From the foregoing, it may be seen that the "special projects" division, in any espionage organization that has such a thing, is likely to grow to enormous proportions and eventually cut the area divisions down to mere service organizations. In the CIA's espionage branch, the trend has progressed so far that the SPD's budget is now as large as those of all the area divisions put together,* as is its production of information. And as the new Director, William Colby, cuts down the size of the espionage branch even more than Richard Helms had already cut it down, the SPD may eventually *be* the Agency's espionage branch. Some of the management consultants who look at the espionage branch from time to time have argued all along that it should have been organized on a functional rather than a geographic basis. The Vietnam war threw the whole geographic arrangement out of balance, they now argue, and while CIA-supported units in Vietnam are being liquidated the Agency should seize the opportunity to clean house.

The growth and development of the OSO's Special Projects Division has been watched with great interest by the British and the Soviet services, both of which have imitated some aspects of it. There are certain pressures felt increasingly by all intelligence services, even those of the East: a public distaste for espionage—which is by now so great that when a spy case is uncovered the government that perpetrated its feels obliged to apologize to its own people as well as to the government that was its victim; a general loss of confidence in the espionage product on the part of intelligence analysts; the growing belief that, at long last, espionage operations must be *totally removed* from diplomatic establishments; the increased concentration of the espionage branches themselves on "the enemy," and the virtual disappearance of any enthusiasm for

---

* This is true since that segment of the OSO's Far East Division which handled Vietnam was taken out of the OSO entirely and turned over to the Defense Department, except for recruitment, training, and support.

operations against neutrals. The response to these pressures will not only bring a further diminishing of the espionages branches, but bigger and better SPDs.

Should organizers of the Soviets' KGB ask the advice of any reputable management expert, they would probably be told that they don't need an espionage branch at all. It so happens that the hordes of KGB officers under cover in Soviet embassies throughout the world get such high percentages of the information they seek through simple overt methods that they now do very little spying*—possibly the reason that they have recently botched up several operations. The Americans and the British will undoubtedly need their espionage operations for years to come, but they will be so intensively concentrated on the U.S.S.R. and China that operations in other areas will be few in number and small in importance.

---

* In a special report entitled *The Peacetime Strategy of the Soviet Union* (London, 1973), the Institute for the Study of Conflict points out that in NATO countries three out of four Soviet diplomats are "intelligence officers"—presumably meaning that three out of four are members of the KGB, because *four* out of four diplomats are quite literally "intelligence officers," as are four out of four American or British diplomats. But the study goes on to say that these "intelligence officers" acquire most of their information without having to spy—e.g., by attending American conventions, by corresponding with scientific and business groups, by reading trade journals, and by attending Congressional hearings. (It might be added that the Soviets sometimes employ "agents" not to spy for them, but to ask questions in places where they themselves might be less than welcome—e.g., the Lockheed plant, to which they sent a Swedish colonel. The information acquired by the Swede was not secret, but Lockheed officials might have been reluctant to give it to Russian visitors.) This very interesting study goes on to give examples of Soviet diplomats who have been expelled from the United States and other countries for attempts at true espionage—all of which were so clumsy as to suggest that they were committed not by KGB officers but by overly zealous "straight" diplomats.

"THE COMPANY"

But whatever the functions, like everything else that goes on in the world, they are ultimately run by "the company."

WHEN I toured the United States in 1970 to lecture to university audiences, I found that the most vocal students in all parts of the country saw the Central Intelligence Agency as representative of all that is wrong with "the rotten society we live in." Question periods were all taken up by heated discussions revolving around the Agency's supposed intrigues in all capitals of the world, including Washington and London; its backing of right-wing totalitarian regimes; and its "working for the large corporations rather than for the American people." At one Western university, I asked, "How many of you think the CIA could have been responsible for the assassination of President Kennedy?" and well over half the audience held up their hands.

Back at the hotel there was another story. I was deluged with calls from students wanting to know how to join up.* When I got back to London I had floods of letters asking the same question, or merely requesting my advice on the pros and cons of joining the Agency. Some of the requests, I noted, were from students who had dominated the question periods with their denunciations of the Agency. ("I suppose you could call

---

* To anyone reading this book who wants to join the CIA, may I suggest that he simply write to "Director, Central Intelligence Agency, Langley, Virginia," enclosing the dust jacket of this book.

it 'building cover,' " said one student when I challenged him on this.)

Although a high percentage of the students who sought me out to discuss the possibilities of a career in intelligence were straightforward types who thought almost entirely in terms of practical advantages, either for a lifetime career or as a stepping-stone to something else, even more were romantics—Walter Mittys, in fact. ("See that little man over there?" said Inspector Hargreaves. "You wouldn't think it to look at him, but he has all the secrets of the world in his head.") Whatever the motives, there are thousands of young Americans who would give their eyeteeth to be employed by the CIA or, simply, to "get into the intelligence business," as one student put it to me, and by "intelligence" he clearly meant the spookier side.

Compared with joining the CIA, getting a job with Soviet intelligence is easy. The applicant needs only the ability to hold down some job in a U.S. Government agency that houses secrets of interest to the Soviets, plus the necessary clean record to get a U.S. Government security clearance. The pay is good—and steady—and once the agent has established himself, he can depend on the Soviets to make all reasonable efforts to spring him from jail if he is caught. Although we have no way of knowing for certain, there are many indications that the American FBI and the British MI-5 catch less than 30 percent of the agents planted in our governments.

On the other hand, one might regard a two-out-of-three chance of surviving one's career as prohibitively risky, and in recent years there has been such a wave of defectors coming Westward, not only from the Soviet Government but from Bloc governments which cooperate with the Soviets in their espionage operations, that even the perfect espionage operation is likely to be uncovered.

For reasons that are beyond even our best Kremlinologists, the Soviets seem not to have sufficiently mastered "need to know" principles. An American or a British defector to the Soviets can give only a segment of his organization's secrets.

But a Russian defecting Westward can often give masses of information, much of which is outside what he needed to know to perform his job. By now the annual number of Soviet defectors is so great that even when the information they give us is fragmented, we are able to put together fairly accurate pictures of what penetrations of our governments the Soviets have managed.

Penalties for getting caught spying for the Soviets can be great. There are the lucky ones, like "Emily," who get off lightly because it is in our national interest to leave them alone. Then there are those who get relatively short prison sentences, and others who escape to the U.S.S.R. to live out their lives in utter misery in Moscow.* Finally, there are the Soviet spies who are quietly liquidated—and under circumstances that are so terrifying as to defy description.

Although neither the CIA nor the SIS has seen fit to turn over to me the statistics on American and British agents behind the Iron Curtain, there is reason to believe that Soviets, Czechs, Poles, etc., who spy for the Western services in many ways fare much better than their counterparts on "the other side." The case of one retired CIA agent I interviewed is probably typical.† For just under twenty years he had served the

---

* There are currently some two hundred American, British, Australian, and Canadian defectors living in an émigré colony in Moscow, and we have it on firsthand authority that they are both physically and psychologically miserable. Of the number, no more than six or seven were for any length of time agents of the Soviet intelligence service. They are treated comparatively well, but even the highest-ranking of them (e.g., Donald Maclean and Guy Burgess, who died a few years ago) have shown themselves to be suffering from acute depression. The others, some twenty-odd who were not agents but who took valuable information with them when they defected and the rest who are odds and ends whom the Soviets accepted for propaganda purposes, are treated with utmost contempt by the Soviets—who, after all, are a highly xenophobic people.
† I should make it clear that those ex-agents of the CIA and SIS whom I managed to interview were reached entirely on my own, and without the cooperation of either of those services. Also, the information that I managed to acquire which enabled me to corroborate or evaluate the information was likewise independently acquired. Only one assertion under this heading came to me from a CIA official: that "only a handful" of

CIA without incident, first in a Soviet embassy in a Middle Eastern capital where he was recruited and trained, and later in Moscow. He had subsequently fled the country, taking his wife and daughter with him, under arrangements made by the CIA which, it is relevant to note, were both expensive and operationally elaborate. He now lives in retirement in a large American city, plays oboe in a symphony orchestra, enjoys round-the-clock security protection from private detectives hired by CIA through a "front," and receives a pension which is high even by American standards. "If I had it to do all over again," he told me in his Berlitz English, "the retirement advantage as I now know it would have been enough to make me decide the same."

But there were career disadvantages, he said. The main one was having to live in Moscow, instead of one or another of the foreign diplomatic posts into which he could have finagled an assignment. Also, it was not pleasant to live in a constant state of fear. Although he never felt he was in danger of capture (in one instance, he participated in an investigation of a fellow employee whom the KGB suspected of being a CIA agent), the penalties for those who were caught were so terrible that he was constantly worried. He said he had good reason to believe that not one of those whom the Soviets sent to Siberia for spying was actually guilty, but that this belief did nothing to relieve the strain on his ulcers.

BECOME AN INTELLIGENCE OFFICER!

The most sensible way for an American or British national to get into the espionage business, of course, is to become an officer of the CIA or SIS assigned to the espionage branch. It is, however, not easy. Although every one of the thousands of

---

the hundreds of Soviet citizens who have been arrested for spying for the CIA or the SIS were in fact agents for one or the other of these services. Information to corroborate this assertion was hard for an independent writer to come by, but I found enough to convince me that it is the truth.

letters of application that reach the CIA headquarters at Lang-ley, Virginia, is given serious consideration, the attitude of Agency recruiters is generally one of "Don't call us; we'll call you." The mere fact of offering one's services to the CIA is regarded as ground for suspicion. And for good reason. An analysis of these letters shows clearly that many of them were prompted by motives other than patriotic ones, a chance to "have a look at the inside so that I can write a book about it later" being a particularly prominent one.

The CIA keeps what must certainly be the largest card file in existence of possible recruits for its organization—university students, members of certain professions, and people having certain special qualifications. A person may find himself propo-sitioned by a CIA recruiter because some area division chief has asked for "a man, age early twenties, who has a back-ground in electronics, who speaks Hungarian although is not of Hungarian ancestry, and who can meet the Agency's criteria for career officers." He is more likely to be approached, how-ever, if he is simply a senior in "one of the better American universities" (i.e., one that has a minimum of student demon-strations) with a B average, an absence of left-wing affiliations, and a record of sound emotional health. The CIA employs pro-fessors and graduate students at "the better American universi-ties" to canvass members of senior classes, either in the name of the CIA itself or through some "front," commercial or insti-tutional.

And then, as is the case with the SIS, the CIA has its "old boy net." Getting a recommendation from someone who is al-ready in the CIA and who has a particularly good record is still the best way to get into the organization—especially the espio-nage branch. In early 1973, James Schlesinger spent his few months as Director of Central Intelligence trying to put an end to the "old boy net," but the nature of the business is such that the net was able to get rid of him before he could get rid of the net. When this "old boy net" goes, a new one is sure to take its place—and to be pretty much like the old one. The fact that the organization is made up largely of friends, and friends of friends, is what gives it what Allen Dulles used to call its "family character."

Once you get in, you will find yourself in a whole new world. The CIA's recruiters do their best to screen out the romantics and to select only young men and women whose motivations are entirely practical; but I would say that 99 percent of those who join the Agency are at least partly attracted by the glamour. Even those few who are entirely blasé when they first get into the Agency are certain to be dazzled by the indoctrination. Of every group of trainees, I am told, about one out of a class of thirty-five decides that the intelligence business is not for him; about two are eliminated because the instructors and evaluators decide they are not for the intelligence business; and another three or four are regarded as "doubtful" and are kept on probation. For those who survive for as long as a year, the attrition is much less than that of any major private corporation, or of any other Government service except that of the State Department's career diplomats.

Those who spend their lives in the Agency, especially in the espionage branch, feel they belong to a private and special world. I remember well my own feelings when, as an Army sergeant undergoing the discomforts of the Louisiana maneuvers of 1941, I was awakened in my pup tent and called to the Division Commander's office in the middle of the night to be given secret orders assigning me to "the Corps of Intelligence Police"; $250 with which to buy civilian clothes; and a first-class train ticket to Washington, D.C. I hadn't the faintest idea what my new life would be like, except that it would be vastly different from anything in my past.

My mood was captured exactly by another sergeant who in civilian life had been a credit investigator. In certain circles, he told me, he enjoyed a reputation for being "the most powerful witch in Louisiana." It appears that at the age of eighteen he had had a terrible fear of the dark. Every night he would lie awake in his parents' house deep in some Louisiana swamp, surrounded by mists, frightened out of his wits at the mysterious sounds coming from the darkness. One day, in a burst of inspiration, he thought: "Why don't I become a part of the darkness? Instead of lying here shivering with fright with blankets pulled up over my head, why can't I *be* a force of the night?" His fear suddenly gone, he climbed out of bed, dressed, went out into the swamp, climbed a tree, and sat there all night hooting like an owl. The next morning at break-fast his older brother told him how he had had nightmares for half the night, and had spent the rest of it with blankets pulled up over *his* head, scared by "one goddam owl that sounded almost human." He had decided it was a kind of werewolf.

My new friend told me that he had played hooky the next day to do some research about witchcraft at the library. Later, he joined a "coven," and at the time he rode with me toward Washington, he was the Grand Master of the witches' associa-tion of Louisiana, Tennessee, and Alabama.

This is sort of a crazy story, but no crazier than my own feelings when I first entered intelligence. Friends of mine in the CIA to whom I have told this story, including several younger members, tell me that they felt the same way. The witch, incidentally, went from the Corps of Intelligence Police to the OSS about the same time I did, and stayed in the re-mains of the OSS until the formation of the CIA. He could not pass the CIA's security screening, however, so he left Govern-ment service to run for Congress. He was elected, and he is now one of the Agency's most troublesome critics on Capitol Hill.

The Agency's training was impressive even in its early days when, as a contract consultant, I was helping to develop courses. But in recent years I would say that there is nothing in the world to compare with the effectiveness of its indoctri-nation. When a new employee finishes his first two general courses, he may have learned only a few procedures that he can use in his job, but he will have a whole new set of criteria by which to judge what is and what is not normally permis-sible in dealing with friends and enemies of the United States.

The first training undergone by young CIA employees who are "officer material" takes place in the modern, streamlined buildings at Langley, Virginia. Much of it is concerned with routine matters such as forms for reports, how to grade information, how to use registry, etc., but there are also many exciting exhibitions. Experts from "the Kingfish's" unit put on demonstrations of how to pick locks, plant microphones, steam open letters, forge documents. Then there is a positively frightening series of lectures, complete with slides, charts, and photocopies of secret official Soviet documents and Communist Party correspondence, which is delivered with such authority that it would convince anyone not only that the Cold War still goes on, but that it holds greater and greater dangers which can be thwarted only by an alert and efficient intelligence system. Finally, there is a display of the "national security machinery"—or "the *real* Washington," as one instructor calls it— which shows how, despite all the bumbling that is inevitable in any large organization, the U.S. Government does manage to protect the nation's interests and how, at the same time, it has a system of "fuses" which ensure that no element of the "machinery" can acquire an excess of power. This part of the course is most impressive. Even the most anti-Government cynic comes out of it with the conviction that the nation faces dangers to national security which are more awful than even the gloomiest columnist imagines, and that the machinery of which the CIA is a part has means of combating them which are so sophisticated and powerful as to be beyond the comprehension of all but those who are part of them.

The second part of the indoctrination takes place at a country estate, a few hours' drive south of Washington, known as "the farm." * Here the new CIA employee gets a taste of what it is like "out in the cold"—i.e., in the danger areas where persons in clandestine services supposedly operate: on the border between East and West Germany, on the Soviet–Iranian border, in "reception" areas in Communist China. In one "night exercise" the trainees black their faces and try to cross a bor-

* For an amusing account of training at "the farm," see Patrick McGarvey's book *CIA: The Myth and the Madness*.

der protected by charged barbed wire, dogs, electric eyes, traps, floodlights, and border patrols. When they are caught, as they inevitably are, they are put through an interrogation by "East German security officials" played with enormous realism by the Training Division's actors. In another "field exercise," the trainees go into a nearby town to "case" restaurants and other places to determine their suitability as meeting places for agents; in another, they keep under surveillance an espionage agent on his way to meet his principal; in another they set up a "transfer"—i.e., the passing of secret documents from an agent to a principal so as not to be observed by the surveillance team on their tails. Some of the trainees do parachute jumps, one in the daytime and one at night, after which they have to hide their parachutes in the approved manner. Only a few of the trainees will ever have to do any of these things in real life, of course, and those few take additional training, but they are given a feel for the problems they may later assign others as they sit comfortably at headquarters planning operations.

The most impressive part of this initial CIA indoctrination is the attitude toward loyalty, security, precision, attention to detail, and healthy suspicion that it manages to implant in the minds of the trainees. "Because of my indoctrination," writes Patrick McGarvey in his *CIA: The Myth and the Madness,* "I still get a visceral twinge—and have qualms of conscience about writing this book." Although one cannot detect any signs of reticence in Pat McGarvey's book, I know what he means. The fact is that this aspect of the indoctrination has been designed by some of the nation's best psychologists, employing the most modern techniques of "motivational research." Certainly it achieves its purpose. The psychologists resent the insinuation that they are engaged in "brainwashing," arguing that the effect of what they have contributed to the training is exactly the opposite of brainwashing as practiced by the Chinese. Instead of conditioning a person so that he can accept only "approved" ideas, it sharpens his instincts and critical faculties so that he can recognize specious political reasoning when he encounters it. Also, the psychologists believe their course imparts a strong sense of mission, which is lacking in other branches of government. With certain reservations, I think they are right. Lord knows, there are plenty of jokes about CIA training, and there is plenty of accidental comedy even in the grimmest courses. But it is certainly true that Agency employees work longer hours, put up with more inconvenience, and devote more off-hours thinking to their profession than any other employees in Government. The absorption of CIA employees in their work, in fact, is so great as to be a security problem. It is the reason why many of them relax only with other CIA employees. In mixed groups they tend either to be tongue-tied, or to go off into a corner with a colleague and spend the evening talking shop.

These two indoctrination courses, the one in the Langley headquarters and the one at "the farm," are just the beginning of CIA training. The CIA's Training Division is a huge enterprise. The "TD's" Green Book lists over four hundred courses which can be assembled in a hundred different patterns and adapted for a wide variety of trainees—from high-ranking civil servants outside the Agency who need to be familiarized with its activities, to residents, principals, agents, and others who require individual instruction. A career officer of the CIA spends a great deal of his service in courses—"retreading" every year or so to be brought up to date on recently developed methods, provided with language training, and given in politics, revolution, counterrevolution, and counterinsurgency, among others. An officer who has reached the upper-middle level of the service may get a year at some peaceful university just to "regroup intellectually," as a former chief of the TD used to say.

A word about the so-called spy schools: there aren't any. In the first place, the CIA's espionage specialists believe the secret of success is simplicity. What the agent has to do should be simple and natural, and should require little training. In the second place, a spy school, complete with classrooms, dormitories, and all the rest, would expose agents. The day when agents work together in "networks" is past, even for the Soviets. When Harry Houghton, the British Naval clerk who spied for the KGB, gave the testimony that sent him up for a fifteen-year jail sentence, SIS officers attending the trial were appalled to hear him say, "One of the most attractive features of my espionage work was the warm feeling of working together as a team it gave me." There is no "team spirit" among American and British spies—and probably no longer any among Soviet spies either, now that they see what a mess it has made of their operations of the Fifties.

Residents, principals, and sometimes utility agents may get quite extensive training, but it is always individual, and it is usually combined with lengthy security debriefings, including sessions with the lie detector.

In most occupations, the managers tend to take on many of the characteristics of the employees down the line, and vice versa. This is not true in the espionage business. While agents are lone operators, to whom "the organization" is largely a mystery, the managers (the case officers, the station chiefs, and the head of desks and divisions at headquarters) are a very clannish lot. They are so clannish, in fact, that even other intelligence officials find it hard to break into their circle. Like the priests at Delphi, they perpetuate mystiques which only they can interpret. And they protect one another. I remember back in my old consultancy days when the OSO's first chief, Colonel Artemus Galloway, used to fire me from time to time for some act of "subvision," a term invented by some of us for "the art of getting things done despite interference from above." I forgot most of the rules, but one of them was "Never carry out an order the first time you receive it. It may turn out to be merely the result of some flap at the morning staff meeting which will be forgotten long before you finish carrying it out." Each time I ran into trouble, a wonderful man named Bill Tharpe would save me by the simple process of changing my pseudonym. After each change, the name of "Joseph Q. Thornquist," or whatever my current pseudonym was, would disappear from the cable traffic, to be replaced by "Herbert J. Appleby," my new pseudonym. And Colonel Galloway would

265

be happy until "Appleby" committed some breech of conduct worthy of "Thornquist."

There is another remarkable difference between the attitudes of agents and staff personnel. An agent is, by definition, a traitor to his own country and inclined to lie, cheat, and steal. A staff officer, however, is likely to be excessively patriotic and lean over backward to disassociate himself from the lying, cheating, and stealing despite the fact that it is the very business of his organization. I have worked with many different kinds of organizations, and the espionage branches of the American and British intelligence services are the only organizations I know in which padding of expense accounts is unthinkable. At present, some of my best creative writing goes into the composition of my expense accounts, but when I was a consultant to the CIA I sometimes claimed *less* reimbursement than I was entitled to, simply because of moral pressures. The nation's specialists in "dirty tricks" happen to be the most puritanical people imaginable: those who are not somehow don't make out at the Agency and wind up involved in Watergate scandals, working for detective agencies specializing in divorce cases, and in other such pursuits.

The first job of a new recruit to the CIA's espionage branch is likely to be as assistant to a "desk officer"—at the Iran Desk, the Low Countries desk, or any one of thirty to forty others. His duties will mostly involve servicing requests from "the field"—for a new automobile, for special equipment of various kinds, or for an adjustment in some accounting mistake. He also will from time to time be required to pull together all extant information on this or that "operation" and study it for flaws in security or effectiveness. Such duties will bring him into contact with personnel of other desks and with "the staffs"—those advisory groups which sit close to the DDP (the Deputy Director, Plans) and which, on the DDP's behalf, harass the area divisions. As the result of such duties, he "gets to know the place," as the Chief of Personnel is fond of saying. Above all, he will spend a considerable amount of time preparing for the overseas post to which, it is presumed, he will eventually be

266

assigned. The first step upward of the new officer is not from assistant desk officer to desk officer, but from assistant desk officer to assistant case officer in some field station. For at least a year, but usually longer, an assistant desk officer is fairly sure of what his field assignment will be, and he and his wife spend a great deal of time reading travel folders, studying the local language, making friends at the Washington embassy of the country, and reading State Department literature on protocol and diplomatic behavior.

It is in the field that the up-and-coming espionage specialist first sticks his neck out. He will be entirely at the mercy of his chief of station, and, as is well known, a good chief of station is a master at the art of taking personal credit for everything that goes right and blaming his subordinates for everything that goes wrong, while giving the appearance of doing just the opposite. In any case, the relations between the chief of station and the new officer, will be both close and stormy, though the station as a whole will stand as one in its frictions with the rest of the embassy. The resulting suspicions, emotional upsets, and back stabbing forge the Agency's OSO into the tightly knit cabal that it unquestionably is.

I have already spoken of the relationship between CIA station personnel and "straight" embassy employees. With several notable exceptions, the station chief makes it a point to have near-perfect relations with the ambassador. It is OSO policy to arrange assignments in such a way that the station chief at each post will have been in the country longer than the ambassador—for example, by keeping him there for a double term (e.g., four years at a two-year post, and six years at a three-year post) and by changing station chiefs only at times preceding the change of ambassadors. When a new ambassador arrives at his post, he will in almost all cases find the station chief an invaluable ally, a source of all sorts of assistance he couldn't get from his regular staff. Unless the deputy chief of mission has been smart enough to cultivate the station chief, the station chief will make a point of showing the ambassador highly secret information which, by enforceable regulation, the ambassador cannot discuss with other members of the embassy, even the DCM (Deputy Chief of Mission). "Every day I give my ambassador his little secret," a successful station chief once told me, "even if I have to make it up." Since most DCM's *are* smart enough not to go into competition with the CIA station chief, the "country team" composed of representatives of all the U.S. Government departments in the embassy is normally dominated by the DCM and the CIA station chief.

As for the rest of the embassy, relations vary from post to post. Normally they are bad. To start with, it is common practice for the CIA station chief to tighten up his cover by "tying the can" onto some other embassy officer whom he doesn't like, who is for one reason or another conspicuous in the eyes of the local populace, and who could be passed off as "the CIA man in the embassy." I know of at least two cases in which the careers of "straight" diplomats were set back because, in moments of crisis, the local government turned hostile and decided to expel the "CIA man" for "plots against the state." Once a can is tied on, it stays on. When the various Arab countries broke relations with the United States at various times over past years, it was always those diplomats with "cans on their tails," never true CIA men, who were declared personae non gratae.

"Straight" embassy officers strike back, of course—sometimes by queering the cover of station personnel, and sometimes by simple social snubbing. The friction between station personnel and the "straight" diplomats normally rises from one condition of "cover" policy: a CIA man of rank exactly equal to that of a regular diplomat is always placed in a cover job which is at least one notch lower than that rank. Thus, the diplomats and their wives—especially their wives—absorb the fiction that station personnel get better pay and allowances than they do. It is true that an Agency employee gets better retirement benefits —as he should, since "cover" considerations prevent his lasting for as long in the service as officers in other services and because his work, for all the precautions, involves certain personal dangers. But an Agency employee and a State employee of equal *real* rank, as opposed to cover rank, get exactly the same pay and allowances.

British diplomats are under strict instructions not to tell their wives of the identity of SIS station personnel in their country, and those who break the instructions impress on their wives that if *they* break them the punishment will be immediate and stern. American diplomats, however, have only the weakest sort of instructions regarding cover or station personnel, and even if they abide by them their wives are likely to break them. After all, it takes only one indiscretion to expose a CIA officer for all time.

It is in the social life of *le corps diplomatique,* however, that straight diplomats and their wives work hardest at making life miserable for their CIA colleagues. When the OSO requests an embassy "slot" in which to place an OSO officer, it will ordinarily request one commensurate with the actual rank of that officer—for example, a "GS 13" at CIA should be a "first secretary" or a fairly senior attaché in an embassy. State, however, after complaining loudly that *no* slot is available, will finally with great reluctance agree that the CIA officer may have a "second secretary" slot, and only on condition that he not have a career designation. So the CIA officer goes to his overseas assignment looking and acting like someone of rank higher than second secretary, driving a larger car and living in a more expensive house than a second secretary could afford, and throwing his weight around as though he were the DCM. Even though all this is inside the embassy compound, the impression he makes somehow leaks through the garden walls, and the community at large soon gets the impression that he is more than he seems. Despite the fact that at official gatherings he is trampled in the rush by his straight colleagues who want to show to one and all that they are ahead of him in protocol, the local officials, as well as members of other embassies, begin overwhelming him with invitations. While his straight colleagues and their wives turn green with envy, he is the darling of the British, French, Italian, and South American diplomats, of the local socialites, of senior local officials, and of the press

—to whom he is relaxed, natural, and informative, unlike his cautious straight colleagues. If all this comes about in months, think what his situation is likely to be after he has been at a post for six years. Regular diplomats can hardly be blamed for spending high percentages of their waking hours trying to cut him down to size.

While a senior OSO officer, one at the station-chief level, may stay at a post for as long as six years, the junior officer rarely stays more than one tour—two years at some posts, three at others. Then he returns to the States for two months' leave, a round of refresher courses, and his second desk assignment—possibly this time as desk officer for some small country, or as assistant to the desk officer of a larger one. With firsthand knowledge of the field and its problems, his value to the Agency has increased tremendously, and he is now treated with something like respect. Provided he has sufficient private means to afford it, his social life in Washington is suddenly rosy. Washington is full of diplomats and ex-diplomats he met in the field. He soon develops a reputation as an "old hand" of his assigned country and soon receives invitations from other embassies. Even those State Department types who were his blood enemies in the field, and who have also been transferred back to Washington, drop their grievances now that their respective situations are regularized. The young officer is now on his way to becoming an "upward mobile."

Still, the real ambition of the CIA officer in training is to get bigger and better assignments between headquarters and the field, in as wide a variety of places as possible. Here is the "ideal career" that one young OSO officer described in response to a form questionnaire:

> —Two years on a headquarters desk—preferences Iran, Argentina, and Austria—in that order;
> —Two years in a field station in Teheran, Buenos Aires, or Vienna;
> —One year on a desk in the best position obtainable (Iran, Argentina, or Austria);

—Two years in a general-area division job, or on a "staff";

—Two (or three) years as chief of station in some small to middle-sized post;

—One year in specialized area training, preferably Russian;

—Five years in Denied Areas Division, advancing upward in the hierarchy promotion by promotion;

—Four years as deputy chief of station in Vienna, or any other station that has both local and "denied area" interests (e.g., Berlin, Ankara, or Teheran) or chief of station in any South American country;

—Indeterminate period in any senior headquarters position offering as wide a scope, by area, as possible;

—Six years as chief of station in London, Paris, Bonn, Tokyo, or any other "Class A" station;

—Division chief, any area, in the OSO, or transfer out of the OSO to CIA management staff.

These assignments, added up, would occupy a thirty-to-thirty-five year career—e.g. from age twenty-five, which seems to be the average age for officer recruitment, to fifty-five, which is the average age of retirement. It is typical of what an intelligent, competent and ambitious young officer with Organization Man inclinations might expect.

But it is not the only way to build a career in the CIA's clandestine services. Cord Meyer, whom I may call by name because he has been exposed by various other writers including himself, made a career out of a single specialty, international organizations. Another officer I know of made himself the world's greatest authority on Deception and was easily as successful as the upward mobile who became a division chief. Then there are the old-timers like Jojo and the Kingfish who grew with the organization and made themselves indispensable by mastering their respective specialties—while seeing to it that no one else learned anything about them. There is only one kind of career that is *not* practically possible for an OSO officer: that of remaining an area specialist, in the manner of that

SIS officer I mentioned in an earlier chapter who, upon retirement, was knighted for being the SIS's last word on Afghanistan. CIA officers are not allowed to stand still. The Agency wants "generalists," not specialists.

But what happens to an organization whose members are all "upward mobiles" and which has a low attrition rate? To make sense organizationally, any group of people working together must have a complex of relationships that can be graphed as a pyramid. An organization of people who all move upward with none dropping by the wayside is graphed as a rectangle set on end, and is an administrative monstrosity. There must be means for letting out the members who bump their heads on the setbacks of the pyramid, yet not cause unwholesome feelings of insecurity in the ones who stay in. The answer to the problem of the CIA as a whole is the academic world: an Agency researcher, psychologist, or scientist can always get a good job teaching in a university, with a yearly "alumnus" bonus from the CIA for spotting potential recruits.

An OSO officer who is likely to have been tainted by his association with clandestine activities has a harder time. The answer in this case is "unofficial cover"—which is needed for genuine cover purposes and can also provide means for employing high-quality Agency personnel who have outgrown the system. When the OSO began setting up business organizations in the early Fifties in response to the State Department's appeal to "get the spies out of the embassies," a number of OSO officers who would otherwise have left decided to stay on.

The worldwide network of companies that the SPD has built up not only gives the OSO all the unofficial cover it needs; it also provides "slots" for aging OSO officers who have outgrown official cover. A case officer begins his career at just under $10,000 per year, and if he is at all successful he will reach a salary of between $20,000 and $25,000 by the time he reaches fifty. If he serves abroad, he is likely to be blocked in his *cover* position at about $16,000, since, with one or two exceptions (London, Paris, Rome), there are no slots above that level available for official purposes. He gets his $20,000 or $25,000, but he gets it secretly, so that he enjoys none of the prestige which goes with such a salary. The wife and children of an OSO officer serving in a series of foreign posts see him apparently blocked at the upper-middle level of the diplomatic service, while his "straight" colleagues move up and up eventually to become ambassadors; they conclude that he is a failure. Oddly, it is this consideration which, more than any other, makes an upper-middle-level OSO officer start thinking in terms of the SPD's unofficial-cover arrangements.

Not all OSO officers are qualified, but those who can successfully hold down cover jobs in commerce comprise as impressive an array of operational talent as is to be found in any business or government organization in the world. The SPD's unofficial-cover arrangement, working with the worldwide network of stations under official cover, provides the U.S. Government with a tremendously powerful international espionage facility.

To appreciate the CIA's espionage potential, one might consider a fairly typical setup in a major city that contains targets of CIA interest—Cairo. There was no U.S. Embassy in Cairo between the 1967 Arab–Israel War, and the American–Egyptian rapproachement of 1973, and the "American interests section" of the Spanish Embassy was so closely watched by the Egyptian police that the OSO had to operate totally through unofficial means. Yet the OSO's coverage of the whole town was so complete during this period that a "subject" could be checked with a minimum of moving surveillance. Through a network of observers—hotel doormen, taxicab drivers, newsstand operators, barmen, waiters, uniformed policemen, and individual members of the Egyptians' own security police—the OSO resident could maintain such complete coverage of the "subject" that it was almost impossible for him to conceal his movements. Had the subject employed any one of the known tricks for shaking surveillance—suddenly reversing his tracks;

getting on a bus, then jumping off again just as it is about to start; etc.—he would have alerted some component of the "city eye," as the stationary surveillance system is called, which might otherwise have failed to notice him. A year or two ago, when an American VIP visiting Cairo was missing for a few hours when he was being urgently paged all over town to receive an important international telephone call, the OSO's apparatus found him before the friendly Egyptian secret police could. In at least two instances, prominent Americans have been whisked out of brothels by OSO agents intent on saving them from blackmail.

Most of those who constitute the "city eye" are unaware that they are working for American intelligence; they have no idea whom they are working for, or they think they are working for their own secret police. Maybe they *are*, but then, through some cutout arrangement, it is for all practical purposes an OSO facility. When President Nasser, in the last year of his life, ordered an investigation into the CIA's surveillance facilities in Cairo, the major part of the investigation fell to a group of officers who, without Nasser's even suspecting it, made up a component of these facilities.

I should emphasize, though, that in most countries of the world, including Egypt, the OSO's local capabilities depend to *some* degree on the open cooperation of the local authorities. Even those countries which profess to hate the United States have honest and patriotic officials in their governments who see advantages to cooperating with the CIA. The OSO long ago learned how to make the most of this fact. By a system of "quarantine," as it is called, segments of local security services that fit into OSO "city eye" capabilities are so controlled that double-dealing with the Soviets or with any other power can be instantly spotted.

There are many countries of the world in which there is no OSO coverage; but in all cities that are crossroads of international movement—Cairo, Beirut, Istanbul, New Delhi, Tokyo, Manila, and a dozen others—the OSO can accomplish any of the following:

274

—Get passport and/or identity-card information on any person entering or leaving the country;

—Determine whether or not any particular person has spent the night in any local hotel;

—Maintain watches on all border posts—land, sea, or air—so as to spot the arrival or departure of any "subject";

—Get photocopies of any airplane manifest;

—Achieve surreptitious search of any hotel room, or of almost any office or private residence, or open search of any person, place, or possession under some plausible pretext;

—Smuggle *anything* into or out of the country—money, documents, equipment, a person, even a Rolls-Royce automobile;

—Carry out burglary, theft, or any other kind of petty crime;

—Plant evidence on anyone, for the purpose of "framing" him into being arrested, or even prosecuted.

In Khartoum, which is hardly a world crossroads, the OSO chief of station in 1961 stole funds being sent to the leftist leader Antoine Gizenga in the Congo, arranged for guns being sent to him to be "accidentally" smashed as they were being transferred at the port, and otherwise demolished the Soviets' attempts to help Gizenga take over the government. In Czechoslovakia, OSO agents arranged for errors to be made in shipments of small arms to Syria, so that ammunition and spare parts wouldn't fit the weapons. In numerous cases, OSO agents have planted contraband in KGB officials' suitcases so that they were arrested for smuggling, and Soviet relations with this or that country have frequently been strained by "frames" put on visiting Soviet officials. There have been many instances in which the OSO's "city eye" has operated with such effectiveness that attempts by the Soviets to retaliate have been spotted and turned against them. The purpose of the "city eye" is the acquisition of information, not "action," though it occasionally has to perform "action" operations of the kind just mentioned because no one else has the capability.

Periodically, the very effectiveness of the surveillance system has drawn criticism. While Richard Helms was DDP before becoming Director of Central Intelligence, the Agency made the mistake of using OSO information to warn errant Congressmen and prominent journalists that their behavior in certain instances might make them liable to blackmail. One Congressman visiting Beirut was enticed to the apartment of a notorious female blackmailer, and was whisked out of it by a U.S. Embassy official, acting on an OSO tip-off, just as local "private detectives" were about to sweep into the room to photograph him in Kama Sutra poses. An American columnist with an international reputation was warned away from a homosexual who wanted to seduce him for political purposes. In both cases the embassy was thanked, but the gentlemen charged back to Washington screaming to find out what other information the CIA had about them.

Of late, the OSO has been so aware of the fear that its capabilities can generate that it rarely uses them any more in missions of mercy. In the recent wave of political kidnappings, the OSO has refused to pass along information that might have led to the kidnappers and their hideouts.

In truth, there are many safeguards to keep the CIA from abusing its power. Its charter confines it to the collection of information "related to national security"; it has no mandate, as some of its seniors assume, "to safeguard American interests." It cannot act *against* American interests, and the position of its espionage branch, the OSO, is so sensitive that it must interpret "American interests" broadly—to include the Chase Manhattan Bank, ITT, the major oil companies, and the international airlines as well as private individuals traveling abroad, philanthropic institutions, missionary societies, and schools.

At least one Government agency, the U.S. Information Agency, interprets "American interests" even more broadly. Once when I was visiting a Caltex refinery in the Middle East, I wandered by mistake into the employees' auditorium— to see a film in progress on "How to Organize a Strike." On inquiring about the source of the film, I learned that it had come from the American Embassy in Beirut. When I mentioned the matter to the Ambassador, he replied that "labor unions are just as American as the corner drugstore, apple pie, baseball . . . and your oil company," and that our cultural contribution to Lebanon would not be complete were we to omit instruction in so American a subject as the labor-union strike.

In the process of forming SPD commercial enterprises, OSO representatives make the rounds of business, philanthropic, religious, and cultural organizations typical of those which might be affected, to ensure that the effect will not be adverse. For the purpose, the OSO has arranged for "need to know" security clearances to be given to key officials in a representative number of such organizations. These gentlemen make up a sort of informal body of "honorary members" whose advice enables the OSO to keep itself from crossing wires with "straight" concerns.

Do these "honorary members" sometimes seek to take advantage of their connection with the OSO to further their own ends? Indeed they do. And the OSO's attitude is that as long as their ends are consistent with the aims and interests of our country as a whole, they are entitled to its help. Major American corporations and philanthropic, religious, and cultural organizations almost all refuse to help the OSO in the one respect in which it most needs help—i.e., by giving cover to OSO staff personnel. But there are dozens of other ways in which they can give boosts to OSO operations—and at their own expense. Thus, the OSO potential consists of its assets under official cover, its assets under the SPD's unofficial cover —*and* the assistance of its "honorary members," known as "Marines," who are in senior positions in some of the nation's largest industrial organizations, banks, airlines, religious organizations, publications, cultural societies, and many more such entities. Quite apart from the espionage information which this combination makes possible, the OSO winds up with a pure *power* potential—or "lobby" potential, as applied to individual countries—which is many times what is imagined by left-wing writers who fear and hate the CIA. It is so well monitored, by individuals whose integrity and patriotism are above question, that the danger of its being misused should be minimal. In fact, thanks to a system of "fuses" and "trip alarms" built into it, even the President of the United States could not mobilize it for a purely selfish purpose.

In this chapter I have written almost entirely about the CIA, with only bare mention of the SIS, the KGB, or any other intelligence agency; but I conclude by saying that the clandestine arms of the British, Soviet, and even Chinese intelligence agencies maintain relationships with the outside world that are comparable to those of the CIA. The British SIS quite frankly has the job of "safeguarding British interests," and were it to be given the job of assisting in the overthrow of a South American government that was confiscating the assets of a British company, it would undertake the job without feeling that, in the event of exposure, it had anything for which to apologize. Moreover, the SIS is so well integrated into the community of British interests that the question of its having undue power does not arise.

In the Soviet system, the KGB is so prominent that it is quite literally the *principal* arm of the U.S.S.R.'s peacetime strategy—with almost three-fourths of Soviet officials serving abroad being KGB members. While only a few are engaged in espionage, it is obvious that with the KGB playing such a significant role, specialists in espionage are the core of Soviet peacetime offensives.

Inside the CIA, the employees use the term "the company" variously to mean the CIA itself, the OSO part of the CIA, or the OSO plus its "Marines." Sometimes, when Anglo-American cooperation is at its thickest, they use "the company" to mean the combined assets of the British and American services and their "Marines." And to those deep inside the intelligence establishments, both East and West, it often seems that the term "the company" should apply to all of them considered together. Considering that the interplay between them is what determines the future of the world, they may have something.

SOME CONCLUSIONS

Finally, one must wonder, is it all worth the trouble?

No OTHER event has ever shaken the American intelligence community so much as the Watergate affair, with all of its sideshows. "At least," said Mother, "it has brought out all the public misconceptions of what we do. We have taken far too much for granted. We always thought we might one day be criticized for not doing what we are supposed to be doing. Instead, we are being criticized for *doing* what we have been explicitly ordered to do, but in fact haven't done."

Although the outburst of accusations against the Agency has erupted *since* Watergate, most of them relate to sins it is supposed to have committed before. They range from the assertion, stated as an accusation, that the Agency has asked friends among university faculties to be on the lookout for suitable recruits to the allegation that the Agency tried to prevent the election of President Allende in Chile, and collaborated with a private corporation in the effort. The Agency is supposed to have approached Americans who were about to visit the U.S.S.R. and to have asked them to be on the lookout for certain information—thereby making "spies" of them. A Washington columnist made much of the fact that the Agency furnished information to the White House, thereby "influencing policy"; another, that the Agency had furnished training in counterterrorism to police departments of major American cities, and

279

was therefore interfering in the internal affairs of the United States—as it is expressly forbidden by its charter to do. Almost all of the accusations, say Agency officials, reflect a truly fundamental misunderstanding both of what the Agency is supposed to do and of what it is in fact doing.

Like other Government agencies, the CIA has a public relations department, and it is better than most. Its head, a tweedy Scottish-American named Angus Thuermer, is a very tough, highly experienced former OSO officer who is that rarity in the Administration, an official who doesn't feel that he has to *apologize* for his organization. His normal response to an accusation is either "Hell yes, we did it, just as we were supposed to do" or "No, we didn't do what you accuse us of, but we *should* have done it and we are ashamed of having let the country down by our failure." Washington newspapermen who are strongly disapproving of the Government's policies toward Southeast Asia have told me that Thuermer's defenses of the Agency's actions in Vietnam, Cambodia, and Laos are "almost totally convincing." "If we could print all of what he tells us," one of them told me, "it might put the Agency in a different light—but it's poor taste these days to go around saying nice things about a spy organization."

A spy organization! Whatever Angus Thuermer may say— for that matter, whatever *I* may say, in this book or elsewhere —journalists and their publics will persist in thinking that "intelligence" and "espionage" are largely synonymous, and that intelligence organizations engage exclusively in "dirty tricks." "To say otherwise," a Washington columnist explained, "would be writing dog-bites-man stuff." Agency officials are reconciled to this attitude. Whether they like it or not, and whatever the true character of the CIA's operations, they feel they must defend the Agency as though it were exclusively in the business of clandestine activities.

If they can defend it at all, that is. With respect to specific accusations it can "neither confirm nor deny," because to deny one is to admit the others. The job of the CIA's public relations office is not to build a warm, lovable institutional image such as is sought by General Motors or Coca-Cola, or even to convince the public that it behaves responsibly in pursuit of legitimate objectives of national security. It is to give an impression that it does *not* behave irresponsibly—in other words, as far as it is possible, to get the Agency out of the public mind altogether. Agency officials appear to believe that the best way to do this is to have its public relations office give discreet, off-the-record "backgrounders" to selected journalists—not to persuade them to an Agency point of view, but merely to acquaint them with certain unpublished facts which they should take into account as they write their stories, and to do the same with a cross section of Congress.

For example, Thuermer's office gave the inside story of the Chilean Presidential election to several Washington newspapermen, many of whom were unsympathetic to the Agency, with the result that the only attacks on the CIA for its alleged involvement in this election were made by correspondents known for making wild charges. At the same time, the CIA officer in charge of Congressional relations, Jack Maury, was taking Congressmen aside to tell them the story. Maury, a Southern gentleman of great charm, has a simple formula. When appearing before committees, he provides a carefully worked-out story that contains no untruths, yet reveals no information that would damage the Agency should it leak out to the public. With demagogues, he takes them aside and tells them "nothing, and lots of it, and with an air of great secrecy." Finally, with the most respected Congressmen, he tells them the whole truth, thereby passing on to them the responsibility for deciding whether or not what he confides should go any further. Thanks to Thuermer and Maury, the Agency's "image" is probably as good as it could be.

Still, even those journalists who have had a large share of Agency confidences are far from clear on the Agency's true policies with respect to "dirty tricks." The Agency has made no explicit statements on the subject, even in private. It has not even explained that "dirty tricks" are but a small segment of its repertoire. All we may know on the subject comes from Agency officials who have spoken to college audiences, although not as CIA officers but as representatives of State or Defense "on liaison duty with the CIA." In their lectures, they present the following arguments, which constitute the nearest we are likely to get to a CIA apologetic:

1. The CIA, complete with its "department of dirty tricks," is essential just as an army is essential. Even the most peace-loving country in the world cannot do without an army as long as it has reason to suspect that one or more of its neighbors are not so peace-loving and that the absence of an army would make them even less peace-loving.

2. But unlike our army, the CIA is *now* in a struggle. While the outside world happily sees an "age of détente," those in the CIA, whatever their personal political persuasion, see unmistakable signs of moves in the world intended to destroy us.

3. Although the intent of the U.S. Government is entirely defensive, and in no way born of a desire to take what is not ours, the nature of the dangers is such that "the only possible defense is a strong offense"—that is, we can't protect every person, place, or thing that might be a target of our enemies' offenses, so we must go on the offensive ourselves.

4. The enemy is hidden, so the offensives against him are largely a matter of seeking him out and learning in advance of his plans to attack us. Unavoidably, this involves invading the privacy (by wiretaps, "bugs," and other surveillance devices) of a wide range of suspects, most of whom turn out to be innocent. They also involve "dirty tricks," for eliminating our kind of enemies, which can be effectively accomplished only in secret.

5. We cannot forego invasions of privacy and "dirty tricks" without giving the enemy advantages that would constitute a grave risk to our national interests, but at least

282

we can ensure that their commission is *exclusively* in
the hands of agencies which are totally incorruptible,
of the highest possible professional competence, and
capable of carrying on their activities with such secrecy
that the possibility of harm to innocent people is eliminated. The FBI, which is responsible for fighting the
dangers internally, and the CIA, which fights them
outside the United States, meet these qualifications.

Informed journalists who are unsympathetic to the Agency
regard these arguments as "simplistic and illogical," as one of
them told me following a lecture by a "liaison" official that we
attended together at Georgetown University, but they don't
deny that they represent the line which the Agency's top officials would present were they able to present any line at all.
Also, they agree with the assertion made privately by some
Agency officers that most of them *don't like* these arguments.
After all, most Agency officials are liberal intellectuals. What
they know, by virtue of their jobs, hampers their idealism.
"Whatever our ideals," an officer told me who had served the
Agency since the days when it was supporting the Algerian
revolutionaries, anti-Portuguese guerrillas in Black Africa, and
Ho Chi Minh in Vietnam, "it is impossible to read, day after
day, the intelligence that comes across our desks without capi-
tulating to the idea that even our dirtiest tricks are necessary."

A half-hour contemplation of the CIA's public relations problems is enough to put any loyal American, whatever his politics,
in a state of gloom. One's spirits may be revived, however, by
a visit to Langley headquarters on "substantive" business. My
last visit, made during the Watergate hearings, was for the
purpose of exchanging information on Palestinian terrorists, a
subject on which I pass for an expert. It took place in a building a quarter of a mile from the main gate which is approached
through a tunnel of about that same length. At the end of the
tunnel, is a thickly carpeted area backed by a pair of huge
mahogany-doored elevators guarded by a squad of athletic

young men wearing gray flannel suits, unfashionably short haircuts, and .38 revolvers. They looked me over; then one of them smiled, greeted me by name, and escorted me to an unnumbered top floor, probably a penthouse.

The "miscellaneous projects" office, where the meeting took place, so taxes credulity that only Ian Fleming would have dared to put it in a novel. Although the building itself has ordinary floors, standard-size offices, fire escapes, and all the other normal features, this particular office is fitted out as a spacious hunting lodge, with beams crossing a slanting ceiling, which is twenty feet high at the upper end. There is a well-stocked bar—this being the only place in Langley besides the Director's private dining room where hard liquor is allowed.

Rising from a huge leather armchair flanked by two greyhounds was—Mother! Mother is now just nearing sixty and has gray hair, but he has kept his weight down and he wears a heavy coat of tan that makes him look like a ranch owner in a television Western. It is he, rather than the Director of Central Intelligence, who really runs the counterterrorist effort. The Director sets policy, establishes the broad lines along which policy will be carried out, and gives valuable advice based on his considerable experience in "working diplomacy." It was Mother, however, who organized the "Octopus" system by which the world's terrorist groups are identified, their members "ringed" and carded, and their movements monitored. He makes constant revisions to the system, and supervises day-to-day counterterrorist offensives. He is also responsible for the direction of a hundred-odd specialists in the field, and for maintaining contact with the many security services that cooperate with the CIA in the worldwide effort.

Mother was expansive but impatient, clearly wanting to get on with the business at hand, but he allowed a half-hour for visits from old friends. While I was there, "Groundhog" came in to say hello. Groundhog was—as it turned out, still *is*—a Chinese-American OSO officer who disappeared in the course of one of Steve Meade's missions to innermost China and was generally believed dead. "When did *you* get out?" I asked. "I'm still 'there,'" he said—meaning that he was still assigned to the China mainland. He was only on home leave recuperating from eight years of third-rate Cantonese food, and after getting his booster shots, he would be returning to his base in a remote village of Kwantung. Yearning for a sight of the shiny new Langley headquarters, he had persuaded Mother to let him in "black" (i.e., the way I had just come in), and after a peak at the place he would be whisked out to some Lower Manhattan "safe house" where he would be reintroduced into his special underworld to make his way back to China.

I reminded Mother of the old days when, in the OSO school, he would refuse to pass a technical student who couldn't enter a room blindfolded and install a microphone *in less than one minute*. In those days, standard procedure was for *one* technician to enter a "target" room, leaving only *one* lookout outside. At Watergate, Jim McCord, who had undergone training and knew the procedure, had entered the Democratic offices with Abbott, Costello, the Four Marx Brothers, and the Keystone Cops, and horsed around for almost half an hour—*without* a lookout. "What happened at Watergate?" I asked. "Let's talk about something else," he said.

A specialist in Palestinian affairs was brought in, and we settled down to discuss Palestinian terrorism. "Tell us about Julian Manyon," a young staff member asked. I explained that Julian was a BBC radio producer who at age twenty-two was already one of Britain's leading investigative journalists. He was currently collaborating with me on a study of the Palestinians' "Black September" movement. I gave a rundown on his background and specific qualifications—all of which information, it turned out, was already on a yellow card headed MANYON, JULIAN (BR.) with holes punched in it.

"Did he meet with a Palestinian by the name of 'Abu Humad'?" the staff member asked. I explained that we never knew whom we were meeting. We simply got the word around that we were looking for Palestinians who were informed on

"Black September," and those we wanted to see came to us—usually under aliases. Abu Humad could have been one of these.

"What did he look like?" I asked. The staff officer glanced at the yellow card, which looked like an ordinary library card for a book; then pressed some buttons on the arm of his chair like those on a modern-type telephone. In less than a second, the lights dimmed and a larger-than-life color slide of Julian talking to a Palestinian was flashed on the opposite wall. There are several million cards of suspected terrorists in CIA computer banks, yet it takes less than one second for a photograph of any one of them to be retrieved and flashed onto a huge television screen. In the case of "Abu Humad" there were perhaps a dozen pictures, taken in different places and from different angles. There were also pictures of Julian talking to various persons, men and women, who looked like Palestinians—and, of course, of me. There was one of me talking to "Tutu" Antonius, the beautiful Palestinian liberationist, at an indoor buffet luncheon given by another Palestinian who couldn't conceivably have any connection with the CIA, and where I would have sworn there was no one wandering about with a camera.

All very impressive. I was told that various press stories on the extent of CIA coverage were, if anything, an underestimation of the true state of affairs. In early 1971, a so-called "Citizens' Committee to Investigate the FBI" stole a thousand or so documents from an FBI office in Philadelphia. Examination soon showed that the FBI was systematically keeping files on persons who posed "a definite threat to the nation's stability and security." The Committee forwarded photocopies to the leading newspapers, and in the months that followed, it was revealed that the U.S. Army's Counter-Intelligence Corps maintained files on "potentially subversive persons"; that the Treasury Department's Secret Service had files "containing names and aliases of five thousand black people," as a report by a sensationalistic Washington columnist put it; that the CIA was maintaining files on Americans who traveled into its "target" areas; and that all of this information on millions of persons was fed into computer data banks where it would stay forever—along with information supplied by police agencies (including records of parking tickets and other such misdemeanors), credit investigative agencies, and banks. In 1971, another columnist published an "admission" by the Defense Department that it had computerized security files on twenty-five million Americans and that the files included not only information on persons regarded as threats to security but on public figures, such as Governor George Wallace of Alabama and Presidential candidate George McGovern, because "—because, well, why *not?* It's better to have the information than not to have it," a Pentagon spokesman told a member of the Senate Subcommittee on Constitutional Rights. The spokesman admitted that the Defense Department kept files on organizations, "incidents with security implications," and "subjects relevant to problems of national security" and that the files were in constant use—with the computers being "questioned" an average of twelve thousand times a day.

In investigating the situation, London *Daily Telegraph* correspondent Ian Ball discovered that the computerized files of the Bureau of Narcotics in Washington contained the files of three children under three years of age who had been exposed to narcotics by parental neglect. Since computers are "unthinking and unforgetting," the files would still be there twenty or thirty years later—to be "recovered," in the jargon of security investigators, should any one of them apply for a Government job, a Government loan, or simply a passport to visit some country "on the narcotic traffic lanes."

"True, all true," say my Agency friends. The Agency has coordinated into one "availability pool" the resources of American and foreign personality-data files—including, incidentally, files of British agencies whose heads feared some public outcry would force them to destroy their own copies—so as to make of itself the world's largest repository of personality data. By the time the present drive for data is completed, there will be a file of some kind on practically every person in the world who in any way comes to the official notice of his own government or of the U.S. Government. The CIA is also the world's repository of political, sociological, economic, military, and scientific data.

If it isn't already, the CIA may well become "the world's most powerful government agency," as one columnist called it, since it has access to the most knowledge, and the ability to keep that knowledge to itself. Understandably, there are increasing pressures from all directions to destroy both its power and its data banks. Resistance to these pressures is the purpose behind the Agency's modest public relations efforts and the program of Congressional briefings that it has recently launched. As the pressures increase, so will the determination of the Agency to keep key Congressmen informed. "The dangers are increasing," an Agency official told me, "and our power to deal with them is increasing proportionately. But so is the public's fear of us." Although the nature of the dangers is such that the Agency can hardly become less secret in handling its information about them, it can at least put its trust in a representative number of Congressmen. My friends at the Agency tell me that they don't need pressures to make them see this point. They see it better than any Congressman could see it, and they will behave accordingly.

No one in Langley has seen fit to confide in me the details of the Agency's plans for the future, nor will anyone tell even those Congressmen on the "watchdog" committee more than they "need to know," but the broad outlines are clear. Under the prompting first of the emergence of the "new terrorism" and more recently of the Watergate affair, the Agency's espionage branch is in the early stages of "not a reorganization so much as a reorientation," as a friend in Langley put it to me. Every effort will be made to ensure maximum Congressional understanding of the necessity of this "reorientation" and the Congressional support the Agency will need to protect it from the increasing attacks that are sure to be made on it by segments of the public which must necessarily remain uninformed. From my conversations with Agency officials, I infer that the principal points which will be made in Congressional briefings will be these:

The détente, *if there is one, must be meticulously monitored.* Agency officials are reluctant to throw cold water on "the age of détente," but they have information which indicates that the Soviets' gestures of friendship are far from sincere, and that they are pursuing the Cold War as vigorously as ever. Obviously, such information comes from highly secret sources— specifically, from spies in the Kremlin itself. There have been no genuine cases of CIA agents in the Kremlin having been exposed, but the few fake cases of the CIA's alleged spying on the Soviets have brought forth highly adverse public reactions. Some Senators have suggested in all seriousness that the U.S. Government should demonstrate its willingness to meet the Soviets halfway in a spirit of détente by dismantling its espionage operations against them. The Agency has no objection, other than a reluctance to appear foolish in the eyes of the Soviets as well as of sophisticated people everywhere, to pretending to agree to such a suggestion—who would know what it had actually done?—but it will argue to those Congressmen it takes into its confidence that these operations should be increased and improved, as in fact is being done. It appears that in the future the Agency will downgrade its "denied area" operations in the U.S.S.R., and possibly try to give the Soviets the impression that it is undertaking a general cutback of anti-Soviet operations, but it will at the same time develop more and better penetrations of the policymaking bodies of the Soviet Government.

Collection of data on international terrorist groups must be expanded and improved even further. While many Agency officials in their hearts sympathize with the outcries of liberals who argue that facilities such as "Octopus" constitute a gross infringement on the rights of privacy, their briefings of Congressmen will show that any curtailing of "Octopus" might invite worldwide outbreaks of terrorism, resulting in the takeover of other countries either by "revolutionary" groups bent on destroying American interests or by military juntas or right-wing groups claiming to be our friends but behaving in a way that would seriously embarrass us. What we have called "Third World operations" will be overhauled so as to take this fear into account. In the past, the Agency's espionage branch accomplished its missions in the Third World by recruiting individual agents of its own, or by gaining control of segments of local security services by recruiting their chiefs as agents. Such means will continue to a limited degree, but the emphasis will be shifted to gaining the open-and-aboveboard official cooperation of these services. Despite protests, the Agency will continue its policy of offering training and equipment to those security services which cooperate with it, and it will give its contacts in Congress ample information to prove the necessity for so doing.

"The Game" will concentrate more on the protection of strategic materials. I have not been allowed to see the modern version of the "Game Center" in which I worked many years ago,* but I am told that it now resembles the parlor game Monopoly, in content if not in form. There is a huge map of the world, with pins in those places where "strategic materials" are located, and these are surrounded with notations that indicate the relative "strategicality" of the various materials and the relative strengths of the great powers in the areas. The new game sprang into existence when a bright young officer who had memorized all the elements from actinium to zirconium put himself in the place of some imaginary enemy and devised a system of "plays" whereby he could paralyze American industry. He would do this by creating circumstances in parts of the world that would deny us access to certain rare substances which only metallurgists, chemists, and botanists have ever heard of but which are essential to the hardening of steel, to making machinery resistant to high temperatures, and to the manufacture of electronic gadgetry around which our modern industries, utilities, and communications are built. Then he took a look at the world and found that such "plays" were

---

* and which I described in *The Game of Nations*

already being made. They were exactly what they would have been had they been guided by a single strategy bent on developing the capability to bring our whole economic system to a halt.

Needless to say, the "enemy" postulated by the young game player was the U.S.S.R., and the enemy which the CIA's information shows to be behind the real-life moves is also the U.S.S.R.—although unlike the moves set up hypothetically, they were being made in competition with the Chinese. Even with this difference, the chances against mere coincidence are a million to one. Even were they ten to one, the conclusion to be drawn from the young man's experiment was sufficient to cause a very different kind of thinking at the Agency, and to bring about a change of operational emphasis to match. We are very much aware that our Government is disturbed by the Arab cutoffs of petroleum, an important item on our list of strategic materials. To Agency planners, petroleum is only one of many; it is not even the most important one, and our vulnerability is much greater than the public imagines. The CIA's "dirty tricks" department may therefore be called upon to take steps of which the public is certain to disapprove, and it will therefore need Congressional support to an unprecedented degree.

There will be greater cooperation with the multinational corporations. Despite all the briefing of Congressmen, and the support the Agency expects to get as a result, restrictions on its activities throughout the world are likely to increase. Some of them will come about as the result of pressures with which Agency officials sympathize, and some for reasons with which they disagree. In any case, there are many things a Government, as such, cannot do and many places it cannot go. For this reason, the Agency will step up its search for independent organizations with mutual interests through which it can operate. Agency officials believe that whatever anyone may think about it, we are entering an era when the interests of the United States and those of frankly "capitalist" institutions throughout the world so coincide that we have no choice but to take advantage of the fact. If this means cooperation with the unloved multinational corporations, ITT included, so be it. Executives of the multinationals are hardly likely to be enthusiastic about such cooperation, nor will many Congressmen, but Agency officials believe that when their briefings present certain inescapable facts to these gentlemen they will see no choice but to go along.

Removing the dangers inherent in a "powerful" government agency is not a matter of decreasing the power, but of ensuring that those who exercise it are incorruptible and truly responsive to public interest. CIA officials believe that their Agency is already incorruptible, and that despite its secrecy it is as responsive to public interest as any other agency. Because of Watergate, however, they now better understand the public's anxieties and they realize they must offer reassurances. In the interest of national security, the Agency will be required to commit some highly unpopular acts over the next decade. It will resist all pressures to destroy "Octopus" or to discontinue its expansion—and will, in fact, allow "Octopus" to absorb personality data of foreign intelligence services that may be forced to destroy their own systems; it will resist attempts of the Communists to take over governments of those countries which contain rare substances vital to our economic well-being, military strength, and health; it will support politicians, political groups, and governments throughout the world whose objectives are compatible with our own; it will sometimes work with unpopular organizations—American, international, and foreign. All these actions are certain to result in some public outcry, and the extent to which the Agency is able to survive it will depend on the extent to which the public becomes confident that the Agency *really has* unpublishable information necessitating the moves, and is acting entirely in the public interest and not for the gain of individual political figures, political parties, or special-interest groups.

The Agency's behavior throughout the Watergate affair went far to convince the public that the Agency, even without the improvements it intends to make, is already deserving of public

292

confidence. Parts of the story which at this writing have not yet been revealed * are even more to the credit of the Agency. President Nixon's "preoccupation" (a word used by John Dean in his testimony) with the subject of radical groups and their supposed foreign connections became intense in 1969 when, among other things, he ordered the FBI to prepare a special report on groups in the United States receiving support from abroad and the CIA to prepare a report on foreign governments and groups thought to be supporting radical groups in America. The FBI complied; it supplied a "preliminary report," to be followed a year later by a complete study, which alleged that there were indeed foreign influences at work in America, but which was weak on specifics. The CIA, however, submitted a straight-faced report in which its experts admitted that they had as yet uncovered *no* evidence that foreign groups had succeeded in establishing contacts in America, although some foreign groups were believed to be trying. The White House found the CIA report "theoretical" and "academic." An Agency friend of mine told me that its writers hadn't set out to prove anything, but simply to "call it as it is," and since there weren't many facts to "call," "a little theorizing was necessary to fill it out." From both points of view it was a disappointing paper, but it was all the Agency could do on the basis of information on hand at the time.

During the next two years, the Agency furnished the White House with a series of papers on the subject which were increasingly informative, but they included little that would pass for positive proof that foreign groups were aiding U.S. dissidents. The writers could only express "strong suspicion" that contacts between foreign groups and certain domestic groups were in the process of being established. The White House—

---

* Although the picture of the Agency's role in Watergate politics which I put together here is the result of numerous individual items of information coming from a wide range of friends at CIA and other parts of the intelligence community, I wish to make it clear that the compilation is entirely my own, that it in no way represents an official Agency view, and that no single source subscribed to the whole.

or, rather, its chief of staff, H. R. Haldeman, to whom the reports were sent—found the reports "too much maybe-this–maybe-that." Worse, they contained references to the possibility that "normal social unrest" might be a factor contributing to the existence of radical groups—a comment that never failed to infuriate the President. The Agency has since dropped this line—not to please the White House, but because the experts came to believe it was beside the point—but the harm was done.

The exchanges with the White House on radical groups were no more satisfactory from the Agency's point of view than from that of the White House. The Agency's Director then, Richard Helms, went over to the White House several times to give oral briefings on the subject, and on each occasion he limped back to Langley with tremendous feelings of frustration because, as he told one of his subordinates, "The President keeps asking the wrong questions" and was otherwise showing that instead of understanding the truly dangerous nature of terrorist groups, he persisted in seeing them in terms of campus disturbances, antiwar demonstrations, and other such nuisances. That wasn't all. As election time drew near, it became clearer that the White House wanted reports from the CIA and from everybody else to support conclusions already formed, and that the conclusions were ones which, with a little embellishment, could be made highly embarrassing to the Democratic Party.

All the while, the CIA's reports on radical groups throughout the world were getting better and better—that is, they contained more hard information which added up to a picture that made sense—but the summaries of those reports sent to the White House were more and more perfunctory. At the same time, the Agency's "theoretical" reporting on the international relationships of the groups was shaping up nicely: for example, those reports which grew out of studies of "word patterns" in Maoist training manuals, speeches of New Left leaders, articles and editorials by writers suspected of New Left associations, and so on, were beginning to suggest group-to-group and person-to-group connections, which were confirmed by follow-up inquiries. One conclusion of a report resulting from a word-pattern study was that a member of Senator McGovern's staff used words and phrases in a way peculiar to secret Soviet manuals for the guidance of propagandists and that his talk and writing reflected certain knowledge that could have come only as a result of intensive study of those manuals.

This finding—or, rather, this "tentative conclusion," because proof to back it was never found—signaled the end of any serious reporting the CIA might have done for the White House on the subject of radical groups. Had a report of that sort come to the attention of President Eisenhower during his first term of office—that is, a report suggesting that one of Adlai Stevenson's aides might be a Communist agent—the first person he would have told about it would have been Mr. Stevenson. Dick Helms and others at the Agency suspected that if they sent Nixon a report suggesting that Senator McGovern might have a Communist in his camp, the Senator would be the *last* to hear about it, and under circumstances that would embarrass him the most.

By that time the White House had organized its own investigators into a special unit later known as "the plumbers." To the FBI and the CIA, the plumbers at first admitted only one function: to sniff out leaks to the press emanating from the White House. One of the plumbers, however, Howard Hunt, admitted to friends at the Agency that the main reason for the formation of the unit was the President's dissatisfaction with the reporting of the FBI and the CIA on radical groups. Hunt also said that the unit was to identify leaders of radical groups that were particularly embarrassing to the President, to get derogatory information on Democratic Presidential aspirants and to carry out certain "black" operations to see that the Democratic campaign went the way President Nixon wanted it to go. Hunt confided to his friends at the CIA that there would be no quibbling over the fact that the plumbers' unit was at the same time working for the White House and for the Committee for the Re-election of the President—"CREEP"—since it was re-

295

garded by Haldeman, Presidential adviser John Ehrlichman, and the others as being "among the resources of the incumbency"—i.e., one of the natural advantages enjoyed by a candidate running for an office he already has.

I am told that Hunt passed on this information sometime before the Agency's Deputy Director, General Vernon Walters, lent him all that equipment. Although General Walters didn't know about the confidence, and lent the equipment on good faith since he knew Hunt was under orders of the White House, I'm afraid this excuse doesn't let the Agency off the hook, because more than one Agency member admitted to me that the thought of Hunt's breaking into the office of Dan Ellsberg's psychiatrist wearing that red wig would have been irresistible—"simply *too much*," as "Lady Windemere," the OSO cosmetician, put it to me over Sunday-afternoon tea in her Georgetown apartment. From what I heard about Hunt, I'm sure *I* wouldn't have been able to resist—especially since there was every possibility that he would make the entry in some Abbott and Costello fashion and get himself and his associates caught. The frightening thing about the affair is that the White House would hire Hunt for *anything*.

As I remember Howard Hunt, he is a nice guy with such a romantic turn of mind that he would possibly *like* to have a criminal mentality (it would help in his writing of novels), but he is deplorably lacking in one. He has never been a CIA agent; he was a desk man whose operational experience consisted of kibitzing, from an administrative standpoint, some of the operations into Cuba. "I wouldn't have trusted him to steal an apple from a fruit stand," one of his former superiors told me, while swearing that the White House employed Hunt without bothering to ask anyone at the Agency about him. "If Haldeman or anybody else had called to ask, 'What about Hunt?' we would have laughed," he said.

The same goes for the other key figures in the Watergate break-in—except Jim McCord. McCord is entirely a "security wallah," as Summaries people call those faceless men who make the rounds of Langley offices after working hours checking to see that desks are clear and safes locked. McCord was their overall supervisor, and he brought considerable imagination to what is normally a totally routine job—for example, he set the traps that caught a secretary in Summaries red-handed in the act of removing papers to take to a crusading Washington columnist. Also, he distinguished himself once when a Dutch manufacturer of electronic gadgetry was trying to outshine that Japanese company I wrote about in Chapter 2. The Dutch salesman announced that over twenty items of gadgetry had been hidden in the exhibition room, and invited his CIA guests to find them. They looked and, as on the occasion of the Japanese demonstration, they couldn't. Then the Dutchman set about to uncover them, and *he* couldn't find them! Jim McCord had sneaked into the room before the demonstration, found them all, and removed them. "Jim is one fine operator," said Helms, who was guest of honor on the occasion.

So what was a fine operator like McCord doing spending thirty minutes in "hot" premises with a lot of idiots, and no lookout outside? Although no one at Langley would come right out and admit it, there are suspicions that McCord was a double agent. Whoever it was at the Agency that put him up to it possibly didn't foresee the ultimate consequences, but the Agency—and, specifically, the Agency's specialists in operations of this kind—had a lot to gain from sabotaging the plumbers. The ultimate consequences were probably too high a price to pay, but after all, it wasn't the Agency that had to pay it.

Suppose the Agency had itself got so out of hand as to attempt a crazy operation like Watergate? This is where the system of fuses would have become operative. Let us say, for the sake of example, that the President orders the Director, CIA, to send some of his boys out to follow Senator Ervin as he makes the rounds of Washington nightclubs. The Director, let us say for the sake of example, is a weak chap who prefers holding on to his job to being sent off to Teheran as Ambassador, so he says, "Yessir, Mr. President," and returns to his office to comply. Since he can hardly be expected to conduct the surveillance personally, he passes the order to the chief of some division most likely to have surveillance facilities inside the United States. Like the Director of Central Intelligence, the division chief cannot himself conduct the surveillance, so he has to call in some members of his staff to make plans for the surveillance, and someone else to choose the personnel to carry it out. Moreover, since he can't move or equip personnel without the concurrence of the overall operations officer who works directly for the Deputy Director, Plans, or DDP—the head of the "dirty tricks department"—he has to bring yet another four or five officers into the operation. If he *doesn't* do all this (if, for example, the DCI has instructed him to bypass the usual procedures), the personnel who are to conduct the actual surveillance will refuse to move—since every one of them is working for the CIA as an organization and not the Director as a person, and knows full well that taking action without a "trip ticket"—i.e., a written order endorsed by some four or five "controls"—is a sure way of getting fired.

So what happens? The DCI, hot from the White House, calls in the Chief of Division X and orders him to get cracking on a surveillance of Senator Ervin. The Chief of Division X, also a weakling who likes his job (let us say), calls in his plans officer and his operations officer and passes the word on to them. And so on and so on. Sooner or later, at least *one* officer down the line either says "No," with adequate means at his disposal for making the "No" stick, or "loses the papers," as the old-timers say. And since those in the act are certain that at least one of their number will act as the fuse and "blow," it is quite possible that they will *all* blow. Anyhow, the word goes back to the DCI either: (a) that the operation was launched, but ran into difficulties and had to be abandoned; (b) that it couldn't be run except in a way that would involve risks of disclosures which might embarrass the White House; (c) that the operation has been launched, when in fact it hasn't, but isn't producing anything worthwhile; (d) that—well, any one of a dozen or more excuses: the more farfetched the better, since the boys down the line wouldn't want to run the risk of causing the Director to *believe* their excuses. Once he has caught the point that they are only trying to protect him, along with the Agency, they can sit down with him to concoct an excuse plausible enough for the White House. But they never, never explicitly refuse to carry out his command, or tell him anything that would "involve" him, as that ominous word is now used around Washington. It is a sort of "Who-will-rid-me-of-this-turbulent-priest?" treatment in reverse.

I am told that the press has uncovered only a fraction of the "requests" made of the CIA by the White House. Among others, the Agency was asked to follow up investigations the FBI was supposed to be making but was found out *not* to be making; it was asked to have prominent Democrats followed when they were abroad; it was asked to "cooperate" with the Internal Revenue Service in maintaining surveillance of num-bered Swiss bank accounts—presumably in hopes of spotting the odd Democrat in the act of "laundering" his funds. On one occasion, Jojo's office was asked for an LSD-type drug that could be slipped into the lemonade of Democratic orators, thus causing them to say sillier things than they would say anyhow. To this day, some of my friends at the Agency are convinced that Howard Hunt or Gordon Liddy or somebody got hold of a variety of the drug and slipped it into Senator Muskie's lemonade before he played that famous weeping scene. After long harassment by such requests, it is easy to imagine that when Howard Hunt asked for a false beard the deputy shrugged, said "What the hell," and gave it to him.

The CIA did tighten up. It resisted all White House re-quests that the Director and his staff considered in any way improper, stalling and making excuses, until the White House realized that the stumbling block was not just Helms, but the "gentlemen's club."

President Nixon and his White House aides apparently never really understood that the "gentlemen's club" is essential to the system of fuses. On individual missions an Agency employee has plenty of room for individual initiative, although subject to postoperational inspection, but inside the Agency action is taken not by individuals but by teams of individuals. Because of the Agency's system of personnel selection and clearance, the chances of there being a corrupt, irrational, or irresponsible individual employee are small, but the chances of there being a whole team of such employees are infinitesimal; as the number of its members increases arithmetically, the chances of its doing anything dishonest or irresponsible decrease geometrically. But to ensure that such interdependence of individuals doesn't simply result in all actions getting bogged down in disagreement, it is essential that members of the teams *like* one another, and respect one another as men of integrity and intelligence. Hence the "gentlemen's club." Under Mr. Nixon, the White House never got the point.

That the point was missed is illustrated by the behavior of James Schlesinger during his brief stay in Langley as DCI. A weakness of a club of any kind is that it is difficult for one member to discharge another. Dick Helms, being not only a charter member of the Agency's "gentlemen's club" but one whose very success was due to the affection in which the other members held him, couldn't bring himself to discharge the deadwood which had been accumulating at the upper levels for some time and which was so blocking positions that there were no vacancies for competent younger officers to be promoted into. The Agency was genuinely in need of a house-cleaning, and when Dick Helms was replaced by Mr. Schlesinger the stalwarts in the Agency rejoiced—even though they liked and respected Helms, and knew that among the President's reasons for firing him was that he had blown several fuses in the course of the Watergate affair. Schlesinger had been a systems analyst for the Rand Corporation and, later, head of the Atomic Energy Commission, and had established good records in both jobs. He had written several "think pieces" which many of the Agency's philosophers regarded as sound. On the occasions when he had sat on interagency committees with Agency representatives he had made a good impression, and they liked him. The Agency was all set to receive him warmly; its officers believed that his arrival would signal a new era in CIA history. But the honeymoon lasted only for as long as it took him to enter his new office, announce to the departing Helms that "This is a gentlemen's club and I am no gentleman," and then demonstrate the fact by acknowledging an introduction to Mrs. Donlevy, Helm's secretary of twenty-five years, by saying, without looking up, "I won't be needing her": in other words, less than a minute.

When Schlesinger began his housecleaning, it quickly became obvious that he was not so much getting rid of deadwood as removing the fuses. For reasons which were no doubt honest, he believed that anything which stood in the way of the Agency's being totally "responsive to the needs of the White House," to use another of John Dean's phrases, had to go. To him, this meant the removal of anyone who refused to take orders for *any* reason, even for the reason that the orders were patently improper. He even tried to fire Mother and Jojo (the Kingfish, Lady Windemere, and the others went into hiding—and, I am told, managed to conceal their existence from Mr. Schlesinger altogether), and Personnel had to resort to several changes of their "funny names" to keep them on the books. The only result of his firings and attempts at reorganization was to force most of the espionage branch to go underground where he couldn't find it, thus crippling his ability to govern. His experiences at the Agency and the brevity of his stay proved the point: the fuses are especially effective when it is they themselves which are under fire. In the future, when the system of which they are a part has Congressional sanction, they will make of the Agency a body that is as untouchable as the Supreme Court.

James Schlesinger—or "Mr. Schlesinger," as he was known to friends he left behind at the Agency—has been replaced by a true professional, William Colby, who ran the famous—or infamous, depending on how you look at it—"Phoenix" operation in Vietnam. How Mr. Colby stands as a club member is not known, even by those who work with him most closely. He has had but few Washington assignments during his career, and is so far pretty much of a mystery man at headquarters—

having only enough of a reputation to be regarded as "the kind of man who goes to *Oh! Calcutta!* to look at the audience." He has so far made an excellent impression on Agency personnel, however, and the stalwarts appear convinced that he will develop policies that are consistent with Agency philosophies on the organization's integrity. "He's a tough baby," Mother told me, "and he's not going to be anybody's figurehead, but we can depend on him not disturb the fuses." He has disturbed some of the senior officers by sticking to his own ideas as to which of those who were fired by Schlesinger should be brought back and which should stay fired, but this appears not to have disturbed his relations with "the cabal," as some Agency members unashamedly call the inner circle— while making it clear that he is in no sense its "boy." He is unquestionably the leader, and he will no doubt lead with a strong hand.

At the same time, he is building from the bottom. Once a week, he has lunch in the Agency cafeteria with a group of young men chosen by one or another of the division chiefs as being representative of the young talent that is growing up in the organization. He encourages them to air their views and their complaints, and he has by now convinced them that this is no public relations gesture but is born of a genuine desire to learn, and to establish rapport with them for the future. By this and other practices, he is inculcating in the younger members a "sense of central mission" and a thorough understanding of the motto "Always keep in mind whom you are working for" —meaning it's not for the President of the United States as a person, not for the Director of the CIA, but for the CIA *as* an instrument of the American democracy.

A young lieutenant coming out of West Point has been told that if his colonel gives him an order he considers improper he must proceed immediately to the nearest inspector general to report, but he soon learns that this would be a very foolish thing to do. Not so in the CIA—especially in the post-Watergate CIA under Bill Colby. From now on, to *fail* to question a doubtful order will be a very foolish thing to do—possibly even in the eyes of the person who gives it. Many orders will be given by senior officials under pressure who know they can count on someone down the line to "lose the papers." The officer down the line who fails to spot incidents in which he is supposed to lose the papers will, as before, be beyond explicit punishment, but he will thereafter suffer "inconveniences." Since there are no careless or stupid people in the Agency, it will be assumed that malice, not genuine oversight, is behind his failure. Mother tells me that at the time of a recent routine flap, brought on by some Congressman's sniffing out the existence of chemical-warfare weaponry in Government warehouses, he had issued an order to destroy all the CIA's supplies of truth drugs, hallucinators, aphrodisiacs, and other operational chemicals and that "some smart-ass kid in Support" had proceeded to the Agency depot in Rosslyn, Virginia, and done just that. Mother "inconvenienced" him severely, knowing that the young man was smart enough to have known what was expected of him and could only have been practicing a kind of mischief which the CIA sometimes practices on the State Department or the White House: "The subtlest form of insubordination," goes the saying, "is to take a stupid order and carry it out to the letter." This sort of mischief, Mother assured me, is a thing of the past.

"Restrictions, restrictions!" complains the Agency staff officer who has followed all the discussions about the future of American intelligence. The morale at Langley is not all it should be; there is a fringe of discontented officers who are getting out of the intelligence business altogether, or who are fading into CIA "associate" organizations where they will build new careers for themselves and, at the same time, provide occasional help to their old love as "loyal alumni." It seems to these officers that the New Look envisioned by Bill Colby and the intelligence "reorienters" will be more concerned with avoiding wrong than with doing right, and that negativism will be the order of the day. On the other hand, they see encouragement from quarters from which they have least expected it: the Third World, where a high percentage of those who advocate "the people's war against imperialism and capitalism" might be expected to reside. Already, the cooperation of Third World security services is increasing tremendously; the nearer the chiefs of these services get to the terrorist movements, even those with which they must sympathize in public statements, the more they regard them as their own enemies as well as ours.

That is not all there is to it. To an extent that liberals in the Agency find frightening, *most* governments in the Third World, especially their security services, are dropping *all* their leftist associations, and appear to be doing so not only because of their secret right-wing yearnings but because they believe they are responding to their equivalents of American and British "silent majorities." All at once, as if called upon by some magic signal, *most* governments of the Third World have begun a pronounced swing to the right, and in ways that they imagine will put them on "our side."

What seems to be happening in the world—especially in the Third World, where terrible economic and social problems are becoming a matter of stark reality and not just something for socialists to theorize about—is that even governments which are nominally Communist are becoming impatient with the so-called "people's war." As governments in power, *they* are finding themselves targets of "the people"—especially when they fail, as they inevitably must, to carry out the extravagant promises they made in order to gain power. Moreover, they see that "the people," as that term is used to indicate those who are fighting the "people's war," haven't a chance in hell of winning, and that it would be a terrible thing if they did.

To put it bluntly, they want to be on the winning side. Anyone who has spent as much time as the CIA's counterterrorism experts have spent in negotiating with local security authorities throughout the Third World—including those who are loudest in their denunciations of "imperialism and capitalism" —must know that the only people left anywhere who still doubt who is going to come out on top in this turbulent world are those political theorists on *our* side who are at a safe distance from the problem.

The up-and-coming young men and women of the CIA make no apology for their confidence that ours is the winning side, that it *should* be the winning side, and that those who "lose" to us will be far better off, in freedoms as well as in economic benefits, than would be the case were they by some fluke to find themselves "winners." They see their Government—the one we've got now and any that might conceivably replace it —as maintaining the leadership in the drive to find new sources of energy, to figure out ways of feeding the world's starving peoples and to give them better lives, to cure cancer and the common cold, and to deal with all the other tremendous problems which require mature and intelligent competence, and constructive energy rather than revolutionary zeal. Even the CIA's most dedicated liberals see their organization as an essential part of the machinery which our Government needs to protect itself so that it can get on with the job. "After all," said the young CIA officer who escorted me to my car after I finished my meeting with Mother, "somebody has to protect the strong from the weak."

AFTERWORD

In writing this book, I have had to figure out a way in which I could tell enough about the business to convey a fundamental understanding of it (or at least enough to correct most of the common popular misconceptions) without giving away secrets essential to the safety of the systems. I have imposed a number of restraints upon myself which prevent me from giving away information concerning ongoing British or American operations in either espionage or counterespionage, and also from revealing any tricks or techniques that have not already been made known to the Soviets by Kim Philby and his like. Where I have described actual operations I have in many cases changed details and the identities of those taking part in them, so that the reader can only guess at the realities on which I have based my account.

APPENDICES

APPENDIX A

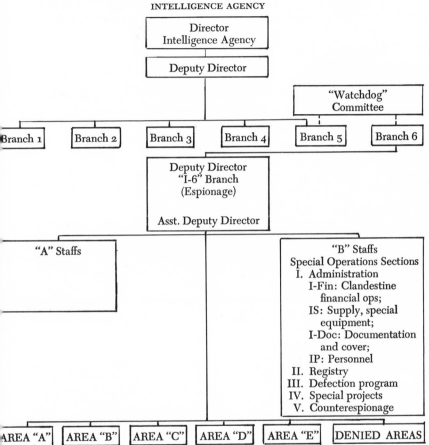

Notes:
The I-6 Branch is under the command of a Deputy Director who
reports straight to the Director of Intelligence, free of guidance by
the various staffs at the director level. Instead of staff guidance,
there is a "watchdog committee" (in some agencies internal, in

some external—e.g., Congressional) whose function is to be on the lookout for possible instances of indiscretion, abuse of power, or malfeasance.

The "A" staffs are advisory only. They deal with the area divisions only through the Deputy Director or the Assistant Deputy Director. The "B" staffs have supervisory powers, sometimes limited and sometimes absolute, over the area divisions on all matters coming under their various specialist jurisdictions.

In some espionage organizations, Branches 5 and 6 are under the same deputy director, but their operations are kept entirely apart.

APPENDIX B

AN INTRODUCTION TO ESPIONAGE OPERATIONS

The following is an Instructor's Guide for a lecture to newly employed intelligence staff officers of Defense, State, the NSA, and the CIA, given under CIA sponsorship at its "country school" during the summers of 1971 and 1972. It is not an official CIA paper, but it has nonetheless been so sanitized that publication in its present form in no way violates Government security regulations.

1. Introduction: The Uses and Abuses of Espionage

First, make it clear that espionage is a very specialized form of information procurement, that it is expected to cover only a very small portion of the overall intelligence-requirement schedules, and that it is used *only* under the following circumstances:

a. When the required information is vital to national security (more explicitly, when *not having* the information would endanger the national security);

b. When alternative means of information procurement are inadequate.

The first of these points, "a," should be supported with examples to show what is meant by the phrase "vital to national security" and the various kinds of requirements that do and do not meet the criterion. Also, show that there are numerous borderline cases, and indicate that when in doubt the planners of espionage operations prefer to err on the side of *not* undertaking a requirement. Should apparent exceptions be pointed out, show that espionage operations do procure information that is not vital to national security, but only as a by-product of efforts to procure information that is.

It should be made clear that espionage operations are conducted against friendly countries only in the rarest of circumstances and on a basis of Executive Order. Wherever there is a question of weighing the dangers of loss of goodwill, confidence, and prestige against the dangers incident to being without information believed to be vital, judgment must be made by authorities above the [espionage branch] and its parent Agency.

2. Acceptance of an Espionage Assignment

Apart from restrictions that may be placed on the [espionage branch] with respect to the acceptance or initiation of espionage operations, there are those which the [espionage branch] imposes upon itself. Espionage risks lives and reputations, of nations, agencies, and individuals, and the risks are best known to [espionage branch] officers themselves. Therefore, before undertaking the development of an espionage operation, these officers must demand answers to the following questions:

a. Do we really need the information?
b. What obstacles must be overcome to get it?
c. What risks are involved in overcoming the obstacles?

Do we really need the information? The [espionage branch] has learned to be wary of research offices and requirements staffs and their application of the criterion "vital to national security." Even those researchers who are normally most opposed to the use of espionage sometimes lose their perspective when they are absorbed in their favorite researches. (Give examples.) Therefore, wherever there is the slightest doubt about the importance of a particular requirement, it is incumbent upon the [espionage branch] to ascertain from higher authority that fulfillment of the requirement is vital. Remember: the assignment of a requirement by a research office or requirements staff of any Government agency, even of the [espionage branch's] parent Agency, does not relieve it from the responsibility of ascertaining that an operation is in pursuit of truly vital information.

What obstacles must be overcome? In some countries there are no obstacles because there are no officially protected secrets. In such countries the act of espionage is not possible, because simple observation is all that is required to obtain local information. (Note:

313

This would not include foreign embassies in that country, of course, because these have their own protections.) In other countries, information is denied to some categories of visitors and not to others: for example, an Israeli visiting Egypt with a false passport would be guilty of espionage just by being there, although his observations were the same as those of any visiting American. In such cases the only obstacle is that of overcoming the local capability to recognize false passports and to establish true identities. In *most* countries— the United States, Great Britain, and most countries of Europe, including some of those in the Soviet Bloc—"espionage," as a legal term, applies only to the acquisition and communication of information which is officially and explicitly designated as "secret" and which, for the most part, lies within physically secured areas to which only authorized persons have access. It is in this latter category of countries, of course, that the obstacles are the most formidable and that the acquisition of intelligence information requires the particular skills which an espionage organization is expected to have.

What risks are involved in overcoming the obstacles? Obviously, the risks incident to an espionage operation vary from country to country in accordance with the different circumstances just described. The question of whether you are or are not committing espionage in a particular country revolves around these three questions:

a. *Who* you are;

b. The nature of the *information* you seek;

c. The *communication* of the information.

If you are an Israeli citizen and you are in Egypt you are legally a "spy" because, apart from the fact that you are carrying a false passport, there would be the fair assumption that just by being there you will see and hear things you are not supposed to see and hear, and the equally fair assumption that you will eventually report it all to Israeli intelligence authorities. The particular information you acquire is of no importance, since you are not entitled to *any* information; proof of communication is also unimportant, since it is assumed that one in your circumstances will somehow communicate. All that is relevant is the fact that you are an Israeli: under Egyptian law, the only law that counts under such circumstances, that is enough to get you labeled as an espionage agent.

If you are a citizen of Egypt or of a country acknowledged to be "friendly" to Egypt you may commit espionage only by the unauthorized acquisition of information that is regarded as "classified" by the authorities. The mere proof that you acquired the information intentionally, bypassing security controls in order to get it, is enough to cause you to be labeled an espionage agent.

Even then, however, you may escape prosecution if you had no intention of *communicating* the information to a foreign power. The illegal acquisition of information is a crime in Egypt, but it is not the crime of espionage unless there is the intent to communicate. The intent to communicate is presumed in the case of a citizen of an enemy state, but with all others it must be proved.

Egypt has its laws; other states have theirs. Needless to say, it is the laws which are in fact in force in a particular state that are relevant and the only ones that are taken into account by planners of espionage operations as they weigh the risks. The question of risk weighs most heavily on these planners as they seek "alternative means" which might obviate the need to run espionage operations.

3. *"Alternative Means"*

There are four general categories of what espionage specialists call "alternative means":

a. *"Overt"*: Speaking literally, all of the "alternative means" are to some extent "overt": that is, they are totally or partly aboveboard. In this context, however, the designation "overt" applies only to such sources as newspapers, trade journals, official records, and other publications that are accessible to the public. It also applies to the open observation of subjects of intelligence interest—e.g., the observation of military parades by military attachés. (Note: The innocent observations of ordinary tourists in the Soviet Union are "overt," even though the tourists are questioned in detail upon their return to their homes. But they are *not* "overt" if the tourists were briefed beforehand on what to be on the lookout for.)

b. *"Creative intelligence"*: Ordinary researchers, working quietly in their offices, are often able to infer highly secret information simply by drawing intelligent conclusions from the juxtaposition of many items of nonsecret information. Changes in the geographical disposition of scientists with known specialties combined with easily observable changes in the flow of equipment, supplies, and raw materials might suggest important new policies, shifts of operational emphasis, or new inventions. More items of information, also nonsecret and seemingly unrelated, might enable a competent researcher to center in on specifics. The issuance of winter clothing to soldiers, plus a step-up of winter maneuvers, might give an indication of military intentions in northerly climates. (Give other examples, but caution against the possibility of "disinformation" and "Deception," subjects of other lectures.) Recently the use of computers to correlate and analyze masses of details, each of which is nonsecret, has raised the effectiveness of inferential intelligence to an incredible level of effectiveness.

"Gaming" comes under the heading of creative intelligence. By imagining themselves in the places of decision makers of another government, "game players" who have carefully studied the personal peculiarities of those decision makers and who have absorbed the intelligence (whether right or wrong) that must be available to them are often able to interpret their current actions and predict their future actions with amazing accuracy. (Suggested examples are the ETOUSA "game room" in London during World War II, and the Army War College's successful "gaming out" of the Japanese attack on Pearl Harbor.)

Another form of creative intelligence is propaganda analysis, which includes the analysis not only of material that is obviously propaganda but of any spoken or printed word (official statements, political speeches, "news" articles in a censored press) that may have purposes besides the simple dissemination of information. The creative analyst regards *any* public speech, statement, or report (or even a news item, if in a government-controlled newspaper) as possibly having such other purposes. Sometimes the mere *selection* of items, all truthful, may indicate purpose. In any case, skillful examination of controlled information will often indicate purposes that are in themselves concealed and secret. Or it may uncover problems which the spokesman and his employers wish to conceal.

c. *Diplomacy and liaison:* Contrary to general belief, officers of the [espionage branch] have the greatest respect for "straight" diplomats and their ability to acquire highly secret information through means that are entirely legal. Senior officials, even of governments generally believed to be hostile to the United States, will often confide important secrets to an American ambassador whom they like and trust as a person. A competent attache—military, Treasury, commercial, or other—will almost always be able to expand his liaison with his opposite number in the local government, as well as with those in other embassies, far beyond the routine exchange of nonsecret information. Even ambassadors and attachés who are not particularly competent but who have reputations for being discreet will acquire large amounts of secret information merely because they represent a powerful and influential government. Officers of the [espionage branch] fully appreciate this, and they refrain from employing the means of espionage in lieu of ordinary diplomatic contact—not only because ordinary diplomatic contact is often more effective for intelligence purposes, but also because it is more desirable for a host of other reasons. A suspicion of espionage, even a faint one, may endanger feelings of trust and personal goodwill which are more important to our national interest than intelligence.

d. *Technical sources:* This lecture cannot cover the wide variety of technical sources—satellites, seismographs, "sniffers," telespectroscopes, and tens of others—by which, singly or in combination, we can examine almost any facet of human activity, no matter how far away and no matter how concealed. It can, however, convey the point that these sources now supply, in quantity, over 99 percent of the raw information required for the formulation of intelligence related to national security and, in quality, as much as 50 percent (i.e., as much as all other sources put together) of what goes into the President's daily and weekly summaries. Give examples: One satellite turn of the world is sufficient to show the existing status of all industrial and military installations within its range; a series of turns, over a year or two, will give photographic interpreters all they need to know about changes in those installations, which indicate their progress or lack of it and the probable cause. Also, show how dependable camouflage is no longer possible: camouflage techniques have not kept up with the development of techniques by which to penetrate them.

All of these technical devices are installed, maintained, and controlled by units of the Government's intelligence system other than the [espionage branch]. But there is one item on the list which is related to the [espionage branch's] operations and which brings the [espionage branch] into an unusual measure of cooperation with one or another of the intelligence agencies controlling it. This is the "sneaky." A "sneaky" differs from the other technical devices in that it is planted inside an intelligence target, and its use may therefore be in violation of the espionage laws of the country where the target is located. For this reason, the planting and on-the-spot servicing of sneakies is the responsibility of the [espionage branch]. But the decision as to where and when to use sneakies belongs to the agency that developed them. Once the enemy is in physical possession of a sneaky, or has otherwise acquired complete technical information about it, the decision may be permanently delegated to the [espionage branch]. Until then, however, stringent efforts will be made to conceal from the enemy the fact that sneakies of various kinds exist, that they are used by the U.S. Government's intelligence agencies, and the details of their manufacture, distribution, and use; responsibility for these efforts falls to the [agencies having responsibility for technical gadgetry used in intelligence].

[The next two paragraphs have been omitted, because they contain classified information that cannot be sanitized. They give examples of sneakies in current use, of which the following can be mentioned: chemically treated handkerchiefs which pick up factory gases for analysis; ordinary household and office items which emit high-frequency sounds not audible to human ears and which can transport "parasite" sounds over great distances; minuscule microphone-transmitters which escape even the most penetrating police searches; a whole range of items which look totally harmless even to an expert observer, and which can be distributed so widely that running them all down would be an around-the-clock job for the target country's whole police force. These, used in conjunction with cameras and receiving sets carried in satellites and intermediate stations of other kinds, make it possible for our intelligence to identify almost any target of interest, to determine its composition and progress, and to learn much about the intentions of those who control it. Remarkably, thousands of these units operating inside the Soviet Bloc and Communist China have gone undetected for years.]

With the complete range of technical surveillance equipment now at the disposal of American intelligence agencies, from "general survey" mechanisms such as around-the-world missiles with cameras having the capacity to photograph automobiles in a Moscow street to "on the ground" devices capable of testing the octane of the gasoline they burn, the [espionage branch] can now be freed of a high percentage of the requirements formerly assigned to it. On targets above the ground—factories, transportation facilities, military installations—we can learn almost all we need to know by technically "smelling" the fumes they exude, by measuring their size and shape, by noting the size, shape, and weight of what is shipped into and out of them, and by keeping track of the personnel they employ and their skills. Even beneath-the-ground targets may be examined by technical methods, including observation of the target itself, because our scientists have developed counter-camouflage measures which can "see" through any presently known kind of concealment, including that network of deep caves in the Ural Mountains, which is supposed to conceal the central communications control base which, according to their present plans, the Soviets intend to use if another world war breaks out. And none of this, as previously, requires espionage. The role of espionage is now reduced to support only.

4. What Is Left for Espionage?

The mission of the [espionage branch] is by now greatly reduced. But there is still plenty for it to do. The five categories of requirements to which its present efforts are confined are as follows:

a. *Information on foreign espionage organization, activity, and personnel:* Partly for historical reasons, partly for empirical reasons, and partly for practical reasons, this requirement continues to be the one that occupies the most man-hours of [espionage branch] personnel.

b. *Early-warning information:* To provide information indicating a forthcoming attack on the United States is an essential part of the mission of all elements of the intelligence system, including the [espionage branch].

c. *Drawing boards:* By now, each side in the Cold War is so aware of the other's capabilities that "alternative means" are quite sufficient to follow all scientific progress. But *plans* for progress remain a requirement of the [espionage branch].

d. *Supplementary information on denied areas:* Those vast areas of the U.S.S.R. and China to which Western observers are denied access are now adequately covered by technical means. But there are still considerable gaps in this information which can be filled only by on-the-ground observation. Since on-the-ground observation in these areas constitutes "espionage," the duty falls to the [espionage branch].

e. *"Pieces":* The same is true of all other types of information which, in recent years, is procured in adequate amounts by "alternative sources." Nonetheless, there continue to be missing pieces to the "jigsaw puzzle," and these are filled by espionage operations —as explicitly requested by requirements units *outside* the [espionage branch].

f. *Operational data:* "Operational data"—i.e., information required by technical intelligence agencies and others for the planning of their own operations—is ordinarily a requirement placed on the [espionage branch]. Also, in many cases the [espionage branch] is called upon actually to install or to assist in the installation of certain technical devices, and thereafter to service them.

5. Functions of the Espionage Service

In order to fulfill these requirements, the [espionage branch] occupies itself with certain carefully delineated fields of activity which are normally its exclusive responsibility. They are:

a. *Penetration of targets in enemy governments.* The recruitment and employment of espionage agents within the policymaking offices of governments that may become hostile toward the United States is the exclusive responsibility of the [espionage branch].

b. *Counterespionage.* Also, operations designed to penetrate foreign intelligence agencies, to gain control over their espionage agents, and to pass information to them ("disinformation") which it suits the U.S. Government for them to have are the exclusive responsibility of the [espionage branch].

c. *Liaison with foreign security and intelligence services.* To the extent possible, the [espionage service] utilizes the assistance of the security and intelligence services of friendly countries. Sometimes liaison is maintained with these services entirely on the basis of exchanging information. In some cases, the basis of the aid is organizational, technical, and material aid supplied by the [espionage branch] to a local service. It is the responsibility of the [espionage branch] to develop and expand mutual interests with security and intelligence services around the world, and to gain as much valuable information as possible through the liaison arrangements which are set up for the purpose.

d. *"Third World" operations.* Although there are but few targets in the so-called Third World that contain information under the categories of requirements assigned to the [espionage branch], there are nonetheless certain activities which, for a wide variety of reasons, the United States Government has to undertake in the Third

World and for which the [espionage branch] is the logical assignee. (Give examples.)

e. *Special projects.* There are also various other activities which are assigned to the [espionage branch] for no reason other than the fact that they have to be carried out and the [espionage branch] is the most logical unit to manage them. Dealing with defectors is one such activity; monitoring the activities of émigré groups against governments of their former countries is another. Also, as was the case during the Vietnam war, the [espionage branch] may be called upon to organize certain types of tactical espionage operations for military commanders.

6. The "Monopoly" over Espionage Operations

Because of the constant necessity to weigh dangers against possible advantages, it is essential that the nation's espionage operations be economically run and tightly controlled. To this end, only one intelligence unit, the [espionage branch] of the Central Intelligence Agency, is authorized to conduct such operations. Other agencies may build close personal relationships with officials of other governments and gain quantities of secret information from them. Under certain limited circumstances, other agencies may even utilize casual informants and reward them with money or favors. But they may not employ "agents" as that term is defined in current Intelligence Directives.

APPENDIX C

THE DOUBLE-TALK GUIDE

The following instructions pertain to the use of a simple means of sending messages so as to make them look normal. It was used by a commercial concern in the Middle East that provided cover for an Anglo-American espionage unit in sending messages of low security classification. The words and phrases were chosen so as to appear normal in the light of the cover business and the known personal interests of its partners.

Remember, this is a "double-talk" system, not a code. Should a message that makes use of it fall into the hands of a cryptanalyst, it will be easily broken. Its purpose is to give secret messages such an appearance of normality that it will *not* fall into the hands of the security authorities and their cryptanalysts. Therefore, in using this system the following rule must prevail: *Use it only when the resulting message looks entirely normal.* If, upon completing a message and reading it over, you see that it has an odd look about it, you must rework it until it looks normal. If you are unable to make your message look normal by means of this system, you should revert to official communications.

Section One: Introductory Signals

These are words and phrases introduced into normal correspondence to alert the reader to the presence of double-talk, or to draw the attention of an unauthorized reader away from items that might otherwise excite his suspicions.

"DOUBLE-TALK COMING": In an otherwise normal letter, postcard, or telegram, any of these words or phrases should be taken to indicate that all that follows *in the same paragraph* is double-talk: *approximate, approximation, correct the grammar, an abbreviated version.* For example, "His approximate version of what happened was . . ." "Mind you, it's only an approximation, but . . ." "I'm submitting my remarks in rough draft. You can correct the grammar, make any additions you think appropriate, and . . ." "The report is too long, so I'm sending you only an abbreviated version."

"REAL NAME WILL BE REVEALED IN MY NEXT MESSAGE": If you wish to avoid giving someone's true name in your report, and you also wish to avoid giving the impression that you are trying to be secret, either of the following phrases will indicate that the name mentioned in the first paragraph of the next message, by whatever means sent (including the telephone), will be the correct name: *"His name has totally slipped my mind"* or *"A very old friend of Sam's."* For example, "His name has totally slipped my mind, but it doesn't matter anyhow. What is important is that he . . ." "A very old friend of Sam's told me . . ." In the follow-up communication, the first paragraph could include a sentence such as the following to indicate that the person referred to is, say, John Smith. "I'm sorry I couldn't get you the recipe you asked for, but I'm sure you can find it in that cookbook I saw in your kitchen, the one by John Smith."

Or, if the name is an unusual one—e.g., Outerbridge Horsey—the following phrase can be used to indicate that it is broken up into two parts, the given name to be found in the first paragraph of the follow-up correspondence and the family name to be found in the second: "*A young man whom I'm fairly certain you've never met.*" (Note: It doesn't matter whether, in reality, Outerbridge Horsey is young or old, or a man or a woman. The word "young" is nonetheless essential to the signal phrase.) For example, "I heard from a young man whom I'm fairly certain you've never met who . . ." In the follow-up communication, the first paragraph could contain the sentence "There is a village near here called Outerbridge," and the second could contain the sentence "Old Horsey didn't like it, but I think it did him good."

"THIS REPORT IS URGENT": To indicate that the content of a message is urgent and should be rushed posthaste to the Central, you should begin it with the word "*Greetings,*" followed by one or two cheerful personal sentences, before getting down to the real message. The rest of the paragraph following "Greetings" should be regarded as meaningless, as mere padding included to make the message appear natural.

"ALL THAT FOLLOWS IS HOKUM FOR THE BENEFIT OF ANY UNAU-THORIZED PERSON WHO MIGHT SEE THE MESSAGE": If you are afraid that some government censor might read your message and examine it for antigovernment sentiments, you might ease his suspicions by beginning your last paragraph with the phrase "*In my care-fully considered opinion*" and follow it with any progovernment nonsense you think he might believe. For example, "In my care-fully considered opinion, the Government of South Africa is doing a better job than the U.S. Government in improving the economic lot of its native population."

"THIS MESSAGE MEANS EXACTLY WHAT IT SAYS": The word "*Amen,*" coming at the end of your message, will indicate that it contains no double-talk and should be taken literally. (Such an assurance is needed more often than one might think, since even straight messages can sometimes have an inadvertent sound of double-talk.)

Important: The above phrases must be used *exactly* as given, without variation. Also, in *all* correspondence between persons using this double-talk system, whether frequently or infrequently, care must be taken to avoid using one or another of these signal phrases innocently. These phrases should be eliminated from your normal vocabulary.

Section Two: Elimination of Provocative Words and Phrases

To the extent to which you are able to justify so doing in terms of your cover work, you should speak plainly and avoid the use of double-talk. Remember, you are in a politically conscious part of the world and it would be unusual for anyone, even an ordinary businessman or a well-informed housewife, not to convey *some* political news and views. But if your reports go beyond the ordinary in sophistication or knowledge, you may sometimes find the following substitutions helpful:

1. For "military forces" substitute "engineers."
2. For the United Nations use some phrase including "power commission"—e.g. "some kind of a power commission."
3. For "intelligence officers" substitute "merchants." For "espionage agents" substitute "salesmen." For the local security authorities substitute "tradesmen."
4. For "anti-Western factions" (in general, or of any kind) substitute "manufacturers."
5. For "information" (or "intelligence") substitute "cost estimates." For "report" substitute "summary." "Confirm a report" may become "Broaden the summary."
6. For "rioters" or "terrorists" substitute "tourists"; for "moderates" substitute "accountants."
7. For "intervention" substitute "investment." For "election" substitute "auction," and for "to influence an election" substitute "sell at auction."
8. For "coup d'état" substitute any of the following: "powwow," "credit investigation," "thinkfest," or "orgy."
9. For "to defect" and "defection" substitute "to confute" and "confutation" respectively.
10. For "politics," "political," and "politician" substitute "sports," "sporting," and "sportsman" respectively.

Section Three: Names of Persons, Organizations, and Places

[Omitted. In the prototype, which was used in Beirut, Lebanon, during the crisis of July, 1958, prominent persons such as Egypt's President Nasser, Lebanon's President Camille Chamaoun, the United States, British, Soviet and Egyptian ambassadors, etc., were given cryptonyms such as "Charley," "Bill," "Wilfred," etc., and the powers involved in the struggle (Egypt, Syria, Lebanon, the United States, etc.) were given such cryptonyms as "the beach," "the mountains," etc. The same for political parties, intelligence agencies, etc., with a choice of cryptonyms most likely to appear natural in an innocent text.]

Section Four: A Special Code for Names Not Listed in Section Three

Purpose: The purpose of this code is to make possible the transmission of names in such a way that they are not obviously coded. For example, were we to use some code wherein "Smith" comes out as "Ygovj," anyone reading one of our cables containing that combination would realize that we were using a code word of some kind. In the code described in these paragraphs, "Smith" comes out as "McVath"—which may look a bit strange, but not so much as to cause the cable clerk to refuse to accept the cable.

When to use this code: This code is to be used in only those rare cases when (a) there is no other sufficiently speedy, secure, and dependable way of conveying identities and (b) the code *happens to work*. This second condition is most important, because there are many names which simply cannot be put into anything but a hodgepodge of queer syllables. (For example, "Eisenhower" comes out "Eutorlewod.") In cases where the code will not work on a name, think of a substitute (e.g., for "Eisenhower" write "President Ike"—encoded as "Krata-Gonsapo"), and if even that looks a bit strange, you can adorn it with some suitable descriptive phrase (e.g., "that old Japanese mystic, Krata-Gonsapo").

How the code works: The following guide sheet should be explanation enough; but before trying to use it you should examine the examples included after it.

ENCODING

	First Letter in Syllable		Independent Consonant in the Middle of a Word (vowel on each side)	Last Letter in Syllable		Auxiliary After a beginning consonant or before an ending consonant
	If followed by a consonant	If followed by a vowel		If preceded by a consonant	If preceded by a vowel	
B	F	F	F	B	F	B
C	G	D	C	C	W	C
D	D	G	G	G	G	D
F	B	B	B	F	B	F
G	C	C	L	D	G	G
H	L	L	H	H	H	H
J	M	M	J	J	J	J
K	P	P	P	K	P	K
L	N	H	N	N	M	L
M	V	V	R	M	L	M
N	N	R	M	L	R	N
P	K	K	K	P	K	P
QU	—	Y	QU	WU	Y	QU
R	J	J	Z	R	D	R
S	S*	T	T	T	T	S
T	W	W	S	S	N	T
V	R	N	V	V	V	V
W	T	S	W	W	S	W
X	QU	X	X	X	Z	X
Y	Z	QU	Y	Y	A	Y
Z	Y	Z	D	Z	X	Z

Vowels	Diphthongs		*S
A—I	AE—AO	IO—OI	SC —McC
E—O	AI—IA	IU—UO	SH —McL
I—A	AO—AE	OA—OU	SK —McP
O—E	AU—EA	OE—OU	SL —McN
U—U	EA—AU	OI—OA	SM —McV
	EI—EU	OU—UE	SN —McR
	EO—OE	UA—UI	SP —McB
	EU—EI	UE—UA	SQU—McW
	IA—AI	UI—IE	ST —McT
	IE—IO	UO—IU	SW —McK
			Mc or Mac—Van

326

Suppose you wish to encode the names "Nixon," "Ford," and "Simpson." Here is what you would do:

a. NIXON: Take the Encoding instructions, run your eye down the first column to the letter "N," and then across to column 3, which, you will note, is headed "First Letter in Syllable—followed by a vowel." This will give you the letter "R." Write down the letter "R" as the first letter in your encoded name. Next, look under "Vowels" to see how to encode the letter "I," the second letter in "Nixon." You will see that "I" is encoded as "A," so you write down "A" as the second letter in your encoded name. Next, you deal with the "X," which, according to the system, is defined as an "Independent Consonant" (column 4), since it is not used with any other consonant and is located somewhere in the middle of the name, not definitely either ending or beginning a syllable. From this column you will see that "X" is encoded as "X." Finally, you encode the "O" as "E" (from the "Vowels" list) and the "N" as "R" (see column 6) which is headed "Last Letter in Syllable—preceded by a vowel"). This all adds up to the encoded proper name "Raxer," which is at least barely plausible.

b. FORD: In encoding this name, you do the "F" and the "O" the same as the first two letters in the name "Nixon." The "R" is encoded as an "auxiliary" consonant (from column 7), since it is used in connection with a "key" consonant. (Note: a "key" consonant is one that either ends or begins a syllable.) It is therefore encoded as "R." Finally, you encode the "D" from column 5 ("Last Letter in Syllable—preceded by a consonant) as "G" and you get the encoded name "Berg."

c. SIMPSON: In encoding this name, you handle the first two letters and the last two letters just as you did in the previous examples, but you run into something new in the fact that there are three consonants all together. When the addressee gets the encoded name and starts decoding it, how is he to know whether to deal with the threesome as though the first two consonants *end* the first syllable with the third one starting the last syllable, or as though the first consonant, alone, ends the first syllable and the last two consonants begin the last syllable? The answer is this:

Encode it *however it looks the most normal,* and leave it
to the addressee to figure it out. He will try it out all ways,
and take the decoded name that is intelligible. For example, when he receives the name "Tampter" (which is
what "Simpson" encodes into) he may first regard the "M"
as ending the first syllable and "P" as beginning the last
one, in which case he will decode "Tampter" as "Silkton."
He then tries it the other way, and gets "Simpson" which
he knows is the correct answer since it is a more likely name
than "Silkton."

Other pointers: A doubled consonant with vowels on either side is
regarded as an "independent" consonant. (For example, "Galloway"
is encoded as "Cinnesia.") The letter "S" at the beginning of a word
and followed by a consonant is encoded according to the special
"S" code (e.g., "Smith" is encoded as "McVath" and "Stern" as
"McTorl.") "Mc" or "Mac" at the beginning of a name becomes
"Van" in the encoded name—e.g., "McClintock" is encoded as
"Van Glarweck."

How to indicate that the code is being used: Ordinarily, we will use
this code only in connection with the identity cables described elsewhere in these instructions. For example, should you wish to cable
the name of "Getty" you would first send a cable containing the
"very old friend of Sam's" signal, and follow it with a cable containing the name "Cossy," which is "Getty" encoded. You would
signal the fact that "Cossy" is an encoded word rather than a
straightforward one by putting "Doctor" in front of it. If your
cable omits the "Doctor," the recipient will assume that "Cossy"
really is the name of the subject, and he will not try to decode it.

How to give your cables a normal appearance: Remember, any
cable containing a coded proper name is *only* for the purpose of
conveying that name and not to send any other information. In
other words, if you receive a cable containing a proper name you
know to be coded (i.e., because of its general layout and the use
of the title "Doctor"), you can assume that anything else in the
cable is only for the purpose of making the cable look normal. For
example, the sender may write a fifty-word cable just to hide the
strangeness of some encoded proper name. As long as you see that
there is an encoded name in such a cable, you should disregard
the rest of the forty-nine words. They are for the censor's benefit,
not yours. Here are some specific pointers:

1. The first task of the cable is to convey the *last name* (the family name) of the identity. Therefore, you can assume that the first encoded grouping you see in an identity cable is *all* concerned with the identity's last name. This is true whether the grouping is one word or is broken down into two or three separate words or is preceded by or includes initials. For example, should you receive the encoded name "Doctor Jeeto Nols" you would know that you have one surname and not a surname preceded by a given name. It simply happens that "Jeeto Nols" is more normal-appearing than "Jeetonols." Decode it and you get "Roosevelt." Suppose the sender wants to send the first name "James" as well. He does this by including the name "James" in the next phrase —either in the clear or encoded, whichever appears best under the circumstances. "James" is a common name, so encoding would probably not be worth the bother, but "Mirot," the way it comes out in the code, might better serve some conceivable purpose. You might say, "Doctor Jeeto Nols, brother of Mirot Nols." (There are other ways of breaking down a name to make it appear more normal: e.g., "Rhoades" comes out "Jhougot," and can be made to appear more normal "Doctor J. Hougot," which is a perfectly plausible French name. "McTuarotins"— "Stuyvesant" encoded—can be made reasonably plausible as "the McTuaro twins," counting on the good sense of the decoder to disregard the redundant "T" in "Stuyvestant," the decoded name.

2. The next problem is to explain away the oddness. In the case of "Jeeto Nols" one might say something like the following: "Doctor Jeeto Nols, a Hungarian obstetrician and brother of Mirot Nols, has just written a long article in some French newspaper saying the Pill is no longer necessary. I do hope you know enough not to believe Hungarians." Another example: Suppose you receive a cable saying: "Unable to determine full name of very old friend of Sam's but he is a doctor and his nickname is Lizo which I gather is short for Lizard." You should disregard all the padding and understand that the sender is simply trying to get across the name "Hare," which is what you get when you decode "Lizo."

3. Sometimes you will want to send a long name, complete with titles and with a company name of some kind—for example, "Raymond Johnston, Beirut representative of Getty Oil Com-

pany." Sending all this will be troublesome, but sometimes it is necessary. A bit of imagination at both ends will overcome some of the awkwardness. You might convey this particular identity by sending a series of cables, as follows: (1) PLEASE RENDER ALL COURTESIES TO ROBIN ANDREWS WHO WILL CALL YOU UPON ARRIVAL BEIRUT EARLY AUGUST. HE IS VERY OLD FRIEND OF SAMS. (2) DON'T MISS ARTICLE LAST WEEKS SUNDAY TIMES BY DOCTOR MEHLSTER ON THAT RELIGIOUS LEADER NAMED JIA VENG. IF THIS DOESN'T CONVERT YOU YOU ARE BEYOND SALVATION. (3) DOCTORS CONNECTION IS COSSY COMPANY WHICH INEXPLICABLY NOT LISTED TELEPHONE DIRECTORY. Such a series would slip by a censor if sent only rarely, but if a succession of similar ones becomes necessary in any one period it will be obligatory to send a number of additional messages merely to make them add up to a credible, if fictitious, story.

4. Finally, remember that you can take small liberties in the spelling of some names if it will make encoding more natural. An example was "Stuyvestant." For another example, if you encode "Bissell" you get "Fattomm," and the double "M" at the end of the word looks strange. It should not confuse the addressee too much should you drop the second "M." "Fattom" will be decoded as "Bissel" and regarded as a simple misspelling.

Decoding: Decoding is simpler than one might think, despite the complicated instructions. Once you know you have a cable containing an encoded identity, all of the preceding instructions become unimportant. You simply seek out the words you know are to be decoded, underline them, and go to work on them. Here is an example:

IN SPITE OF FACT GISTER IS VERY OLD FRIEND OF SAMS AND HAS DOCTORS DEGREE BELIEVE ASSOCIATION WITH MICK RENDERS PROJECT RISKY. WISH DO ALL POSSIBLE FOR ANY OLD FRIEND OF SAMS BUT WISH YOU WOULD EXPLAIN TO HIM TACTFULLY THAT UNDER PRESENT CIRCUMSTANCES WE MUST REGARD ALL FINANCIAL VENTURES THIS AREA AS VISIONARY.

When you get such a message, the first things you note are the "friend of Sam's" signal and the word "doctor." From then on you know you are dealing with a cable that has but one purpose: to convey to you somebody's proper name. You underline the "Gister" and the "Mick" and go to work decoding, disregarding all the rest of the cable.

From there on, decoding is simply a matter of using the chart headed "Decoding." You may find it difficult here and there trying to decide what to do with combinations of consonants, but by trial and error you should be able to figure out what the encoder intended. Here are a few names for practice: T. Hasoberg, Flickster, Redvir, Frewl, Funnod, Dekoning, Mickser, Memot. Note that in decoding "Funnod" you may either regard the double "N" as a doubled "independent consonant" per your Encoding instructions, in which case "Funnod" is decoded as "Buller," or deal with the first "N" as "last letter in syllable preceded by a vowel" and the second "N" as "first letter in syllable followed by a vowel," in which case you get "Butver." You must then deduce the correct spelling on the basis of extraneous evidence.)

> Despite its flaws and the confusion it sometimes caused decoders, and *because* of its low security classification, this double-talk system survived many much more sophisticated systems and deluded code breakers for years. The very fact that messages containing it were normal in appearance, and buried in masses of genuinely normal messages, caused analysts to overlook them.

DECODING

| | First Letter in Syllable | | Independent Consonant in the Middle of a Word (vowel on each side) | Last Letter in Syllable | | Auxiliary After a beginning consonant or before an ending consonant |
	If followed by a consonant	If followed by a vowel		If preceded by a consonant	If preceded by a vowel	
A	I	See "Diphthongs"	I	I	I or Y	—
B	F	F	F	B	F	B
C	G	G	G	C	G	C
D	D	C	Z	G	R	D
E	O	See "Diphthongs"	O	O	See "Diphthongs"	—
F	B	B	B	F	B	F
G	C	D	D	D	D	G
H	L	L	H	H	L	H
I	A	See "Diphthongs"	A	A	See "Diphthongs"	—
J	R	R	J	J	J	J
K	P	P	P	K	P	K
L	N	H	G	N	M	L
M	J	J	N	M	L	M
N	N	V	L	L	T	N
O	E	See "Diphthongs"	E	O	See "Diphthongs"	—
P	K	K	K	P	K	P
QU	X	Y	QU	QU	—	QU
R	V	N	M	R	N	R
S	S	W	T	T	W	S
T	W	S	S	S	S	T
U	U	See "Diphthongs"	U	U	See "Diphthongs"	—
V	M	M	V	V	V	V
W	T	T	W	W	C	W
X	—	X	Y	Y	Z	X
Y	Z	QU	Y	Y	QU	Y
Z	Y	Z	R	Z	X	Z

Diphthongs		Mc
AE—AO	IO —OI	McB —SP
AI —IA	IU —UO	McC —SC
AO—AE	OA—OU	McK —SW
AU—EA	OE—OU	McL —SH
EA—AU	OI —OA	McN —SL
EI —EU	OU—UE	McP —SK
EO—OE	UA—UI	McR —SN
EU—EI	UE—UA	McT —ST
IA —AI	UI —IE	McV —SM
IE —IO	UO—IU	McW—SQU
		Van—Mc or Mac

APPENDIX D

When telephoning, let the number ring a few times, then hang up. Then call again to state the message. (Note: Don't specify any particular number of rings. The number you hear at your end may not be the same as the number heard at the receiving end.)

The message: "I keep getting the wrong number. What number is this, please?"

The meaning: "Meet your contact at the usual time at the usual place. If this is unsatisfactory, so indicate by giving the correct response."

The message: "Is this . . . just a minute, I'm unable to read this writing . . . 540–1130?" (The number is said slowly, as if being read from poor handwriting.)

The meaning: "Add one day and one hour and thirty minutes to the usual weekly meeting time, and meet at the same place."

Analysis: (1) The first number, 5, means *add* to the usual meeting time. If the first number is 7, you should *subtract* from the usual meeting time.

(2) The 40 means nothing. It is added for the sake of padding. The only meaningful numbers are the first and the last four—whatever the number of digits. (For example, the telephone number 51130, in an area where only five digits are normal, has the same meaning as 540–1130 in area where seven digits are normal.)

(3) The first 1 (i.e., the fourth digit back from the last) means "one day." If the number has begun with a 5, it means one day should be *added* to the normal meeting time. If with a 7, then it should be *subtracted* from the normal meeting time.

(4) The last three numbers, 130, mean one hour and thirty minutes—to be *added* to the normal meeting time.

Illustration: Let us say that your normal weekly meeting is Thursday at 6:00 in the evening. Your telephone rings, then stops. After it rings again you answer, and the caller says: "Is this . . . just a minute, I'm unable to read this writing . . . 736–0010?" This means that you are to meet your contact one hour earlier than the normal meeting time but on the same day—i.e., at 5:00 on Thursday instead of 6:00 on Thursday.

333

The message: "Sorry, but I must have the wrong number. Is this
. . . Oh, never mind." (Hangs up without awaiting a reply.)
The meaning: Meeting cancelled. Await instructions.

APPENDIX E

THE ONE-TIME PAD

One cannot properly appreciate the relationship between espionage and code breaking without an understanding of the limitations
of the latter. The uninitiated believe that any code can be broken—
a simple one by use of the method shown in Edgar Allan Poe's "The
Gold Bug" and more complicated ones by refinements of that method
made possible by use of the computer. But there *is* an unbreakable
code, and all but low-level codes and codes used in primitive circumstances are based on it. Originally, it was based on sets of letters
randomly chosen and put together in groups of five in line after line,
page after page, in a pad. The encoder and the decoder have identical pads, and they use the lines and the pages in the same order.
Later, it was based on "code machines" which randomly changed
the whole system with the encoding of each letter, but according to
a control "key" at the decoding end which ensured an identical
random selection.

For example: On page 336 we see a few lines from a page of
a one-time pad consisting of six groups, each of five letters, which
provide the basis for encoding and decoding a message. The encoder
wants to send the message:
BELIEVE IDENTITY ABLE INVOLVED [IN] MERCURY. CONTACT ZODIAC
FOR DETAILS PRETENDING IDENTITY WISHES U.S. VISA.

"Identity Able" is, of course, "Identity A" (British and Americans
both use forms of the "Able, Baker, Charlie, Dog" alphabet for
cabled messages) and is some individual who will be identified in a
subsequent message. "Mercury" is a cryptonym for some operation
or a case under investigation, and "Zodiac" is a cryptonym for some
official agency, possibly the local police. The Identity device and the
cryptonyms are used to provide internal security as the message in
the clear passes through the hands of coders and decoders and also
possibly through those of secretaries and file clerks.

To see how the message is encoded, turn to page 336. The

334

first letter of the message is B. So you write B under the first letter of the five-letter group in the pad, which is M, and you write E, L, I, E, V, E and so on under the following letters, L, J, Y, V, A, and M through to the end of the message. (The groupings of five, instead of according to actual word lengths, is to frustrate code breakers' attempts to speculate on words according to their lengths.) Then you use the chart to find the letter for encoding. The first letter of your message is B, and it comes under the pad letter M. Therefore, you scan the top line of the chart until you get to M. You then read vertically down to the line beginning with B, and there you find that the letter under M is O. This becomes the first letter of your coded message. Do the same for all the other letters and you get:

OQVHA WRKAQ QGIQV WLCXC SEDVT ZZLPH MFIKC LAQYI PNQHF
KZSCF OASYK XSNPZ SQBSG KGVPC UUZQB KQAVN WDCKT VNOYA

The decoder reverses the process. He has an identical pad, remember, so he puts the OQVHA and so on under the MLJYV and so on of the pad, and finds the proper letters of the message by use of the chart in the same way as encoding. He runs his eye across the M line until he gets to O, then vertically to the top to see that the O is in the B column, so he writes down the B as the first letter of the decoded message. Then he runs his eye across the L line until he gets to Q, then vertically to the top to see that the second letter of the message is E. And so on until the message is completed.

As you see, there is a whole new code for each letter, and since the new codes are randomly chosen it is impossible to break such a message unless you have managed to steal a copy of the pad or, in the case of a code machine, the "key."

The Message: Believe identity Able involved [in] Mercury. Contact Zodiac for details pretending identity wishes U.S. visa.

MLJYV	AMBWL	CMZWW	VJQST	EIOJX	UVYKP
BELIE	*VEIDE*	*NTITY*	*ABLEI*	*NVOLV*	*EDMER*

JKQLZ	WMWXF	VNBDW	JWMNN	KVYXB	LZXXU
CURYC	*ONTAC*	*TZODI*	*ACFOR*	*DETAI*	*LSPRE*

YLNOX	WZMLX	GAQWC	NHHNI	DIJOK	CMJKW
TENDI	*NGIDE*	*NTITY*	*WISHE*	*SUSVI*	*SAEND*

```
  A B C D E F G H I J K L M N O P Q R S T U V W X Y Z
A B C D E F G H I J K L M N O P Q R S T U V W X Y Z A
B C D E F G H I J K L M N O P Q R S T U V W X Y Z A B
C D E F G H I J K L M N O P Q R S T U V W X Y Z A B C
D E F G H I J K L M N O P Q R S T U V W X Y Z A B C D
E F G H I J K L M N O P Q R S T U V W X Y Z A B C D E
F G H I J K L M N O P Q R S T U V W X Y Z A B C D E F
G H I J K L M N O P Q R S T U V W X Y Z A B C D E F G
H I J K L M N O P Q R S T U V W X Y Z A B C D E F G H
I J K L M N O P Q R S T U V W X Y Z A B C D E F G H I
J K L M N O P Q R S T U V W X Y Z A B C D E F G H I J
K L M N O P Q R S T U V W X Y Z A B C D E F G H I J K
L M N O P Q R S T U V W X Y Z A B C D E F G H I J K L
M N O P Q R S T U V W X Y Z A B C D E F G H I J K L M
N O P Q R S T U V W X Y Z A B C D E F G H I J K L M N
O P Q R S T U V W X Y Z A B C D E F G H I J K L M N O
P Q R S T U V W X Y Z A B C D E F G H I J K L M N O P
Q R S T U V W X Y Z A B C D E F G H I J K L M N O P Q
R S T U V W X Y Z A B C D E F G H I J K L M N O P Q R
S T U V W X Y Z A B C D E F G H I J K L M N O P Q R S
T U V W X Y Z A B C D E F G H I J K L M N O P Q R S T
U V W X Y Z A B C D E F G H I J K L M N O P Q R S T U
V W X Y Z A B C D E F G H I J K L M N O P Q R S T U V
W X Y Z A B C D E F G H I J K L M N O P Q R S T U V W
X Y Z A B C D E F G H I J K L M N O P Q R S T U V W X
Y Z A B C D E F G H I J K L M N O P Q R S T U V W X Y
Z A B C D E F G H I J K L M N O P Q R S T U V W X Y Z
```

Encoded Message:

OQVHA	WRKAQ	QGIQV	WLCXC	SEDVT	ZZLPH
MFIKC	LAQYI	PNQHF	KZSCF	OASYK	XSNPZ
SQBSG	KGVPC	UUZQB	KQAVN	WDCKT	VNOYA

INDEX

Abu Humad, 285–86
Acheson, Dean, 39
Adenauer, Konrad, 58
Afghanistan, 50
Africa, 233, 283
  anti-American sentiments in,
  53
Agent, 106–108, 113
  captured, 181–87, 188–90
  vs. case officer, 110
  categories of, 24
  contacting, 122–23
  and documents, 116, 130–33
  external communications, 135,
    140–46
  internal communications, 135–
    140
  miscellaneous, 33–34
  networks, 112, 113n
  pay and incentives, 146–50
  and principal, 123–30, 133,
    148, 150–52
  recruitment of, 151–54, 259–
    260
  selection of, 119–22, 126–27
  training, 23, 133–35, 261–65

  and traps, 180
  walk-in, 24–27, 155–59
Airline crew members, as cou-
    riers, 145
Airplanes, as dead-letter drops,
    137
Albania, 201
Alcoholics (former), as security
    risks, 166, 166n
Algeria, 74, 98, 99n, 221, 283
Allende, Salvador, 279
Allies, in World War II, 43, 116
"Alpha" case (World War II),
    42–43
Alsop, Stewart, 50, 204–205
Alternative means, 315–19
  CIA and, 59–63
  gaming (creative intelligence),
    57–59, 315–16
  itemized, 65
  journalists as, 50–55
American Federation of Labor
    (AFL), 236, 236n, 237
Amnesty offer, as counterintelli-
    gence, 181
Anderson, Robert, 90

337

Prostitution, and blackmail, 17–18

Protestants (Northern Ireland), 220n

Qadhafi, Muammar el-, 75n, 98, 99n

Quwatli, Shukri, 203, 204, 243n

Raborn, William, 27
Radar, 70
Radical groups, 76–77, 293–95
Radio (clandestine), and external communications, 143
Radio Free Europe, 247
Ramadier Government (France), 236
Ramparts magazine, 230n
Recruitment
of agent, 151–54, 259–60
of foreign agent, 190
of walk-in agent, 158
Religious groups, international, 238–39
Resident, function of, 103–105
Revolution, and terrorist groups, 75–80
Rhodesia, 221
Right-wing terrorism, 96
Rockefeller Foundation, 249
Roosevelt, Eleanor, 47
Roosevelt, Franklin D., 37–38, 108
Roosevelt, Kermit, 205
Rumania, 200–201
Russia, *see* Soviet Union

Sadat, Anwar el-, 95, 116, 234
Schlesinger, James, 45, 259, 300–301, 302
Scientific American (periodical), 44
Scientists, and security, 165n
"Screech," and external communications, 144
Secrecy, and Third World operations, 198–206
Secret police, 95
and totalitarian regimes, 75
Secret Service (Treasury Department), 286
Secret writing, and external communications, 142–43, 145, 145n
Security, 160
duties of forces, 161–62
"father confessor" policy, 163–164, 165
full security investigation, 167–68
lie-detector test, 164, 164n, 165n
"need-to-know" principle, 170–71
personnel investigation, 166–167
physical security, 168–69
Security risks
and blackmail, 165
and lie-detector test, 164, 164n, 165n
Sending sets, as espionage device, 64
Servants, as agents, 121–22
Seventh-Day Adventists (religious group), 239